A Practical Guide to Database Design

A Practical Guide to Database Design

Second Edition

Rex Hogan

CRC Press
Taylor & Francis Group
Boca Raton London New York

CRC Press is an imprint of the
Taylor & Francis Group, an **informa** business

A CHAPMAN & HALL BOOK

CRC Press
Taylor & Francis Group
6000 Broken Sound Parkway NW, Suite 300
Boca Raton, FL 33487-2742

© 2018 by Taylor & Francis Group, LLC
CRC Press is an imprint of Taylor & Francis Group, an Informa business

No claim to original U.S. Government works

Printed on acid-free paper

International Standard Book Number-13: 978-1-1385-7806-7 (Hardback)

Library of Congress Cataloging-in-Publication Data

Names: Hogan, Rex, 1944- author.
Title: A practical guide to database design / Rex Hogan.
Description: Second edition. | Boca Raton : Taylor & Francis, CRC Press, 2017. | Includes index.
Identifiers: LCCN 2017050960 | ISBN 9781138578067 (hardback : alk. paper)
Subjects: LCSH: Database design.
Classification: LCC QA76.9.D26 H64 2017 | DDC 005.74/3--dc23
LC record available at https://lccn.loc.gov/2017050960

Visit the Taylor & Francis Web site at
http://www.taylorandfrancis.com

and the CRC Press Web site at
http://www.crcpress.com

Visit the eResources at
http://crcpress.com/9781138578067

To my wife Cindy, for always being there for me.

Contents

Introduction, xiii

Author, xv

CHAPTER 1 ■ Overview of Databases   1

1.1   WHAT'S A "DATABASE"?   1

1.2   GUARANTEED ACCURACY AND AVAILABILITY OF DATA   2

    1.2.1   Atomicity   2

    1.2.2   Consistency   3

    1.2.3   Isolation   3

    1.2.4   Durability   3

1.3   DYNAMIC ALTERATION OF DESIGN   3

1.4   DYNAMIC QUERIES—ANY DATA, ANY TIME   5

1.5   REFERENTIAL INTEGRITY ENFORCEMENT   6

1.6   BACKUP/RECOVERY   8

1.7   FAILOVER   9

1.8   TYPICAL INSTALLATION   10

QUESTIONS   13

REFERENCES   14

CHAPTER 2 ■ Data Normalization   15

2.1   INTRODUCTION   15

2.2   THE LANGUAGE OF NORMALIZATION   16

2.3   CREATING THE ENTITY/ATTRIBUTE LIST   17

    2.3.1   The *Order Entry* Model   18

2.4   CLEANING UP THE ENTITY/ATTRIBUTE LIST   20

    2.4.1   Problem Type 1—Synonyms   20

    2.4.2   Problem Type 2—Homonyms   20

2.4.3   Problem Type 3—Redundant Information   20

2.4.4   Problem Type 4—Mutually Exclusive Data   21

2.4.5   Problem Type 1—Synonyms   21

2.4.6   Problem Type 2—Homonyms   23

2.4.7   Problem Type 3—Redundant Information   23

2.4.8   Problem Type 4—Mutually Exclusive Data   23

2.5   NORMALIZATION   24

2.5.1   First Normal Form   25

2.5.1.1   *Requirement 1—Keys to Create Uniqueness*   25

2.5.1.2   *Requirement 2—Attributes Can Have Only One Value*   26

2.5.2   Second Normal Form   29

2.5.3   Third Normal Form   31

2.6   CREATING THE DATA MODEL   35

2.7   FOURTH NORMAL FORM   37

2.8   FIFTH NORMAL FORM   37

QUESTIONS   39

REFERENCES   40

CHAPTER 3 ■ Database Implementation   41

3.1   LOGICAL TO PHYSICAL DESIGN   41

3.2   USAGE PATH ANALYSIS   42

3.3   TABLE KEY AND COLUMN DATA TYPES   44

3.4   INDEXES   45

3.5   TABLE CREATION   46

3.5.1   Using Microsoft Access   47

3.5.2   Using SQL Server   56

3.5.3   Using Oracle   72

QUESTIONS   73

CHAPTER 4 ■ Normalization and Physical Design Exercise   75

4.1   INTRODUCTION   75

4.2   CREATING THE ENTITY/ATTRIBUTE LIST   75

4.3   MOVING TO THIRD NORMAL FORM   78

4.4   THE PHYSICAL DATA MODEL   88

QUESTIONS   91

CHAPTER 5 ■ The erwin Data Modeling Tool   93

5.1 WHAT IS A DATA MODELING TOOL?   93

5.2 WHY DO I NEED A DATA MODELING TOOL?   93

5.3 REVERSE ENGINEERING   93

5.4 CHANGE MANAGEMENT   94

5.5 DOWNLOAD AND INSTALL ERWIN TRIAL SOFTWARE   95

5.6 CREATE THE UNIVERSITY LOGICAL DATA MODEL   96

5.7 CREATE THE UNIVERSITY PHYSICAL DATA MODEL   109

5.8 CREATE AN SQL SERVER UNIVERSITY DATABASE   114

QUESTIONS   115

REFERENCE   116

CHAPTER 6 ■ Using Microsoft Access   117

6.1 OVERVIEW   117

6.2 MODIFICATIONS TO THE DATABASE DESIGN   118

6.3 LOADING DATA INTO TABLES   118

6.4 CREATING QUERIES   119

     6.4.1 Create a Customer-Credit_Card Query   119

     6.4.2 Create a Query Using SQL Commands   125

     6.4.3 Filtering Query Results   125

6.5 USING FORMS   129

     6.5.1 Create a Form to Update Advertised_Items   129

     6.5.2 Create a Form to Add a New Customer   141

     6.5.3 Generating a *Master* Screen for Users   146

6.6 GENERATING REPORTS   146

     6.6.1 Using Reports to View a Customer Order   146

6.7 DEPLOYING ACCESS FOR A TEAM OF USERS   153

     6.7.1 Linking to an SQL Server or Oracle Database   155

6.8 THE ROLE OF PASS-THROUGH QUERIES   155

QUESTIONS   156

CHAPTER 7 ■ Using SQL Server   157

7.1 OVERVIEW   157

     7.1.1 Advantages   157

     7.1.2 Change Management for SQL Server   157

7.2	DATABASE CREATION/INSTALLATION	158
	7.2.1 Installation Planning	158
	7.2.2 Software Installation	160
7.3	CREATING DATABASES	170
	7.3.1 Create an SQLSvrLogs Database	171
	7.3.2 Create the University Database	174
	7.3.2.1 Table Definitions	174
	7.3.2.2 Creating Indexes	177
	7.3.2.3 Index Maintenance	180
	7.3.2.4 Referential Integrity Constraints	180
7.4	USER ROLES	184
7.5	AUTHORIZED USERS	186
7.6	BACKUP/RECOVERY	190
7.7	LOADING DATA INTO TABLES	195
7.8	CREATING VIEWS	202
7.9	MANUAL QUERIES AND EDITS	204
7.10	USING STORED PROCEDURES	207
7.11	USING SQL SERVER AGENT	208
	QUESTIONS	210
CHAPTER 8 ■ Using Perl to Extract and Load Data		213
8.1	WHY PERL?	213
8.2	PERL VERSUS PYTHON	219
8.3	WINDOWS VERSUS UNIX	219
8.4	REVIEW KEY MATCHING FEATURES	221
8.5	MONITOR SQL SERVER LOGS	222
8.6	MONITORING WINDOWS LOGS	225
8.7	OTHER APPLICATIONS AND USES	226
8.8	LOADING DATA INTO TABLES	227
8.9	SUMMARY	229
	QUESTIONS	229
	REFERENCE	230

CHAPTER 9 ▪ Building User Interfaces   231

9.1   MICROSOFT ACCESS IN A TYPICAL OFFICE ENVIRONMENT   231

        9.1.1   General Capabilities   231

        9.1.2   Advantages   232

        9.1.3   Disadvantages   232

9.2   USE MICROSOFT ACCESS AS GUI   232

        9.2.1   General Capabilities   232

        9.2.2   Advantages   232

        9.2.3   Disadvantages   233

9.3   .NET FRAMEWORK   233

        9.3.1   General Capabilities   233

        9.3.2   Advantages   233

        9.3.3   Disadvantages   234

9.4   PHP   234

        9.4.1   General Capabilities   234

        9.4.2   Advantages   234

        9.4.3   Disadvantages   235

9.5   JAVA   235

        9.5.1   General Capabilities   235

        9.5.2   Advantages   235

        9.5.3   Disadvantages   235

QUESTIONS   235

CHAPTER 10 ▪ Creating the University Database Application   237

10.1   CREATE TABLES FOR UNIVERSITY ENVIRONMENT   237

10.2   CREATE RELATIONSHIPS TO ENFORCE REFERENTIAL INTEGRITY   241

10.3   DESIGN A SCREEN TO ADD NEW STUDENTS   244

10.4   CREATE A SCREEN TO ENROLL STUDENTS IN A CLASS   260

10.5   CREATE A SCREEN TO ASSIGN GRADES   268

10.6   CREATE SCREENS TO ENTER MIDTERM AND FINAL GRADES   271

10.7   CREATE A "MAIN" MENU   271

10.8   DEVELOPING APPLICATIONS FOR UNIVERSITY
        ADMINISTRATORS   272

QUESTIONS   273

Chapter 11 ■ PHP Implementation and Use   275

   11.1   WHY PHP?   275

   11.2   SYSTEM COMPONENTS   276

   11.3   DESIGN OF WEB-BASED INTERFACE   279

        11.3.1   User Logon Options   280

        11.3.2   User Authentication   281

        11.3.3   Home Page User Options   283

        11.3.4   Review/Check Warning Records   283

        11.3.5   Review/Check Error Records   292

   11.4   SCRIPT LOGIC   292

        11.4.1   Warning Records Logic   292

        11.4.2   Error Records Logic   294

   QUESTIONS   295

   REFERENCES   296

APPENDIX A: WARNING MESSAGES, 297

APPENDIX B: ERROR MESSAGES, 309

APPENDIX C: UNIVERSITY DDL, 321

APPENDIX D: SEARCH FOR TERMS, 405

APPENDIX E: SQL SERVER LOG CHECK, 407

INDEX, 409

Introduction

ABOUT THIS BOOK

This is a book intended for those who are involved in the design or development of a database system or application. It begins by focusing on how to create a logical data model where data are stored *where it belongs*. Next, data usage is reviewed to transform the logical model into a physical data model that will satisfy user performance requirements. Finally, it describes how to use various software tools to create user interfaces to review and update data in a database.

ORGANIZATION OF THIS BOOK

- Chapter 1 describes the functionality of database management systems and how they guarantee accuracy and availability of data.

- Chapters 2 through 4 describe how to define and normalize data requirements to create a logical data model, and then map them into an initial solution for a physical database.

- Chapter 5 describes how to use an industry-leading data modeling tool to define and manage logical and physical data models.

- Chapters 6 and 7 describe how to implement a physical database using either Microsoft Access or Structured Query Language (SQL) Server and how to use Microsoft Access to create windows interfaces to query or update data in tables.

- Chapter 8 describes how to use the PERL programming language to identify and extract records of interest from files and load these records into a database. As an example, it includes a script that identifies and extracts *warning* and *error* messages from an SQL Server log file and shows how to load these records into tables in a tracking database described in Chapter 7.

- Chapter 9 reviews various software tools that are commonly used to create user interfaces to databases to retrieve or update data.

- As with most skills, the ability to design and implement a database improves with practice and experience. Chapter 10 reviews the design and implementation of a database using a much more complex data environment for a University.

- Finally, Chapter 11 describes how to use PHP to build a web-based interface to review and update data in a database.

  The database used in this example is the tracking database created in Chapter 7 and loaded with the PERL script in Chapter 8. Appendices A and B contain the PHP scripts used by this interface to update the status flags in that database.

- Appendix C contains the Data Definition Language (DDL) text file generated by the data modeling tool to create the University database.

HOW TO USE THIS BOOK

User Specialists and Design Teams

- Learn how to create a logical data model where data are stored *where it belongs* by reviewing the material and exercises in Chapter 2.

- Learn how to analyze data-processing requirements to create a physical design model that will satisfy user response times by reviewing the material in Chapters 3 and 4.

Database Administrators

- In addition to the above-mentioned uses, learn how to use an industry-leading data modeling tool by reviewing the material and exercises in Chapter 5. It includes instructions on how to create the DDL statements needed to create a physical database. The DDL to create the University database is included as Appendix C.

- Learn how to implement a physical database using either Microsoft Access or SQL Server by following the exercises in Chapters 6 and 7.

Developers

- Learn how to translate user requirements into a database solution by reviewing the material and exercises in Chapters 2 through 4.

- Chapter 8 shows how to use the PERL language to identify records containing data of interest from external files and load them into a table in a database.

- Learn how to use Microsoft Access to develop user interfaces by reviewing the exercises in Chapters 6 and 10.

- Gain an understanding of software used to develop user interfaces by reading Chapter 9.

- Learn how to use PHP to develop a web-based interface to a database by reviewing the information and code contained in Chapter 11 and listed in Appendices A and B.

Author

Rex Hogan is the author of *A Practical Guide to Database Design* (first edition). In addition, he has written *Diagnostic Techniques for IMS Data Bases* and coauthored *Managing IMS DataBases* with Steve Shapiro and Maxie Zinsmeister.

Rex has more than 40 years of experience as a database administrator and a software engineer. This includes more than 17 years of experience with Southwestern Bell/AT&T where he became their lead database specialist. During this period, he also taught various undergraduate and graduate classes at Washington University's Center for the Study of Data Processing in St. Louis, Missouri. He then worked for TRW/Northrop Grumman in Fair Lakus, VA for 16 years, primarily as a database administrator (DBA)/senior software engineer in the Intelligence Community where he became a specialist in the rapid design and development of database systems and applications. Finally, he worked for five years as a computer scientist for the Air Force Office of Special Investigations, where he developed computer systems to monitor usage of Air Force Internet traffic.

CHAPTER 1

Overview of Databases

1.1 WHAT'S A "DATABASE"?

Today, generally everyone uses a computer in one form or another.

- Home-based computers are frequently used for managing a personal business, update spreadsheets, or complete school assignments. Others use them for email, social interaction with friends and family members, monitoring the Internet for news, or for entertainment.

- Owners of small businesses use spreadsheets and/or software products such as QuickBooks to keep track of personal or business expenses.

- Office environments must gather and store and manage information for a wide range of topics or subjects, such as customers or clients, appointments, or customer orders.

- Business environments must manage a much wider scope of data regarding the information and data needed to run or manage the business.

- Users using computers in government offices need computers to manage their jobs. For those working as analysts in the Department of Defense (DOD) or in the Intelligence Community, the *nature of the job* is continually expanding, requiring analysts to monitor or track new information or data as it becomes available. Analytical teams continually face the responsibility of analyzing new and evolving forms of information to identify and extract information of relevance using software tools available to them. Often, that means having not much more than the desktop Microsoft Office products ranging from Excel to Microsoft Access.

As the data needed by the user or customer community grow in size, complexity, and importance, the *care and feeding* of that data requires the use of a database management system (DBMS) to store, manage, and protect it.

A DBMS[1] is a special software package that is designed to define and manage data within one or more databases. Individual databases, in turn, manage the definition of data objects/tables in a given subject area and provide controlled user access to that data.

Examples of DBMSs include Structured Query Language (SQL) Server, Oracle, and Microsoft Access. An SQL Server or Oracle instance would then serve as host to, for example, a personnel database.

1.2 GUARANTEED ACCURACY AND AVAILABILITY OF DATA

A DBMS is, by its very nature, built to guarantee the accuracy and availability of data as updates occur. Updates are bundled as application *transactions*[2] that apply all data updates within a logical *unit of work*[3] associated with that application. These updates must be made on an *all or nothing* basis; either *all* the updates are applied, or, if a logical or database error occurs, *none* of the updates are applied, leaving all of the data in a clean consistent state from the user and application perspective.

The application software updating the database issues commands to the database to start a unit of work. If all updates complete successfully, a *commit* call is issued to make those updates permanent. If in the process of making those updates some condition is found that prevents the update from occurring, a *rollback* call is made to reverse any updates and put the data back in a logical state representing the data at the beginning of the transaction.

For example, a user might log on to their banking system and start an update to move funds from their savings to checking accounts.

- After logging in and starting the transfer, the software performing the updates first issues a database update to debit the savings account for the specified amount.

- If that update is successful, it issues an update to credit the checking account by that amount.

- Upon successful completion, a *commit* call is issued to commit the changes and release database locks on the rows being updated. An appropriate message would be sent to the user confirming that the funds transfer was completed.

- If, however, the update to the checking account failed (e.g., the user entered the wrong savings account number), a *rollback* call would be made to reverse all updates made, and an appropriate error message would be sent to the user. As a result, the database and the underlying data are left in a clean, consistent state.

The ACID[4] properties (atomicity, consistency, isolation, and durability) of database systems and transactions guarantee the accuracy and availability of data.

1.2.1 Atomicity

The *atomicity* is the *all or nothing* requirement when making updates. Either all updates made during the unit or work succeed or no updates are made. This protection includes updates in a unit of work or transaction, device input/output errors, network errors, and power failures.

1.2.2 Consistency

Consistency requires that transactions take the database from one valid state to another. Any and all updates must conform and enforce any referential integrity[5] constraints defined. (Referential integrity constraints define and control any *one-to-many* relationships between tables in a database.)

1.2.3 Isolation

Isolation of database updates involves mechanisms that enable multiple concurrent users to simultaneously access and update the same data elements within a database.

As database updates occur, locks are transparently placed on updated rows that prevent subsequent users to access or update those rows until the updating process commits those updates and the locks are released. Any processes requesting access to rows being updated are *held*/delayed until the updater's commit point is made.

1.2.4 Durability

This feature/requirement ensures that any updates made by a transaction (i.e., a unit of work completed and updates committed) will survive a subsequent system error or problem, for example, a system failure or a power or disk failure.

Database systems have mechanisms/features that support a full database backup. In addition, database systems log updates to nonvolatile devices (a database log file) as updates are made to the database. If/When necessary, a database can be rebuilt/recovered totally by first using the database backup to recover all data to the point the backup was made, then using the database log to reapply all updates made to the database after that point in time. This subject is covered in more detail in Section 1.6.

1.3 DYNAMIC ALTERATION OF DESIGN

Relational database management system (RDBMS) represent the *third generation* of DBMS products. As one of their key features, these products give the user the ability to dynamically add or drop columns to data or make other changes *live* while the database is online and being updated by users. That provides a significant change over the second-generation *hierarchical* systems that had to be taken down and modified off-line to apply changes. Third-generation systems include products such as SQL Server, Oracle, and Microsoft Access.

Note that MySQL is *touted* as an RDBMS and it has many relational-like features. However, it has significant limitations that, in my opinion, prevent it from being classified as a true RDBMS.

> For example, each table in MySQL is implemented as a *flat file* with indexes as needed to support data retrieval. If/When any changes are required, for example, a column is to be added, MySQL creates a new temporary table with the new column, copies all records from the original file to the new, and then deletes and renames the old and new files accordingly.

In a former role, I prototyped a MySQL implementation for a data collection application running a UNIX (Solaris) server. As the prototype progressed, it was no surprise to find that I needed to add new columns to the MySQL table to help track information about what was being collected. I found that the time requirements to make changes to a MySQL table with a million rows were *anything* but *transparent*.

As a work around, I then made what I hoped was a one-time modification to the table adding *spare* columns (Spare1, Spare2, Spare3, etc.) with the plan of renaming these columns if/when needed to reflect application-specific, meaningful names. That helped, but even then I found that MySQL required/used too much overhead for managing large tables.

The ability to dynamically change table definitions can, in most products, be made using that product's database administrator (DBA) graphical user interface, or by working at the command line by issuing commands using the product's data definition language (DDL). The DBA user interface is much easier and quicker to use, but when supporting mission-critical applications, change management procedures are used to control updates across multiple environments and platforms, each with their own copy and version of the application database.

- A Development platform is used to design, develop, and test individual software components and tables within a database.

- Incremental changes are made by manually running DDL changes at the command prompt.

- All incremental changes are accumulated as they are applied, creating a change package with all modifications needed for that release.

- When all changes have been made and tested for a software release, a Test platform is used.

- With the test system database configured for the older software release, the change package is applied and the software release is tested to ensure all updates have been correctly applied and the software works as intended.

- If errors are found, the change package must be revised as necessary and the entire update process repeated.

- After changes have been successfully applied and tested on the Test system, the change package is ready to be applied to the Production platform.

The careful application and use of change packages on the Test platform allows the scheduling of downtime of the Production system with the expectation of *no surprises* when the updates are applied.

1.4 DYNAMIC QUERIES—ANY DATA, ANY TIME

Although RDBMS products made a huge improvement by allowing dynamic changes, an even more significant enhancement was through the implementation of the SQL language. This gives the user the ability to ask for any data, at any time. For example, any authorized user can connect to the database and, using one of several query managers typically available, issue a command to retrieve data using the command syntax, where {} indicates optional parameters:

```
"SELECT <column name(s)> FROM <table name> {WHERE <column name> =
<value>};"
```

For example,

```
"SELECT First_Name, Last_Name FROM EMPLOYEE WHERE DEPT-NUMBER =
12;"
```

would retrieve the first and last names from the Employee table where that table's DEPT-NUMBER column has a value of 12.

SQL has, of course, many variations to extend the power and flexibility of the commands issued. Some simpler examples are

```
"SELECT * FROM EMPLOYEE;"
```

would retrieve/display all columns in the Employee table;

```
"SELECT COUNT(*) FROM EMPLOYEE;"
```

would display the number of Employees in the Employee table; and

```
"SELECT MAX(Annual_Salary) FROM EMPLOYEE;"
```

would display the highest annual salary found in the Employee table.

The power of SQL is multiplied by creating a "View"[6] of two or more tables that create a *virtual* object to query against. For example, a View can be created named "Department_Employees" that combines the Department table with the Employee table matching the DepartmentID column in Department with the DepartmentID in Employee.

Using this *virtual table,*

```
"SELECT * FROM DEPARTMENT_EMPLOYEES WHERE DepartmentID = 12;"
```

will list all information for employees that are assigned to Department 12.

Developers and users, however, must be aware that SQL implementations *are not all equal.*[7] RDBMS vendors have worked together over the years to define and implement SQL within their products beginning in 1986. However, at the implementation level, SQL commands will vary depending on the RDBMS product being used. The major vendors support the basic SQL standards (i.e., their product will provide some specific functionality), but the details of implementation will be different. For example, SQL provides for a *wildcard* character to allow/support either single character matches or to match any number of characters in a search string. If using SQL Server or Oracle:

```
"SELECT * FROM PRODUCTS WHERE Product_Name LIKE 'DELL%';"
```

will display all information from the *products* table for product names begin with "DELL."

If using Microsoft Access, this command would be

```
"SELECT * FROM PRODUCTS WHERE Product_Name LIKE 'DELL*';"
```

to match the wild card character used in Access.

In addition, each vendor will include their own SQL *enhancements* (features going beyond the standard) to support their products' competitive advantage.

Fortunately, from the developer's point of view, 90%–95% of their SQL *skills* will transfer/apply when working with another RDBMS product.

1.5 REFERENTIAL INTEGRITY ENFORCEMENT

A database will contain multiple tables, each containing information about one type of information to be stored in the database. For example, an employee database might have a table for department, one for employee, and another for employee-deduction. Each table contains detailed information about that particular item/object, each containing at a minimum the following information:

Department

DepartmentID

DepartmentName

DepartmentManagerID

Employee

EmployeeID

EmployeeFirstName

EmployeeMiddleName

EmployeeLastName

EmployeeWorkPhoneNumber

EmployeeHomePhoneNumber

EmployeeStreetAddress

EmployeeCity

EmployeeState

EmployeeZipCode

DepartmentID

Employee-Deduction

EmployeeID

DeductionCode

DeductionAmount

When the tables are loaded, information for each occurrence is loaded as a row in the respective table and each data element/value is associated with its respective column in the table. For example, a row in the department table might have the following content:

DepartmentID	DepartmentName	DepartmentManagerID
SalesArea1	Northern Virginia Marketing	E1005

Looking at the employee table, the first row for an employee assigned to the above-mentioned department might appear as follows:

EmployeeID	EmployeeFirstName	EmployeeMiddleName	EmployeeLastName	...	DepartmentID
E2001	Albert	Alan	Smith		SalesArea1

Note that the relationship between the Department row for the Northern Virginia Marketing unit and the Employee row for Albert Smith is determined by the fact that the DepartmentID, "SalesArea1," is stored as the value for the DepartmentID column in the Employee table. This illustrates the *one-to-many* relationship between Department and Employee and is referred to as Referential Integrity.

Referential Integrity is fundamental to data integrity and is normally activated and enforced by the RDBMS as data are inserted or deleted from individual tables. For example

- Any DepartmentID value assigned to a new employee must match a DepartmentID value in the Department table.

- Any new Employee-Deduction rows must contain a valid/matching EmployeeID.

- More importantly, if/when an employee is terminated, all Employee-Deduction rows will be automatically deleted without the programmer having to remember to perform that function.

1.6 BACKUP/RECOVERY

All DBMSs have, inherently, built-in backup/recovery systems. If the database fails (e.g., the underlying disk drive(s) fail), the database can be restored *to the point of failure*; that is, restored to contain data up to the last unit of work completed before the failure occurred. Depending on the DBMS product being used, backup/recovery services include some combination of the following:

- A mechanism/service to create a complete *cold* backup (i.e., the data are offline and not being updated).

- A mechanism/service to create a *hot* backup (i.e., the database is online and being backed up while the backup is being made).

- Depending on the RDBMS, incremental or partial services may be available to record all *changes* to the database since the last backup was made.

- A logging service to record all updates to the database as they are being made to a log file. In a non-RAID (redundant array of inexpensive disks) environment, the log file(s) should be stored on a different disk drive from that used to store the RDBMS tables to avoid losing both the *data* and the log file if the disk drive fails.

- Depending on the RDBMS, dual log files may be maintained to mitigate problems/ issues if errors are encountered when using the primary copy.

Both SQL Server and Oracle support cold, hot, and incremental backups.

As hot backups are taken while the database is being updated, there are additional technical issues involved to deal with log records created while the backup is being taken.

Backup/Recovery operations consist of the following:

- *Taking a full backup of the database*: This operation takes a complete copy of the database and provides the initial starting point for a future recovery operation. Depending on the size of the database, cold backups could require a significant amount of time.

- *Logging all changes as the database is updated*: Logging operations are a fundamental component of all RDBMSs. To ensure logs are always available for recovery operations, dual logging may be used to create two copies when logs are written to non-RAID devices.

- *Recovering the database*: A recovery operation starts with the last full backup of the database and applies all log updates made up to the point of failure.

- Note that the database must be offline to users during the recovery operation. Depending on the size of the backup and the number of logs required, the time required could be unacceptable to the user community.

- More frequent cold database backups shorten the time for database recovery but normally require more downtime for the user community.

- If incremental/partial backups were taken, the recovery would start with the last full image of the database, apply the latest incremental/partial backup, and apply logs made after the incremental/partial backup were taken. This approach is more complex to manage but significantly reduces the time required to recover the database.

- Note that this operation requires having a full and usable copy of the database. If database backups are taken to non-RAID devices, a second copy should be taken for critical databases to ensure a usable backup file is available if/when needed.

- Recovery operations might also be required in case of extensive user operations/issues. For example, a full backup of the database is advisable before applying a new software release for the user. If the software upgrade causes major issues/problems, the entire system must be restored to a point before the software update was made.

- *Service agreements*: Major database operations require a database recovery plan, which details the use and frequency of full and partial database backups. The plan is included as part of the service agreement drawn up for the user, specifying the acceptable down time to the user community if database recovery is involved.

1.7 FAILOVER

As noted in Section 1.1, a single instance of an RDBMS may, in turn, serve as host to multiple databases. Backup and recovery mechanisms have always been used to guarantee the availability of the data for a database hosted by the RDBMS. Failover mechanisms have more recently been implemented to guarantee the availability of all databases running on that RDBMS in the event of a host or RDBMS software failure.

In setting up a failover environment, a remote copy of the source database is created on another host, either within the same computer complex, in another building, or even in another city. When normal processing on the host resumes, all log updates are recorded on the local log and transmitted to the remote log as well. In the event of a system failure, all connections and processing active on the failed host are switched to the failover host and RDBMS instance and processing resumes.

If the database is important enough to have failover protection, determination of the failover site involves a number of issues.

- A failover environment requires a high speed, secure network connection between the primary host and the failover host to handle the volume of database log activity as processing occurs.

- A failover host in the same building as the primary host is fairly easy to set-up and manage. However, this provides no protection if the building is lost due to storm damage or through an act of terrorism.

- A failover host in a nearby building may be economically practical in the sense of installing a sufficiently fast network but may still be at risk if a natural disaster or storm occurs in the city.

- A failover host at a remote location will of course provide more protection by the physical separation of the buildings, but the cost of a secure high speed network may be cost-prohibitive.

Now let us take a look at the detail involved in setting up and running an RDBMS and its associated databases.

1.8 TYPICAL INSTALLATION

- The first step in creating a database is to install the system software for the RDBMS itself.

- For *light and small* databases, Microsoft Access comes preinstalled as part of the Professional or Enterprise versions of Microsoft Access.

- SQL Server runs in a Windows environment and comes with an installation disk that is very straightforward to use. The installer must of course first choose a disk drive for the system software and later indicate which system options are to be installed.

  As part of the installation sequence, the installer must specify what type of accounts may be used to access the data. The default is for a system/Windows account, but SQL Server accounts may also be used. These are accounts known and managed only by SQL Server, which I personally prefer. As a *senior DBA*, I want total control of establishing account names and controlling *who can access what* and remove all responsibility for database account control from system administrators.

  As part of the installation process, an SQL Server system administrator account and password are created.

  Note that depending on the particular version of SQL Server being installed and the version of Windows software being used, prerequisite software updates may be necessary. If the host computer has an internet connection, any required software will be automatically found and downloaded. If, however, the host computer does not have an internet connection, the installer may have to use another computer to download the update from the internet, *sneaker-net*/copy the update to the computer being used and run the update, then try to continue with the SQL Server installation.

- Oracle runs on both Windows and UNIX. My experience with Oracle has been limited to building and managing high-performance, high-availability systems on Solaris. Windows platforms cannot support the availability requirements of a database that cannot be *down* for more than a couple of hours every year, and of course Windows platforms are prone to security exposures/issues.

Oracle provides a written procedure for UNIX installations that are very straight-forward. There are two steps, however, that require a user with *root* privileges to perform.

After the RDBMS software has been installed, a database can be created. As part of that process, the DBA must make decisions on how many files (or Oracle Tablespaces) will be used to store data, where the various data files will be placed (i.e., what disk drive(s) to use), and where to store the log files needed for database recovery.

All of these decisions must be made with an eye toward performance. Let us take a minute to review how data are managed.

- Rows in a table are stored in a *page*, the smallest amount of data managed by an RDBMS in I/O operations.

  Some RDBMS systems (e.g., Oracle) allow the DBA to specify the page size. A large page size would be chosen if the data in the table are often processed sequentially; therefore, with one I/O operation, many rows are retrieved and can be accessed without requiring another I/O operation. A small page size would be chosen if the rows are processed in a random sequence; the smaller page size would be transferred more quickly than a large one.

  SQL Server, on the other hand, has a fixed page size.

- When a new row is added to a table, the RDMBS will first identify a *most desirable block*. Each table will normally have a unique key column (or set of columns), and the page with the row having the next lowest key value would be the most desirable location to store the new row.

- After storing the new row, one or more indexes must now be updated to record the row just added. Each index, in itself, contains a layered set of values, represented in a tree structure that must be traversed to do a lookup. As a result, for each index, two or three I/Os may be required to make that update. This operation must then be repeated for each index associated with that row.

In summary, the addition of just one row to a table requires multiple I/Os to add the row itself and to update all of the associated indexes associated with that table. The time required to perform these operations can be drastically reduced if the files being updated can be spread across multiple devices so that multiple I/O operations can be performed simultaneously.

If the host computer is built which has multiple disk drives available, the following types of data should be placed on different disk drives:

- The RDBMS software.

- *Data* files for the database tables.

- *Index* files should be placed on a different drive(s) from the data files.

- If at all possible, the RDMBS log file must be on a different drive from data files to ensure recoverability in case the data drive fails.

If the host computer has nothing but a single disk drive, you can, of course, implement the RDBMS, its databases, and log file(s) on that host. Of course, additional disk drives would support a higher performance level and have greater odds of being recoverable should a failure occur.

RAID[8] implementations work well and are used whenever possible to support an RDBMS and its databases. In each case, a RAID configuration is used to support I/O operations as it was one physical drive. The more significant RAID types used are

- *RAID 0*: RAID 0 *stripes* or spreads the I/O activity across all drives in the RAID unit. Although having no protection for device failure, this implementation is used where speed is the primary factor.

- *RAID 1*: RAID 1 implementations focus on disk failure by configuring drives such that every drive used has a backup or copy. All I/Os are targeted to both, and if one drive fails, the second drive will continue to support all I/O activity.

- *RAID 5*: RAID 5 stripes data to support fast performance but includes parity functions that allow operations to continue if a single device fails. A minimal RAID 5 system with four disks would stripe data across three drives and use the fourth for parity. This configuration supports a higher level of performance while providing protection for a single device failure. However, when a file (or table) is updated, additional overhead is generated to make not only the file update but update the parity map as well. If the RDBMS is update intensive, this overhead could be significant.

- *RAID 10*: RAID 10 provides the best of both worlds. Data are striped to support fast I/O, and each disk has a copy to protect against device failure. Expensive, yes, but it supports the highest performance as well as protecting against device failure.

RAID drives are *game changers* when configuring an RDBMS and its databases. A single RAID 5 system could be used to store and manage all data, indexes, and logs, providing performance enhancements through striping as well as recovery protection against device failure. The best possible solution, of course, is to use RAID 10 for everything, totally removing the DBA from concerns about separation of data and indexes and log files.

Given an understanding about how to install an RDBMS and creating the associated databases, the next step involves how to design a database that will meet the user's needs. That is covered in Chapter 2.

QUESTIONS

1. Do you consider MYSQL to be a database? Why or why not?

2. In the context of a database transaction, what is a *unit of work*? Why is it important?

3. What are the *ACID* properties of a RDBMS? Why are they important?

4. In a database recovery operation, what files are used to restore the database? What does each contain?

5. What's the difference between a Table and a View?

6. Given the following table structure, write an SQL query to find the EmployeeID and employee name from the Employee table for those assigned to Department 20.

   Employee

   EmployeeID

   EmployeeFirstName

   EmployeeMiddleName

   EmployeeLastName

   EmployeeWorkPhone Number

   EmployeeHomePhone Number

   EmployeeStreetAddress

   EmployeeCity

   EmployeeState

   EmployeeZipCode

   DepartmentID

7. Are SQL queries identical between products such as Microsoft Access, SQL Server, and Oracle?

8. Write an SQL query to find the number of employees in Department 20.

9. In writing an SQL query, what's the difference between = and *like*?

10. You are part of a team configuring a mission critical database for failover. What are the issues in locating the failover instance in the same building, in adjacent building, or in a nearby location?

11. What are the differences between RAID 0 and 1?

12. You are asked to install a RDBMS on a desktop computer with two internal drives. How would you configure the system across those drives to provide the best possible backup/recovery protection?

13. Why are Referential Integrity constraints important?

14. A new database has a new table for Department and another for Employee as shown in Section 1.5, and Referential Integrity constraints created. Files are available to load each table. Does it matter in which order the tables are loaded? Why or why not?

15. In setting up backup/recovery operations for a database for use by your business, what considerations are there in making/storing external backups for the database?

REFERENCES

1. Database management system, *Techopedia*, Retrieved from https://www.techopedia.com/definition/24361/database-management-systems-dbms (accessed August 18, 2017).
2. Rouse, M., Transaction, Whatis.com, Retrieved from http://searchcio.techtarget.com/definition/transaction (accessed August 18, 2017).
3. Database logical unit of work (LUW), *SAP Documentation*, Retrieved from https://help.sap.com/saphelp_nwpi71/helpdata/en/41/7af4bca79e11d1950f0000e82de14a/content.htm (accessed August 18, 2017).
4. Pinal, D., ACID, SQLAuthority.com, Retrieved from https://blog.sqlauthority.com/2007/12/09/sql-server-acid-atomicity-consistency-isolation-durability/ (accessed August 18, 2017).
5. Referential integrity, *Techopedia*, Retrieved from https://www.techopedia.com/definition/1233/referential-integrity-ri (accessed August 18, 2017).
6. Relational database view, *essentialSQL*, Retrieved from https://www.essentialsql.com/what-is-a-relational-database-view/ (accessed August 18, 2017).
7. Arvin, T., Comparison of different SQL implementations, Retrieved from http://troels.arvin.dk/db/rdbms/ (accessed August 18, 2017).
8. RAID, PRESSURE.COM, Retrieved from https://www.prepressure.com/library/technology/raid (accessed August 18, 2017).

Data Normalization

2.1 INTRODUCTION

The first step in designing a database is to decide what needs to be done by identifying the data requirements of the users. That sounds deceptively simple, and it can be, but it usually is not. Why? It is because users, the people for whom the system is being built, rarely can clearly describe what they need. That is bad enough, but the problems are often compounded quite unintentionally by the data-processing (DP) staff. These good folks, normally quite knowledgeable in the current system, know in detail what data exist, and how the existing programs work. However, what *is* rarely matches what is needed in the future system. Often, in-depth knowledge of how the system functions causes tunnel vision in the DP staff as well as the users and inhibits creative thought in determining the requirements for a new, enhanced system.

In short, the system design team, composed of user representatives, computer analysts, and/or programmers, and the database/data administration team, cannot communicate effectively.

A process called normalization can solve these problems. By using this technique, users describe what their requirements are without the use of the buzz words and terms so common in DP. The DP and data administration staff participate in these discussions, recording data requirements while serving as advisors in the analysis and providing their insight into what the new system might consist of. Afterward, when all data requirements have been identified, the technical staff can then decide on the details for a satisfactory physical database design.

This analysis technique will not be easy for end users to immediately understand and use. However, only a few basic concepts and definitions are required to begin. With the proper introduction and coaching, users can fully participate as members of the design team. Their input is so important to this process that many companies have created full-time user positions as data/database analysts to translate requirements into entity/ attribute specifications for the technical development team.

Oh, and do not let the terms *entity* or *attribute* confuse or bother you. An entity is just a collection of data elements that ultimately may be implemented within a table (when using a relational database management system) or as a file (if implemented in a flat file system). Similarly, attributes refer to what will become columns in a table (when using a relational database management system), or fields within rows when implemented using a flat file system. We are deliberately referring to data elements as entities and attributes in the design phase in large part to avoid terms that might imply physical implementation decisions. It is *much* too early to think about physical design and implementation. Using this process, we will first analyze what data elements we need by creating a normalized data model; next, we will analyze how the data are used; and finally, we will make physical design decisions to product a result that will satisfy user data requirements within acceptable time frames.

How is this technique different from others? The key is in communication. Users can, for the first time, concentrate on something they know and understand—a description of the information they use to perform their jobs—without using any technical terminology. The DP staff also benefit by hearing a description of the user's data requirements in the common language of normalization. At a later point in the design, these data requirements will be translated by the technical staff into a specific list of data elements required for each process (or program).

This technique is often referred to as *entity/relationship modeling*.

2.2 THE LANGUAGE OF NORMALIZATION

To review data and data requirements with user representatives, the terms *entity* and *attribute* must first be defined.

- An entity is something about which information is known. It describes or represents something of interest to the user, such as a person, a place, or a thing. Typical examples of entities include *employee*, *payroll record*, and *department*.

- An attribute provides detailed information about an entity. It helps one to identify, describe, or clarify the entity by providing a value for some quantifiable characteristic or trait. For example, for the entity *employee*, appropriate attributes would be the employee's name, address, social security number, and home phone number. Each attribute describes the employee by providing detailed information about that person. For example, John Smith, SSN 111-22-3333, lives at 2505 Hillcrest Drive and has a phone number of 757-345-1234.

Those of you with DP background have probably matched the terms *entity* and *attribute* with the terms record and field, respectively. That is exactly what they are, or how they may be implemented. The difference is that entities represent what you *might* ultimately implement in terms of record structures and content; they by no means represent a physical design decision. It is far too early for that. Physical design decisions will be made after you have identified all of the data requirements and have analyzed the overall impact of accessing that data to meet user requirements. The entity/attribute terminology focuses on the information needed by the user, detailing the meaning of the information being analyzed. At the same time, these terms help one to suppress the urge of the technical staff to prematurely jump into physical design decisions.

What, then, is normalization? For now, let us say it is a technique for reviewing the entity/attribute lists to ensure that attributes are located *where they belong.* A more comprehensive definition will be given later. For example, an employee entity should contain only attributes that provide information about the employee. If, by accident or oversight, an attribute is incorrectly associated with employee, the normalization process will enable you to identify and correct the error.

In many respects, normalization is simply applied common sense. The end result of the analysis reflects the same type of logic analysts have used for years; this approach merely provides a set of formal rules to avoid mistakes or oversights. We will review exactly what these rules are later in the current chapter.

2.3 CREATING THE ENTITY/ATTRIBUTE LIST

Let us assume that you have formed a design team composed of representatives from the end user, application programming, and database support staff. Your team has agreed to use the normalization approach to data analysis and have defined and discussed the terms *entity* and *attribute.* In getting started, what is done first?

As a starting point, search through existing reports or forms to identify data requirements. If part of the system is already automated, study the file layouts and/or database design. If you have already automated some tasks, you will probably need that data in the new or expanded system. Ask the users what else they need to track. What other information will they be wanting in the future? You want to keep those future requirements in mind, even though the proposed data may not exist for six months or more.

On the other hand, recognize that requirements do change. Most of us who have been around the DP business for any amount of time can recall, for example, a report that has been produced for the last five years and is no longer used. You need to be careful to ensure that the data are still relevant to today's (and tomorrow's) business.

Try *brainstorming* to identify data elements. Less-experienced end users will find the discussion particularly useful because the DP staff can suggest "if you have this type of data, then you can perform these functions." For example, bill of material data for a shop assembly operation would include information on parts that are on order from suppliers. The anticipated delivery date of parts, along with the cost of each item, could be used to forecast account payable information for the finance department. As with any type of brainstorming session, accept all ideas and suggestions without question. Revise and refine later.

You will soon find that a massive volume of notes will be generated, along with the need to get this information organized in some way. The easiest thing to do is to enter these initial entity/attribute lists in a data modeling tool, such as erwin (discussed in Chapter 5).

> Data modeling tools are specialized applications that allow you to capture and record definitions for entities, their associated attributes, and illustrate the association between entities (the *data model*). In addition, they support mapping of logical to physical designs and can generate DDL (Data Definition Language) statements to create tables in DBMS products such as Structured Query Language Server and Oracle.

Once these reports are available, review them to verify that an attribute is precisely and accurately defined. All team participants must agree on these definitions; disagreement often identifies the need for additional attributes to be created. Fortunately, a data modeling tool greatly reduces the administrative tasks required.

2.3.1 The *Order Entry* Model

Let us review the data environment that will serve as the sample problem used to illustrate the database design process.

Assume that you are part of the design team for a company that will advertise and sell merchandise on the Internet.

- Customers will connect to the company's website, search Advertised_Items for sale, and place orders for the items selected. The orders are then filled and shipped to the customer by the stock room.

- Each item advertised has a reorder level. When the number of items in inventory drops to or below that quantity, available suppliers are searched and additional items will be ordered from one of those suppliers on the basis of their current selling price.

The data model to be created will include data requirements to create orders for customers, to fill orders from the stock room, to monitor inventory quantities, and to reorder items from suppliers as needed.

As part of the design team, consider the above-mentioned overview of this environment and try to come up with five or six entities that seem appropriate (e.g. customer). Next, try to identify at least four attributes for each (as in Customer Name, Address, and Phone Number). Be sure to clearly define the meaning of each attribute that you identify.

When you have completed your list, compare your answer to that of Figure 2.1. This will serve as a starting point for the next phase of analysis, as it contains several intentional errors which will be resolved as part of the normalization process.

Attribute	Description
Customer	
CustomerTelephoneNumber	The customer's telephone number
CustomerName	The customer's name
CustomerStreetAddress	The street name associated with the customer's account
CustomerCity	The city in which the customer lives
CustomerState	The state in which the customer lives
CustomerZipCode	The customer's zip code
CustomerCreditRating	The credit rating for this customer
OrderNumber	An order number for this customer
Order	
OrderNumber	A unique identifier for each order
CustomerPhoneNumber	The customer's telephone number
CustomerName	The unique name for this customer
OrderDate	The date when the order was placed
NumberOfDays	The number of days from when the order was placed until shipped
CustomerStreetAddress	The street address for where the order is to be shipped
CustomerCity	The city to which the order is to be shipped
CustomerState	The state to which the order is to be shipped
CustomerZipCode	The zip code associate with the shipping address
CustomerCreditCardNumber	The credit card number used for this purchase
CustomerCreditCardName	The customer's name on the credit card used
StockNumber	The stock number for the item purchased
ShippingDate	The date the order was shipped
Advertised_Item	
ItemNumber	The unique identifier for each Advertised_Item
ItemDescription	A description of the item advertised
ClothingFlag	A code identifying clothing items
HealthFlag	A code identifying items as Health and Beauty
ItemWeight	The shipping weight for each item
ItemColor	The color of the item
ItemPrice	The selling price of the item sold
SupplierCode	The unique identifier for the supplier of this item
OrderNumber	The order number on which this item appears
Supplier	
SupplierID	A unique identifier for each supplier
CompanyName	The unique name for this supplier
SupplierStreetAddress	The street address for this supplier's main office
SupplierCity	The city in which the supplier's main office is located
SupplierState	The state in which the supplier's main office is located
SupplierZipCode	The zip code for the supplier's main office
StockNumber	The unique identifier for each advertised item
Purchased_Item	
ItemNumber	The unique identifier for each item on an order
ItemDescription	The description of the item advertised
QuantityOrdered	The number of items purchased
SellingPrice	The price of the item purchased
ShippingDate	The date the item purchased was shipped to the customer

FIGURE 2.1   The initial entity/attribute list.

2.4 CLEANING UP THE ENTITY/ATTRIBUTE LIST

Before beginning the normalization process, the initial entity/attribute list must be checked for errors or oversights.

2.4.1 Problem Type 1—Synonyms

A synonym is created when two different names are used for the same information (attribute). If an attribute resides in more than one entity, insure that all entities use the same attribute name.

For example, the attributes "SupplierCode" and "SupplierID" below are both intended to represent the unique identifier (key field) for supplier. As they have been spelled differently, this represents an error.

Advertised_Item	**Supplier**
SupplierCode <== error	SupplierID <== error

By using more than one name for the same attribute will cause many problems, including a failure to recognize *one-to-many* (1:M) relationships when the data model is developed.

Advertised_Item	**Supplier**
SupplierID <== correction	SupplierID

2.4.2 Problem Type 2—Homonyms

A homonym is the reverse of a synonym. Just as you cannot use different names for the same attribute, you cannot use the same name for different attributes.

For example, the attribute "CompanyName" under the Customer entity refers to a different data element "CompanyName" under Supplier. This is another error in data definition.

Customer	**Supplier**
CompanyName - The unique name for this customer <== error	CompanyName - The unique name for this supplier <== error

One or both names must be changed to reflect their differences.

Customer	**Supplier**
CustomerName - The unique name for this customer <== correction	SupplierName - The unique name for this supplier <== correction

2.4.3 Problem Type 3—Redundant Information

This problem, in which the same information is stored in two different forms or ways, is a bit harder to spot. One way to check for it is to consider if the value of any attribute is known or is derivable through the other attributes defined.

For example, in an "Employee" entity, storing an employee's age is redundant information when the birth date is also stored as an attribute.

```
Employee
EmployeeAge <== error
EmployeeBirthDate <== error
```

In this example, removing EmployeeAge will eliminate the error condition. When needed, the employee's age can be derived using the EmployeeBirthDate and the current date.

2.4.4 Problem Type 4—Mutually Exclusive Data

Mutually exclusive data exist when attributes occur, all the values of which, perhaps expressed as *yes/no* indicators, cannot be true for any single entity.

As an example, consider an Employee entity with attributes of "Married" and "Single."

```
Employee
Married <== error
Single <== error
```

Errors of this type often represent values of a larger category. Whenever possible, resolve the error by creating the larger categorical attribute.

In this case, these two elements can be resolved by creating an attribute of "MaritalStatus," which would have a value of either M (Married) or S (Single).

```
Employee
MaritalStatus—An indicator of
    the Employee's marital status
```

Study Figure 2.1 and see what suggestions you would make to correct any discrepancies as defined earlier. When you are finished, compare your list with the comments below, and the revised entity/attribute list shown in Figure 2.2.

2.4.5 Problem Type 1—Synonyms

Customer	Order
CustomerTelephoneNumber <== error	CustomerPhoneNumber <== error

Note that the CustomerTelephoneNumber in Customer and CustomerPhoneNumber in Order refer to the same attribute but have different names. CustomerPhoneNumber will be changed to CustomerTelephoneNumber.

Customer	Order
CustomerTelephoneNumber	CustomerTelephoneNumber <== correction

Advertised_Item	Supplier
ItemNumber <== error	StockNumber <== error

Attribute	Description
Customer	
CustomerTelephoneNumber	The customer's telephone number
CustomerName	The customer's name
CustomerStreetAddress	The street name associated with the customer's account
CustomerCity	The city in which the customer lives
CustomerState	The state in which the customer lives
CustomerZipCode	The customer's zip code
CustomerCreditRating	The credit rating for this customer
OrderNumber	An order number for this customer
Order	
OrderNumber	A unique identifier for each order
CustomerTelephoneNumber	The customer's telephone number
CustomerName	The unique name for this customer
OrderDate	The date when the order was placed
ShippingStreetAddress	The street address for where the order is to be shipped
ShippingCity	The city to which the order is to be shipped
ShippingState	The state to which the order is to be shipped
ShippingZipCode	The zip code associate with the shipping address
CustomerCreditCardNumber	The credit card number used for this purchase
CustomerCreditCardName	The customer's name on the credit card used
StockNumber	The stock number for the item purchased
ShippingDate	The date the order was shipped
Advertised_Item	
ItemNumber	The unique identifier for each Advertised_Item
ItemDescription	A description of the item advertised
ItemDepartment	A code classifying the item into one of the various product categories of items for sale
ItemWeight	The shipping weight for each item
ItemColor	The color of the item
ItemPrice	The selling price of the item sold
SupplierID	The unique identifier for the supplier of this item
OrderNumber	The order number on which this item appears
Supplier	
SupplierID	A unique identifier for each supplier
CompanyName	The unique name for this supplier
SupplierStreetAddress	The street address for this supplier's main office
SupplierCity	The city in which the supplier's main office is located
SupplierState	The state in which the supplier's main office is located
SupplierZipCode	The zip code for the supplier's main office
ItemNumber	The unique identifier for each advertised item
Item_Ordered	
ItemNumber	The unique identifier for each item on an order
ItemDescription	The description of the item advertised
QuantityOrdered	The number of items purchased
SellingPrice	The price of the item purchased
ShippingDate	The date the item purchased was shipped to the customer

FIGURE 2.2 The revised entity/attribute list.

The ItemNumber attribute represents the unique identifier for each advertised item, as does StockNumber in Supplier. The same attribute name must be used in both entities as they represent the same information.

Advertised_Item	Supplier
ItemNumber	ItemNumber <== correction

2.4.6 Problem Type 2—Homonyms

In Figure 2.1, the customer's address appears in both the Customer and Order entities with the same attribute names, but they refer to different data elements.

Customer	Order
CustomerStreetAddress <== error	CustomerStreetAddress <== error
CustomerCity <== error	CustomerCity <== error
CustomerState <== error	CustomerState <== error
CustomerZipCode<== error	CustomerZipCode<== error

The Customer address attributes refer to the address associate with the customer's account/ home location, but the Order's address attributes refer to where the order is to be shipped. The Order attributes must be changed.

Customer	Order
CustomerStreetAddress	ShippingStreetAddress <== correction
CustomerCity	ShippingCity <== correction
CustomerState	ShippingState <== correction
CustomerZipCode	ShippingZipCode <== correction

2.4.7 Problem Type 3—Redundant Information

In Order, the NumberOfDays was defined/intended to track the length of time between when the order was placed and when the order was shipped. The same result can be obtained by finding the difference between the OrderDate and ShippingDate attributes. Therefore, NumberOfDays can be eliminated.

2.4.8 Problem Type 4—Mutually Exclusive Data

In Advertised_Item, the ClothingFlag attribute classifies the item as a clothing item, whereas HealthFlag classifies the item as a health/beauty product. They both cannot be true for any single item.

This is fixed by removing both from Item and adding a new attribute ItemDepartment.

Item
ItemDepartment – A code classifying each item into one of the various product categories of items for sale

Figure 2.2 shows the corrections described earlier.

2.5 NORMALIZATION

Now that a *clean* entity/attribute list exists in which an attribute has one and only one name as well as a unique meaning, the normalization process can begin.

More formally stated, normalization is the process of analyzing the dependencies between attributes within entities. Each attribute is checked against three or more sets of rules, then making adjustments as necessary to put each in first, second, and third normal form (3NF). (It is possible you may want to move further to fourth or fifth normal form [5NF], but in most cases, 3NF is not only adequate, but preferred; more later.) These rules will be reviewed in detail in the next section and provide a procedural way to make sure attributes are placed *where they belong*.

Based on mathematical theory, normalization forms the basis for the implementation of tables within relational database systems. In practice, it is simply applied common sense; for example, you should only put attributes in an employee entity (table) attributes (or columns) that describe the employee. If you should find an attribute that describes something else, put it wherever it belongs.

Employee

EmployeeID

DeductionAmount <== error

In this example, DeductionAmount should not be associated with Employee, because it does not provide information about the employee as a person or individual. Instead, it provides additional detail about a payroll deduction for that employee. A Payroll Deduction entity would be created, if necessary, and DeductionAmount moved to it.

Employee	**Payroll Deduction**
EmployeeID <== unique employee identifier	EmployeeID <== identifies the employee involved
	PayrollDate
	DeductionAmount

Practical issues, typically related to performance, may later require you to use tricks of one kind or another when setting up physical structures. But you are not there yet! Place your data in 3NF and do all subsequent analysis with that view of data. Later, when all requirements are known, and after considering usage requirements, decisions will be made regarding physical structures. If at that time non–third normal structures are needed for reasons of efficiency, fine. For now, however, it is far too early to make judgments or decisions related to physical design.

The following steps put the data model into, successively, first, second, and 3NFs. Keep in mind two points. First, although they may appear overly meticulous, they provide the user with specific guidance on how to put the data model into 3NF. Second, after you have developed several data models, the result will appear as common sense to you, and you will tend to *think third normal* and create entity/attribute data models in 3NF automatically. So, although the process appears to be tedious, it really is not.

2.5.1 First Normal Form

In his book, *An Introduction to Database Systems*, C. J. Date gives the definition of first normal form (1NF) as "A relation R is in first normal form (1NF) if and only if all underlying domains contain atomic values only."[1] It is important to note that, in Date's discussion of this topic, it is implied that a relation has a primary key associated with it.

I prefer to rephrase this definition by giving the following criteria. An entity is in 1NF if

1. All entities must have a key, composed of an attribute or combination of attributes which uniquely identify one occurrence of the entity.

2. For any single occurrence of an entity, each attribute must have one and only one value.

2.5.1.1 Requirement 1—Keys to Create Uniqueness

For a specific value for the key attribute(s), there can only be one occurrence of the entity. For example, in the entity Advertised_Item, the ItemNumber is used to identify one unique Advertised_Item. Of course, the key should be unambiguous; there must be no question or confusion on what ItemNumber identifies. In addition, the key must be constant/unchanging over time. If an entity does not have a unique key, one must be created to provide a unique identifier for each occurrence of the entity.

There may, in fact, be more than one within an entity to obtain uniqueness. Analyze each and pick (or create) an attribute that clearly communicates/identifies the associated entity.

In the Customer entity, CustomerName appears to be good choice to identify customers. However, in practice, using names (particularly for businesses) creates many problems. First, different businesses can exist having the same name. In addition, a business may often be referred to by many names; I was once told that there are 27 different ways to spell or refer to AT&T. Although we need a standard spelling for the name for each customer, using CustomerName as a key introduces many problems.

Also in the Customer entity, CustomerTelephoneNumber would uniquely identify each customer but would be a poor choice for a key. First, the number itself does not have much inherent meaning. In addition, if the customer were to move their office to another location, the CustomerTelephoneNumber would change, and data relationships based on the old telephone number would no longer exist.

For the Customer entity, I recommend creating a new attribute CustomerIdentifier, based on an alpha-numeric combination of characters that are of course unique for each customer.

If you do find two candidates for keys, perhaps one can be eliminated. In many cases, however, both may be needed (as in the CustomerName and CustomerTelephoneNumber above). They each are required to provide different information about any specific customer instance. In this example, CustomerName can be considered a secondary key (i.e., an entity that uniquely identifies uniqueness but is not practical to use as a primary identifier).

Review the revised entity/attribute list in Figure 2.2 and identify keys for each entity. When finished, refer to Figure 2.3 in which the key attributes are identified with an "**" indicator.

2.5.1.2 Requirement 2—Attributes Can Have Only One Value

The second requirement for 1NF is often stated as "an entity must have no repeating groups."

To understand what a *repeating group* is, consider the OrderNumber attribute within Customer. At any given moment, the attribute OrderNumber will have multiple values, each reflecting a different OrderNumber for that customer at that moment in time. OrderNumber, therefore, is a repeating group.

As a second example, the ItemNumber attribute in Supplier is also a repeating group because a supplier normally provides multiple times of items that will be advertised for sale.

Customer	Supplier (Revised in Figure 2.3)
OrderNumber <== error – repeating group	ItemNumber <== error – repeating group

In contrast, consider CustomerName in the Customer entity. For a given customer, we create one unique name for that customer. CustomerName, therefore, is not a repeating group.

Whenever repeating groups occur, they must be removed and placed *where it belongs*, moving it to (or creating it within) the entity to which it belongs. To see what that means in practice, consider the following example.

Department	Employee
DepartmentNumber	EmployeeNumber
EmployeeNumber <== error – repeating group	

Step 1: The repeating attribute must be removed from the entity in which it appears, after assuring that the attribute exists in the data model in 1NF.

Attribute	Description
Customer	
**CustomerIdentifier	The alpha-numeric string that uniquely identifies each customer
CustomerTelephoneNumber	The customer's telephone number
CustomerName	The customer's name
CustomerStreetAddress	The street name associated with the customer's account
CustomerCity	The city in which the customer lives
CustomerState	The state in which the customer lives
CustomerZipCode	The customer's zip code
CustomerCreditRating	The credit rating for this customer
OrderNumber	An order number for this customer
Order	
**OrderNumber	A unique identifier for each order
CustomerTelephoneNumber	The customer's telephone number
CustomerName	The unique name for this customer
OrderDate	The date when the order was placed
ShippingStreetAddress	The street address for where the order is to be shipped
ShippingCity	The city to which the order is to be shipped
ShippingState	The state to which the order is to be shipped
ShippingZipCode	The zip code associate with the shipping address
CustomerCreditCardNumber	The credit card number used for this purchase
CustomerCreditCardName	The customer's name on the credit card used
StockNumber	The stock number for the item purchased
ShippingDate	The date the order was shipped
Advertised_Item	
**ItemNumber	The unique identifier for each Advertised_Item
ItemDescription	A description of the item advertised
ItemDepartment	A code classifying the item into one of the various product categories of items for sale
ItemWeight	The shipping weight for each item
ItemColor	The color of the item
ItemPrice	The selling price of the item sold
SupplierID	The unique identifier for the supplier of this item
OrderNumber	The order number on which this item appears
Supplier	
**SupplierID	A unique identifier for each supplier
CompanyName	The unique name for this supplier
SupplierStreetAddress	The street address for this supplier's main office
SupplierCity	The city in which the supplier's main office is located
SupplierState	The state in which the supplier's main office is located
SupplierZipCode	The zip code for the supplier's main office
ItemNumber	The unique identifier for each item
Item_Ordered	
**ItemNumber	The unique identifier for each item on an order
**OrderNumber	A unique identifier for each order
ItemDescription	The description of the item advertised
QuantityOrdered	The number of items purchased
SellingPrice	The price of the item purchased
ShippingDate	The date the item purchased was shipped to the customer

FIGURE 2.3   The revised entity/attribute list with keys.

You cannot just *throw the attribute away*. First ensure that the attribute exists *where it belongs*. Analyze what the attribute describes and, if necessary, create a new entity in 1NF. Once an entity exists (or is identified), move the attribute to that entity and remove the repeating attribute in which it was originally found.

In the above-mentioned example, EmployeeNumber is a repeating group with Department (departments have more than one employee). As EmployeeNumber was also found (correctly) in Employee, the error is resolved by simply removing EmployeeNumber from Department.

Step 2: Next, study the relationship between the entities from where the repeating attribute came *from* and where it moved *to*. Determine if the *from–to* relationship is one-to-many (1:M) or many-to-many (M:M).

In the above-mentioned Department–Employee example, the *from* entity is Department, and the *to* entity is Employee. To determine if this is a 1:M or M:M, ask "for one Department, are there one or many employees?", then repeat the question in reverse by asking "for one employee, are there one or many departments?". In this case, one Department has many employees, but one employee is associated with one department. Therefore, the relationship is 1:M.

When the relationship is 1:M, this is an acceptable relationship and no further adjustments are necessary. If, on the other hand, the answer is M:M, then one final check/adjustment is necessary before you move to Step 3.

In reviewing the OrderNumber entity in the Customer entity, the OrderNumber attribute already exists within Order. It can therefore be removed from the Customer entity. Next, in checking the relationship between the Customer and Order entities, we find that one customer can have many orders, but one order relates to a single customer. Therefore, there is a 1:M relationship between Customer and Order, and no further adjustments are necessary.

However, now consider the ItemNumber attribute with Supplier.

- Where does ItemNumber belong to? As it is the unique identifier for an Advertised_Item, it belongs under Advertised_Item and already exists there. It can therefore be removed from the Supplier entity.

- Is the relationship 1:M or M:M? One item can be purchased from many suppliers, and a single supplier provides many items. Therefore, the relationship is M:M.

- Now, we have a problem. The M:M relationship between Advertised_Item and Supplier requires that we have an entity to hold information (attributes) about one Advertised_Item when purchased from a unique supplier. For example, how much does that supplier charge for that item, and what was the quality of the merchandise received when that Advertised_Item was ordered from a unique supplier?

```
Advertised_Item <<--------------------------------->> Supplier
     **ItemNumber            Reorder cost?          **SupplierID
                    Quality of item last received?
```

If it does not already exist, a new entity must be created to store the attributes common to the entities in the M:M relationship (in this case, Advertised_Item and Supplier); see Step 3.

Step 3: Convert each M:M relationship into two 1:M relationships by creating (if necessary) a new derived entity.

A M:M relationship poses a basic design problem because there is no place to store attributes common to the two entities involved, that is, attributes that lie in the intersection of the two entities.

Creating a new entity to store the intersection elements transforms the M:M relationship into two 1:M relationships and provides a storage location for the data common to the two entities involved.

In the above-mentioned example, create a new entity Reorder_Item, which represents information for items that can be ordered from suppliers. This modifies the data model to include two new 1:M relationships:

```
Advertised_Item <------->> Reorder_Item <<--------> Supplier
     **ItemNumber          **ItemNumber           **SupplierID
                           **SupplierID
                           Reorder_Cost
                           QualityOfItemReceived
```

Study the information contained in Figure 2.3 and make a list of any adjustments you feel are necessary to put the entity/attribute list in 1NF. When you are ready, compare your solution to that shown in Figure 2.4.

2.5.2 Second Normal Form

Mr. Date's definition for second normal form (2NF) is: "A relation R is in second normal form (2NF) if and only if it is in 1NF and every non-key attribute is fully dependent on the primary key."[2]

I prefer a slight modification by stating this additional requirement as follows:

For 2NF, each nonkey attribute must depend on the key and all parts of the key.

If the value of an attribute can be determined by knowing only part of the entity's key, there is a violation of 2NF.

Attribute	Description
Customer	
**CustomerIdentifier	The alpha-numeric string that uniquely identifies each customer
CustomerTelephoneNumber	The customer's telephone number
CustomerName	The customer's name
CustomerStreetAddress	The street name associated with the customer's account
CustomerCity	The city in which the customer lives
CustomerState	The state in which the customer lives
CustomerZipCode	The customer's zip code
CustomerCreditRating	The credit rating for this customer
Order	
**OrderNumber	A unique identifier for each order
CustomerTelephoneNumber	The customer's telephone number
CustomerName	The unique name for this customer
OrderDate	The date when the order was placed
ShippingStreetAddress	The street address for where the order is to be shipped
ShippingCity	The city to which the order is to be shipped
ShippingState	The state to which the order is to be shipped
ShippingZipCode	The zip code associate with the shipping address
CustomerCreditCardNumber	The credit card number used for this purchase
CustomerCreditCardName	The customer's name on the credit card used
ShippingDate	The date the order was shipped
Advertised_Item	
**ItemNumber	The unique identifier for each Advertised_Item
ItemDescription	A description of the item advertised
ItemDepartment	A code classifying the item into one of the various product categories of items for sale
ItemWeight	The shipping weight for each item
ItemColor	The color of the item
ItemPrice	The selling price of the item sold
Supplier	
**SupplierID	A unique identifier for each supplier
SupplierName	The unique name for this supplier
SupplierStreetAddress	The street address for this supplier's main office
SupplierCity	The city in which the supplier's main office is located
SupplierState	The state in which the supplier's main office is located
SupplierZipCode	The zip code for the supplier's main office
Item_Ordered	
**ItemNumber	The unique identifier for each item on an order
**OrderNumber	A unique identifier for each order
ItemDescription	The description of the item advertised
QuantityOrdered	The number of items purchased
SellingPrice	The price of the item purchased
ShippingDate	The date the item purchased was shipped to the customer
Restock_Item	
**ItemNumber	The unique identifier for each item on an order
**SupplierID	A unique identifier for each supplier
PurchasePrice	The current cost of this item if purchased from this supplier

FIGURE 2.4 The first normal form entity/attribute list.

Consider the following definition of a Payroll Deduction entity to record deductions for every paycheck.

Payroll Deduction

**EmployeeID

**DateDeductionTaken

EmployeeName <== 2NF error; dependent only on EmployeeID

DeductionType

DeductionAmount

Here, the EmployeeName is an error for 2NF because the name is dependent only on the EmployeeID and not the date when the deduction was taken.

Any adjustments for 2NF violations follow the same steps as for 1NF errors. First, ensure that the attribute in error exists correctly in 1NF. Next, check the relationship between the entity in error (here it is Payroll Deduction) and the entity in which the attribute is correctly associated (Employee). If there is a 1:M relationship, no further adjustments are necessary. However, if there is an M:M relationship between these entities, verify that the intersection entity exists, and if necessary, create that derived entity.

Almost all violations of 2NF are found in entities having more than one attribute concatenated together to form the entity key. It seems almost trivial to state that, for entities with a single key, nonkey attributes must rely on that key. (For example, in a Customer entity, you would expect to find only attributes that provide information about that customer.) If, when the entity/attribute lists are created, keys were immediately identified and checks made to ensure that only attributes dependent on that key were added, you need only check entities that use concatenated attributes for keys. If that initial check was not done, you should check all attributes in each entity to verify that attributes are dependent on that entity's key.

Take a look at the 1NF solution in Figure 2.4 and determine what, if any, further adjustments are necessary to move to 2NF. When you are finished, compare your results to Figure 2.5.

2.5.3 Third Normal Form

Finally, Mr. Date gives a definition for 3NF as follows: "A relation R is in third normal form (3NF) if and only if it is in 2NF and every nonkey attribute is nontransitively dependent on the primary key."[3]

Once again, I prefer to phrase the requirement differently, adding the following criteria to that for 2NF:

A nonkey attribute must not depend on any other nonkey attribute.

Attribute	Description
Customer	
**CustomerIdentifier	The alpha-numeric string that uniquely identifies each customer
CustomerTelephoneNumber	The customer's telephone number
CustomerName	The customer's name
CustomerStreetAddress	The street name associated with the customer's account
CustomerCity	The city in which the customer lives
CustomerState	The state in which the customer lives
CustomerZipCode	The customer's zip code
CustomerCreditRating	The credit rating for this customer
Order	
**OrderNumber	A unique identifier for each order
CustomerTelephoneNumber	The customer's telephone number
CustomerName	The unique name for this customer
OrderDate	The date when the order was placed
ShippingStreetAddress	The street address for where the order is to be shipped
ShippingCity	The city to which the order is to be shipped
ShippingState	The state to which the order is to be shipped
ShippingZipCode	The zip code associate with the shipping address
CustomerCreditCardNumber	The credit card number used for this purchase
CustomerCreditCardName	The customer's name on the credit card used
ShippingDate	The date the order was shipped
Advertised_Item	
**ItemNumber	The unique identifier for each Advertised_Item
ItemDescription	A description of the item advertised
ItemDepartment	A code classifying the item into one of the various product categories of items for sale
ItemWeight	The shipping weight for each item
ItemColor	The color of the item
ItemPrice	The selling price of the item sold
Supplier	
**SupplierID	A unique identifier for each supplier
SupplierName	The unique name for this supplier
SupplierStreetAddress	The street address for this supplier's main office
SupplierCity	The city in which the supplier's main office is located
SupplierState	The state in which the supplier's main office is located
SupplierZipCode	The zip code for the supplier's main office
Item_Ordered	
**ItemNumber	The unique identifier for each item on an order
**OrderNumber	A unique identifier for each order
QuantityOrdered	The number of items purchased
SellingPrice	The price of the item purchased
ShippingDate	The date the item purchased was shipped to the customer
Restock_Item	
**ItemNumber	The unique identifier for each item on an order
**SupplierID	A unique identifier for each supplier
PurchasePrice	The current cost of this item if purchased from this supplier

FIGURE 2.5 The second normal form entity/attribute list.

If a nonkey attribute's value can be obtained simply by knowing the value of another nonkey attribute, the entity is not in 3NF.

For example, in the Order entity, you see the nonkey attributes CustomerCreditCardNumber and CustomerCreditCardName. There is an obvious dependency between the credit card number and the name on that credit card. A violation of 3NF exists, and CustomerCreditCardName must be removed.

How do we make this adjustment? Once again, repeat the steps covered under 1NF adjustments. Make sure the proper entity exists, then check for 1:M versus M:M relationships. In this case, you need to create a new entity Credit_Card to store information about the credit cards that the customer might use. The key for the entity is CustomerCreditCardNumber, and the CustomerCreditCardName would be a nonkey attribute.

Start from the 2NF solution in Figure 2.5 and see what other adjustments are necessary to get to 3NF, then check your solution against that shown in Figure 2.6.

By the way, try this shortcut expression for the rules of normalization.

For an entity to be in 3NF, each nonkey attribute must relate to the key, the whole key, and nothing but the key.

The entity/attribute list is now in 3NF, and each attribute is *where it belongs*. Nonkey attributes appear only once, in the entity which they describe. Attributes in key fields can (and do) appear in several related entities. These repeated occurrences establish the various one-to-many relationships that exist between entities. This redundancy is required for a relational DBMS, which provides data linkage on the basis of data content only. For example, those entities related to Advertised_Item (Ordered_Item and Restock_Item) must all have the Advertised_Item's key, ItemNumber, stored in them to support access/ data retrieval by ItemNumber.

It is important to keep in mind that the final data structure/design has not been created/finalized yet. The data model is just a logical view of data elements and how they relate to each other. This logical structure *could* be used to create tables and table structures, but the final decisions on database design and table structures will come later, after considering the results of how the data will be accessed. This is covered later in the book.

For now, there is one final step at this part of the analysis, which clarifies your solution by drawing a picture of the data relationships that have been created.

Attribute	Description
Customer	
**CustomerIdentifier	The alpha-numeric string that uniquely identifies each customer
CustomerTelephoneNumber	The customer's telephone number
CustomerName	The customer's name
CustomerStreetAddress	The street name associated with the customer's account
CustomerCity	The city in which the customer lives
CustomerState	The state in which the customer lives
CustomerZipCode	The customer's zip code
CustomerCreditRating	The credit rating for this customer
Order	
**OrderNumber	A unique identifier for each order
CustomerIdentifer	The unique name for this customer
OrderDate	The date when the order was placed
ShippingStreetAddress	The street address for where the order is to be shipped
ShippingCity	The city to which the order is to be shipped
ShippingState	The state to which the order is to be shipped
ShippingZipCode	The zip code associate with the shipping address
CustomerCreditCardNumber	The credit card number used for this purchase
ShippingDate	The date the order was shipped
Ordered_Item	
**OrderNumber	A unique identifier for each order
**ItemNumber	The unique identifier for each Advertised_Item
QuantityOrdered	The number of items purchased
SellingPrice	The price of the item purchased
ShippingDate	The date the item purchased was shipped to the customer
Advertised_Item	
**ItemNumber	The unique identifer for each Advertised_Item
ItemDescription	A description of the item advertised
ItemDepartment	A code classifying the item into one of the various product categories of items for sale
ItemWeight	The shipping weight for each item
ItemColor	The color of the item
ItemPrice	The selling price of the item sold
Supplier	
**SupplierID	A unique identifier for each supplier
SupplierName	The unique name for this supplier
SupplierStreetAddress	The street address for this supplier's main office
SupplierCity	The city in which the supplier's main office is located
SupplierState	The state in which the supplier's main office is located
SupplierZipCode	The zip code for the supplier's main office
Restock_Item	
**ItemNumber	The unique identifer for each item on an order
**SupplierID	A unique identifier for each order
ReorderPrice	The current cost of new items ordered from this supplier
Credit_Card	
**CustomerCreditCardNumber	The credit card number used for this purchase
CustomerCreditCardName	The customer's name on the credit card used

FIGURE 2.6   The 3NF entity/attribute list.

2.6 CREATING THE DATA MODEL

The best way to view the results of this analysis is to draw a pictorial representation of the 3NF data, usually referred to as a data model or a relational view. In this type of diagram, each entity is represented by a box, which is labeled with the entity's name. The *related* boxes are connected with an arrow, such as[*]

In words, there is a one-to-many relationship between Customer and Order, or, for each customer, there are many orders.

This is a fairly easy diagram to draw. Begin by simply drawing and labeling a box for each entity. Then, for each entity, ask "Does the key of this entity exist entirely within another entity?" If so, connect them with a ——● line.

Draw the data model for the 3NF solution in Figure 2.6 and compare your results with that shown in Figure 2.7.

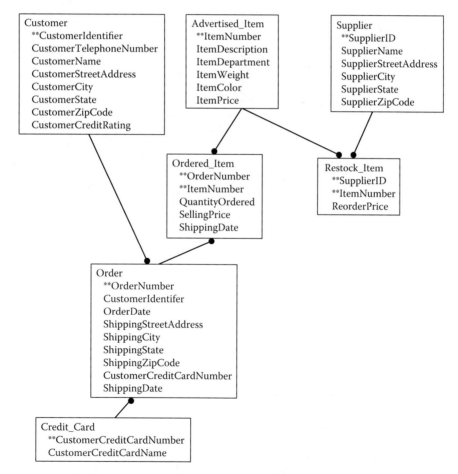

FIGURE 2.7   The initial entity/attribute diagram.

---

[*] Note: 1:M relationships are often drawn using a >-------<< connector line.

Be very rigorous about drawing the 1:M lines and only draw them in which "the key of one appears within the many." When finished, check your diagram carefully to see that it "makes sense." You may find two entities that logically *should* be related but have not been connected by a line. Adjust the data model attributes as needed to allow you to then add the 1:M line.

For example, in Figure 2.7, common sense suggests that there should be a 1:M relationship between Customer and Credit_Card. One was not drawn in Figure 2.7 because the customer's key was not (at that time) in Credit_Card. After reviewing this, it is clear that there *should* be a 1:M relationship between these two entities, so we add the customer key (CustomerIdentifier) to Credit_Card, then draw the 1:M relationship between the two. See the revised entity/attribute diagram in Figure 2.8.

For completeness, I will now review fourth and 5NFs, although in my experience, they have limited practical application for real-world applications/databases.

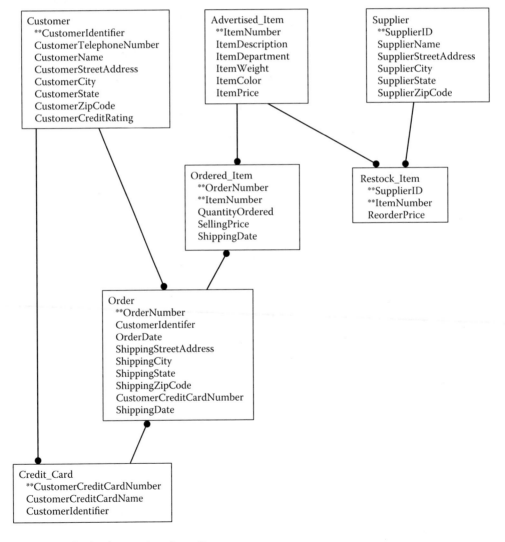

FIGURE 2.8 The final entity/attribute diagram.

2.7 FOURTH NORMAL FORM

Ronald Fagin gives the following definition for fourth normal form. "A relation schema R*
is in fourth normal form (4NF) if, whenever a nontrivial multivalued dependency X -->>
Y holds for R*, then so does the functional dependency X --> A for every column name A
of R*. Intuitively all dependencies are the result of keys."[4]

Wikipedia restates this definition as "A table is in 4NF if and only if, for every one of its
non-trivial multivalued dependencies $X ->> Y$, X is a superkey—that is, X is either a candidate key or a superset thereof."[5]

Their example helps one to clarify the meaning behind this change. They show a 3NF
table containing information for restaurants, pizza variety, and delivery area. Note that the
unique key for this table requires the concatenation of all three columns.

Pizza Delivery

**Restaurant

**Pizza_Variety <== 4NF error

**Delivery_Area <== 4NF error

If a restaurant offers all varieties at all locations, the 4NF issue is that Pizza_Variety
depends only on Restaurant and is independent of Delivery_Area. The 4NF solution
would break the above into two tables:

Restaurant Variety

**Restaurant

**Pizza_Variety

Delivery Area

**Restaurant

**Delivery_Area

Although from the theoretical point of view this might provide a *cleaner* definition/
delineation of data types, in practice it breaks the data into two tables. As a result, when
data about restaurants, varieties, and delivery areas are needed, more I/O is required to
retrieve the same equivalent as opposed to the 3NF solution, and application performance
is degraded.

5NF takes this one step further.

2.8 FIFTH NORMAL FORM

Wikipedia contains the following definition for 5NF. "A join dependency*{A, B, ..., Z}
on R is implied by the candidate key(s) of R if and only if each of A, B, ..., Z is a superkey for R."[6]

Wikipedia's explanation restates this as "A table is said to be in the 5NF if and only if
every non-trivial join dependency in it is implied by the candidate keys."

Once again, there is an example that clarifies the intent of this requirement. The 3NF solution for information regarding traveling salesman, brands, and product information calls for a table with the following design:

Saleman Product by Brand

**Traveling_Saleman

**Brand

**Product_Type

To be in 5NF, this information must be implemented in the following table structures:

Product Type by Salesman

**Traveling_Saleman

**Product_Type

Brand by Salesman

**Traveling_Salesman

**Brand

Product Type by Brand

**Brand

**Product_Type

Once again, an implementation based on 5NF requires that the data be implemented across more tables. Application logic processing these data will generate more I/O activity, and performance will be degraded.

Does this matter? The answer is "It depends."

> I find it interesting to recall that "It depends" is the correct response to almost *any* question on database design or implementation. Then again, after being in this business for more than 40 years, I have seen or been involved in projects ranging from the *smallest* to the *largest*.

For simple, small systems, the additional I/O may not make a difference. In general, however, a large, complex system would (in my opinion) generally suffer from a 5NF implementation. Early prototyping of a solution may be required to predict or measure the performance of a proposed solution to see if performance will be acceptable. Depending on the size and importance of the system being designed, two steps are typically taken.

1. Vendors typically publish performance criteria that reflect how a specified configuration will perform to a standard workload. Mapping the anticipated application data workload against these standards can measure the effectiveness of the proposed configuration.[7]

2. A more accurate benchmark can be done by building a scaled-down version of the database with sample data and running applications or queries to measure database performance.

Does performance matter? For a database of sufficient size or complexity, absolutely. When I last worked for Southwestern Bell Telephone/AT&T, I was a manager on the project to design a database that would support anything the company might sell/offer in the future. Our design team did an in-depth analysis of the associated data and derived a 5NF set of entities for this environment. The resulting design contained more than 500 entities. At this phase, we felt we could not make any performance-related changes in the data model because we did not want to hamper/prevent more sophisticated data accesses if/when new data requirements were identified.

When we finished the 5NF solution, we implemented it and used it with a modified billing program (revised to run against the relational tables) that had to run each night. The *nightly run* took days to complete.

So where are we in terms of database design? In practice, I start with a 3NF design as a hypothetical solution for relational tables. It is my understanding that this, in general, is an industry practice, and 4NF and above are rarely used outside of academic circles.[8] I then analyze data access required to meet application requirements and modify the logical design as needed to a design for physical tables. These steps will be covered in detail in the next chapter.

QUESTIONS

1. Define the terms *entity* and *attribute* and give examples of each.

2. In developing a new data model for Customers, some having multiple offices, a data requirement for a "Customer Location" has been identified. Is this an entity, or an attribute, and why?

Referring to the data model shown in Figure 2.8:

3. If the attribute "PreferredCreditCard" is to be added, how would the entity/attribute list change?

4. If information were to be added to track the quality of items sold by a supplier, what changes would be made to the data model?

5. What is the difference between the ItemPrice in Advertised_Item and SellingPrice in Ordered_Item?

You are asked to participate in creating a logical data model for a physician's office.

6. List five entities you would expect to see in this data model and give a description of each.

7. For each entity, list five attributes that would be appropriate for each.

8. For each entity, what attribute(s) would be appropriate as a key?

9. Develop a data model showing these five entities and their relationships.

You are asked to lead a design team for a new database to be used by your company.

10. Who would you ask to participate as a member of the design team? Why?

11. When developing an initial list of entities for the database, what guidelines would you give the participants on what to consider/not consider?

12. How would you document the entity/attribute lists as they are developed?

13. What do you feel is the appropriate level for data normalization for the entity/attribute lists to be developed? Why?

14. Is the database to be used for implementation a factor at this stage? Why or why not?

15. As the logical data model is developed, should any significant usage requirements be noted or documented? Why or why not?

REFERENCES

1. Date, C. J., *An Introduction to Database Systems*, Reading, MA, Addison-Wesley, 1985, p. 367.
2. Date, C. J., *An Introduction to Database Systems*, Reading, MA, Addison-Wesley, 1985, p. 370.
3. Date, C. J., *An Introduction to Database Systems*, Reading, MA, Addison-Wesley, 1985, p. 373.
4. Fagin, R., Multivalued Dependencies and a New Normal Form for Relational Databases, *ACM Transactions on Database Systems*, 2, 267, 1977.
5. Fourth normal form, Wikipedia.com, https://en.wikipedia.org/wiki/Fourth_normal_form (accessed August 23, 2017).
6. Fifth normal form, Wikipedia.org, https://en.wikipedia.org/wiki/Fifth_normal_form (accessed August 23, 2017).
7. Active TPC benchmarks, TPC.org, http://www.tpc.org/information/benchmarks.asp (accessed August 23, 2017).
8. Fourth normal form, Techopedia.com, https://www.techopedia.com/definition/19453/fourth-normal-form-4nf (accessed August 23, 2017).

Database Implementation

3.1 LOGICAL TO PHYSICAL DESIGN

Let us begin with a review of the (third normal form) 3NF logical data model from Chapter 2 (Figure 3.1).

In theory, we would like to use this diagram to implement a *physical model* conforming as close as possible to this architecture. In other words, we would implement a database with a table for each of these entities with columns for each attribute. The only replications of attributes across entities are those needed to make *one-to-many* associations between entities.

The advantage of this form of implementation is that any piece of information is only stored in one place inside the database and table structure. If/When that information changes, for example, a Supplier's name changes, that name must be changed in only one location. The software application designed for the database is much simpler, and any *database rules* (the software implementation of the company's business rules and their implementation through data relationships) are simpler to implement and maintain.

In practice, however, a 3NF physical data model seldom provides an acceptable performance level. As a first step after deriving the logical model, we need to look at how the user needs to access the data to estimate the I/O requirements for that design/implementation. If we can make changes to the physical model by storing information redundantly, we can drastically reduce I/O requirements to access information with minor changes in the application software.

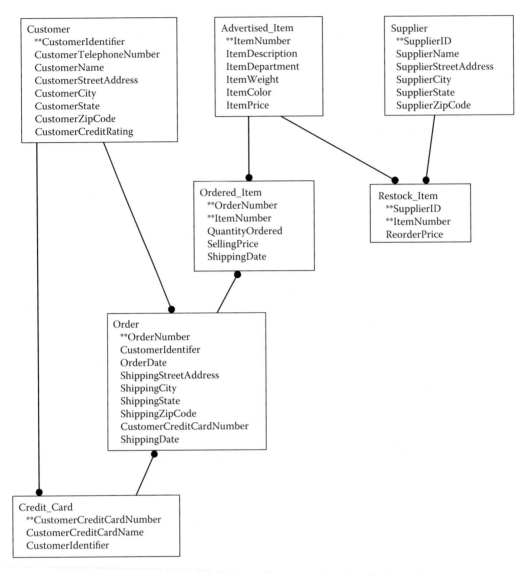

FIGURE 3.1 The 3NF logical data model.

3.2 USAGE PATH ANALYSIS

Using the above-mentioned data model, let us review the accesses needed to satisfy some important, frequently used queries.

- For a specific Customer order, what is the total cost?

Table	Search Criteria	Number of Rows	Why Needed
Customer	CustomerIdentifier	1	To get Customer information to be displayed for verification
Order	CustomerIdentifier	1	To get Order details to be displayed
Order_Item	OrderNumber	Multiple	To obtain SellingPrice to compute total cost

If we change the physical model to add OrderTotalCost to Order, the access paths would be

Table	Search Criteria	Number of Rows	Why Needed
Customer	CustomerIdentifier	1	To get Customer information to be displayed for verification
Order	CustomerIdentifier	1	To get Order details to be displayed and the OrderTotalCost

Note that the OrderTotalCost information must now be implemented in application logic, preferably by using a database *trigger* or stored procedure. Triggers and stored procedures are the preferred methods to implement business rules, rather than embedding them within some arbitrary application software module.

- For a specific Advertised_Item, what is the lowest price currently offered by a Supplier?

Table	Search Criteria	Number of Rows	Why Needed
Advertised_Item	ItemNumber	1	To get Advertised_Item information to be displayed for verification
Restock_Item	ItemNumber	Multiple	To get the ReorderPrice values
Supplier	SupplierID	Multiple	To obtain Supplier information associated with that SellingPrice

If Advertised_Item were modified to include LowestPrice and LowestPriceSupplier, then the above would change to the following:

Table	Search Criteria	Number of Rows	Why Needed
Advertised_Item	ItemNumber	1	To get Advertised_Item information and the lowest price and its associated Supplier code
Supplier	SupplierID	1	To obtain Supplier information associated with that SupplierID

Once again, accesses are significantly reduced at the cost of implementing logic within a trigger or stored procedure to update this information as Supplier price updates are received.

- When Customer information is retrieved, include their preferred credit card number.

Table	Search Criteria	Number of Rows	Why Needed
Customer	CustomerIdentifier	1	To get Customer information
Credit_Card	CustomerIdentifier	Multiple	To find the Credit_Card information with the PreferredOption set

If the Customer table were modified to include a CustPreferredCreditCard column, access change to the following.

Table	Search Criteria	Number of Rows	Why Needed
Customer	CustomerIdentifier	1	To get Customer information as well as their preferred credit card number

The revised 3NF data model now represents a physical data model, showing all tables and the columns to be defined within each.

Design modifications are generally always necessary to provide satisfactory levels for the application. The earlier the performance issues can be identified, the easier they are to address without impacting software or database changes as design and testing progress.

3.3 TABLE KEY AND COLUMN DATA TYPES

In reviewing the physical model for the database, the design team must decide on what to do regarding keys for each table. Normally, this is very straightforward, because the first step of the normalization process involves identifying a key for each entity. However, determining the exact form and value for key columns requires consideration of several factors before detailed physical design decisions can be made.

- Are key column(s) an absolute requirement? In most cases, yes, because database applications inherently store and update data throughout the *life cycle* of the data elements. (This is the time from when data are added to a table until it is deleted because it is no longer needed.) Without uniqueness, we have no way of retrieving or updating a specific row in the table.

  There are, however, exceptions. If data records are being collected and stored in a table that can be analyzed and treated as a group without the need to retrieve and update individual rows, a key identifier/column may not be required. For example, if bulk data are being collected that includes a column for date and time, that column can be used to review and summarize results for that date, and that set of rows can be deleted when no longer needed.

- What data type is appropriate for each key? Are there any inherent business rules that guide or determine acceptable values?

  For example, the Customer table in the physical model has a "CustomerIdentifier" column that will uniquely retrieve one specific row for a Customer. The user may have business rules defining how CustomerIdentifier values are assigned for new Customers. In that case, the storage format for CustomerIdentifier might be "varchar(50)" (i.e., a character field varying in length up to 50 characters).

As an alternative, we could make CustomerIdentifier a large integer number and use the RDMBS feature that uses an ever increasing integer value ("auto increment" in Microsoft Access and Structured Query Language [SQL] Server, and the Oracle "Identity" feature). This is used when the application or data have no inherent business rules dictating how the table's key column is created and you simply need a way to create a unique value for the row's key. This approach is also used when the underlying data are so complex or the column length for a key is very large. In either case, creating a key column as an integer is *much* more efficient to use, especially considering the size of the indexes in the primary and subordinate tables (see the next section for details).

- Next, the storage format/data type for each non-key column must also be reviewed and noted. This information will be used when defining columns for each table in the database.

Note that the design team cannot rush through this step. Each column needs to be carefully reviewed to see exactly what will be stored. For example, for a phone number, will only 10 digits be recorded, or will a character format be used to store number in the form of "nnn-nnn-nnnn"?

After all data types have been reviewed, as one last step before creating tables in a database, you must identify indexes needed to efficiently support relationships across tables.

3.4 INDEXES

As noted earlier, RDMBS systems and SQL give the user or application the ability to ask for any data at any time. For example, the following query will retrieve all Restock_Item rows for a specified Advertised_Item.

```
SELECT * FROM Restock_Item WHERE ItemNumber = "DELL_12345";
```

If the Restock_Item table was implemented without any indexes, the above-mentioned search would still execute and return the correct information/matching rows. However, if an index was created in the Restock_Item table on the ItemNumber column, the index would be used to immediately retrieve only the rows that matched that ItemNumber. The answer to the query is the same, but the index allows for the data to be retrieved without all of the I/Os required to do a table scan.

Identifying and creating indexes, then, are critical in obtaining acceptable performance levels for a database application. As a general rule, indexes should be created in tables for

- The column(s) that make up the primary key for the table.

- Columns that serve as *foreign keys*, that is, those columns on the *many* side of a one-to-many relationship.

- Columns found used as search criteria in the usage path analysis.

These criteria in themselves may not result in the best possible database design, but they will get you off to a good start. In addition, tools are available for SQL Server and Oracle to help you monitor I/O activity while your application is being designed and tested to help you identify and deal with unexpected performance issues.

3.5 TABLE CREATION

After reviewing the composition of keys for each table and identifying the indexes needed, we are now ready to implement those decisions by creating tables in the newly created database. The following sections describe how to create tables for the physical data model shown in Figure 3.2.

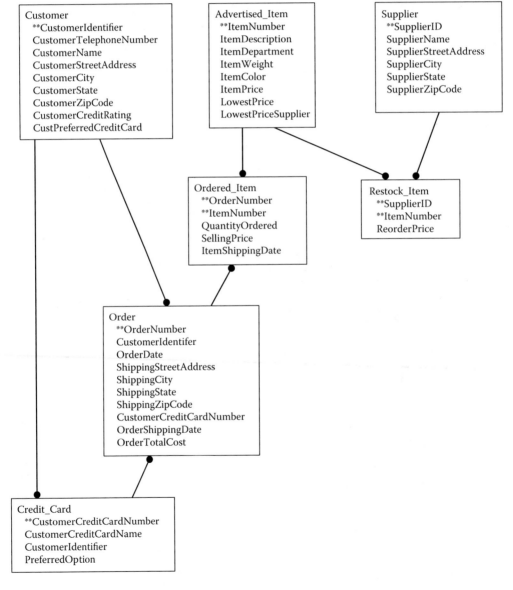

FIGURE 3.2   The physical data model.

3.5.1 Using Microsoft Access

- Create a new database

If you haven not already done so, open Microsoft Access and select "Blank Database" to begin the dialog to create a new database. Next, click the folder to the right of the file name and navigate to the folder you want to use to store the new database. Finally, change the file name to the name you want to use for the database, click "OK;" then, click the Create box. The new database will appear as follows.

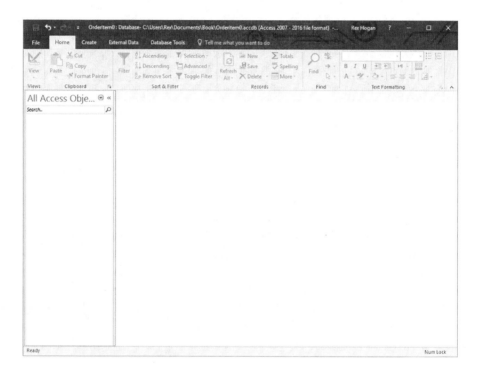

- To define a new table

From the above-mentioned screen, select the Create tab, then click the Table Design item:

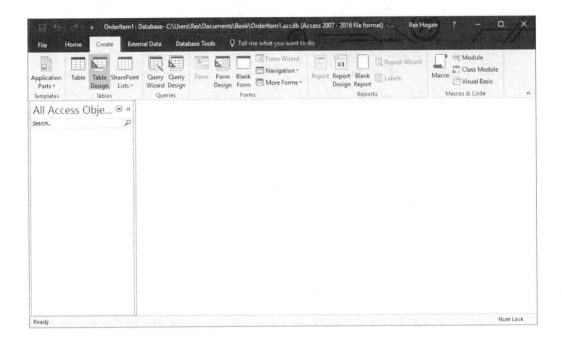

The detailed design screen will open. Under "Field Name," type the name of the first column (in this example, "CustomerIdentifier" in the Customer table), then click the pull-down under "Data Type" and select "Number" to reflect a decision to use the auto-increment feature for this column.

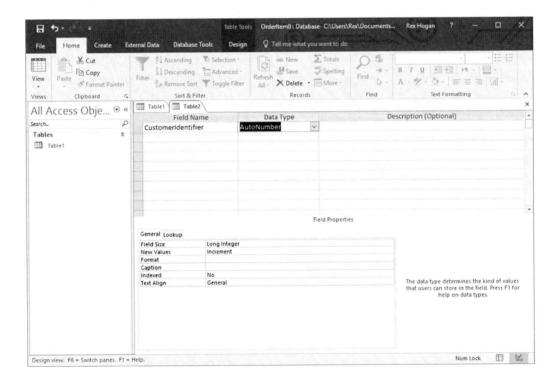

Continue adding column names under "Field Name," entering an appropriate Data Type for each. The design of the Customer table appears as follows.

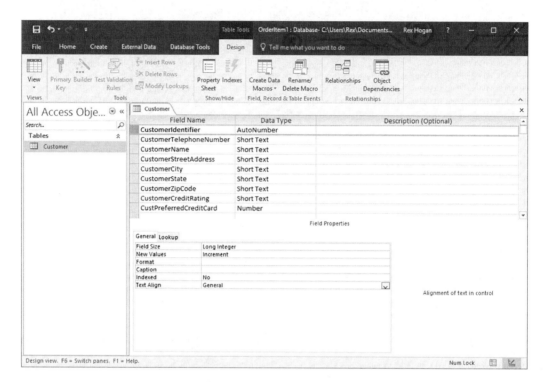

When closing the table's design, you will be prompted to enter the name of the table being saved.

In addition, you will be prompted if you want to have a primary key defined for the table, reply "No."

Finally, edit the table to identify the primary key. Click on the table name, then right click and select "Design View." When the table opens, select the CustomerIdentifier row, right click it, then select the "Primary Key" from the pop-up list. The table can now be saved with that change.

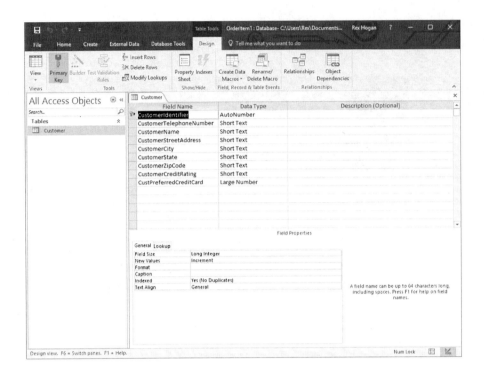

Referring to Figure 3.2, repeat this process to create tables for all items in the diagram. For each column, choose the appropriate data type.

Note that Access does not support varchar data types. If available, varchar data types are much more efficient than a fixed-length implementation. For example, if the string "Wilson Grocery" was stored with a data type of varchar(50), only 14 characters of storage would be needed/used. However, Short Text data types are fixed length. If stored as Short Text with the default of 255 characters, "Wilson Grocery" would use 255 bytes of storage. When using Short Text data types, it is important to change the default length for that column to a lower, more reasonable value. I have changed the length for all of my Short Text columns to 50.

After creating all of the tables shown in the physical data model, the database will look like the following.

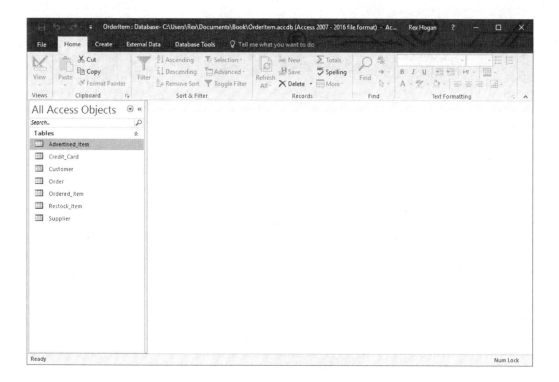

Technically, the database can be used at this moment *as is*. However, to improve processing efficiency and data integrity, we need to implement indexes as well as Referential Integrity constraints.

First, we will modify the database to add the Referential Integrity constraints. Click on the "Database Tools" tab, then choose "Relationships," and the following list will appear.

Selecting all table names in the list and clicking Add produces this display.

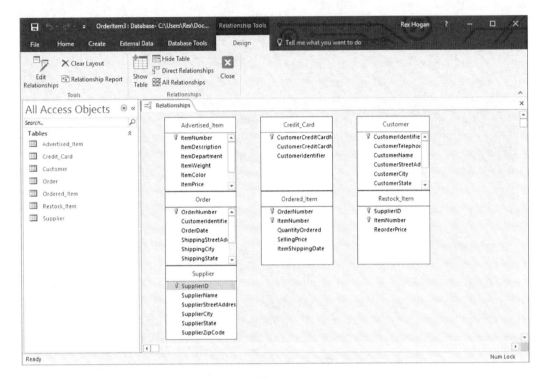

I have rearranged the display of tables in my database to that shown on the next page.

Study the diagram on the next page and confirm that each of these one-to-many relationships exists based on the primary keys as defined.

- Between Customer and CreditCard
- Between Customer and Order
- Between Credit_Card and Order
- Between Order and Ordered_Item
- Between Advertised_Item and Ordered_Item
- Between Advertised_Item and Restock_Item
- Between Supplier and Restock_Item

We are now ready to define the one-to-many relationships shown in Figure 3.2. In this instance, it is simple; we simply ask "does the key for a given table appear within another table?" Whenever that relationship is found, a Referential Integrity relationship must be created. We therefore need Referential Integrity constraints

- Between Customer and CreditCard
- Between Customer and Order
- Between Credit_Card and Order
- Between Order and Ordered_Item
- Between Advertised_Item and Ordered_Item
- Between Advertised_Item and Restock_Item
- Between Supplier and Restock_Item

To create Referential Integrity between Customer and Credit_Card

- Click on the Customer table and select CustomerIdentifier
- Select Customer's CustomerIdentifier, hold the left mouse button down, and drag the arrow to CustomerIdentifier in Credit_Card. Releasing the mouse produces this display:

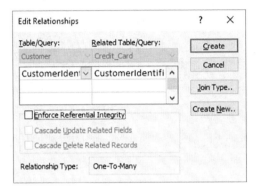

Verify the table and column names selected for the one-to-many relationship, then click the box to "Enforce Referential Integrity" as well as the two cascade options when they appear. Clicking "Create" activates Referential Integrity between Customer and Credit_Card as indicated by the line shown in the following.

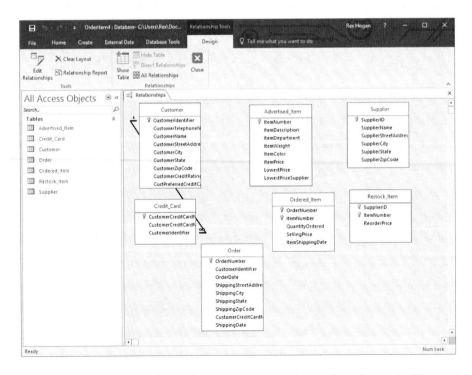

Now repeat that process for each one-to-many relationship shown in Figure 3.2 and compare your results to the following:

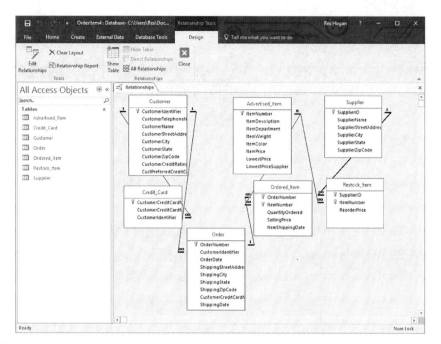

The last remaining task is to create indexes where needed.

- Note that Access has already specified that each table's key column(s) will be indexed.

- For each one-to-many relationship, we want an index on each column serving as a *foreign key* (i.e., those that are keys in another table).

   For example, we want an index in Credit_Card's CustomerIdentifier column. To create that index, open Credit_Card in "Design" view.

Note at the bottom of the display that CustomerIdentifier is not indexed. Change that option to "Yes" and close and save that view.

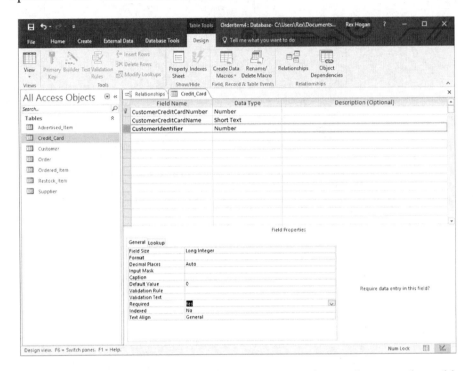

Now make those changes for all columns serving as foreign keys to other tables.

We also need indexes to support significant retrieval for tables using other than the table's key or foreign key column(s).

For example, if we found that we frequently needed to retrieve Customer information using only the customer's telephone number, we can create an index on that column. As we are using a relational database management system (RDBMS), this change can be made at any time, while the database is online or in use.

Indexes are one of the primary solutions to performance problems as they are discovered in application development and testing. Remember that most RDBMSs have monitoring and tuning tools that can help discover issues as testing progresses.

Now let us look at how to implement the physical data model using SQL Server.

3.5.2 Using SQL Server*

- Create a new database

Use the SQL Server Management Studio to create and manage all databases on this system.

---

* Note that the installation instructions for SQL Server are included in Chapter 7.

From the Windows "All Programs" "Start" icon, navigate to the Microsoft SQL Server folder created for this software installation and choose SQL Server Management Studio. Optionally, type "sql server" in the search window and select "Sql Server Management Studio."

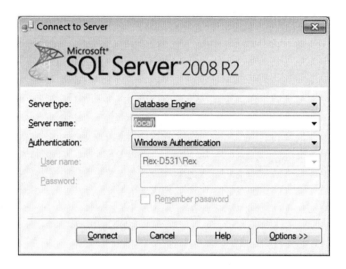

After verifying the log on information is using a Windows account that was authorized as an SQL Server administrator, click "Connect" to log on.

You will be presented with a menu displaying the different types of services available.

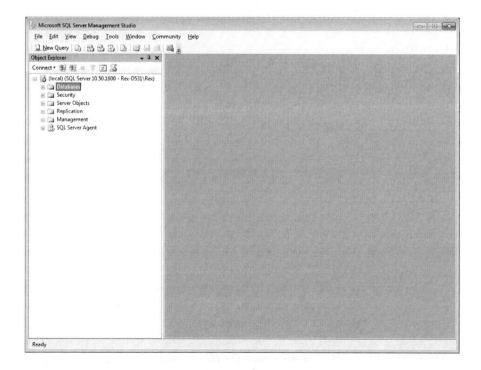

Put the cursor on "Databases," right click and select "New Database." You will then be presented with the following screen showing details of installation options.

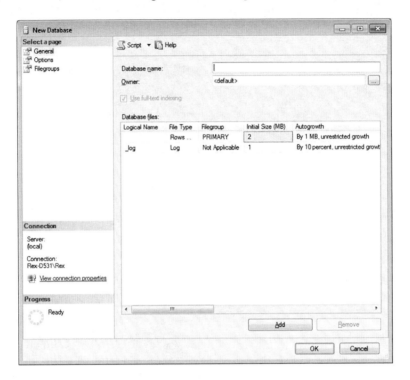

Enter the name of the new database in the "Database Name" block.

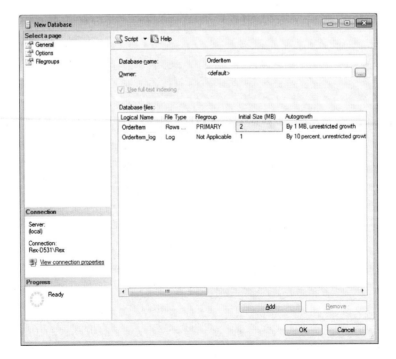

Next, use the scroll bar at the bottom of this window to move to the right to show where the database will be installed.

Change the default configuration details as appropriate.

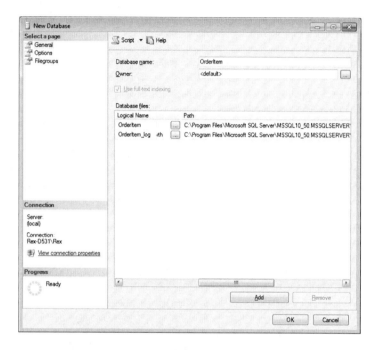

Double click on "Databases" and again on the name for the database just created.

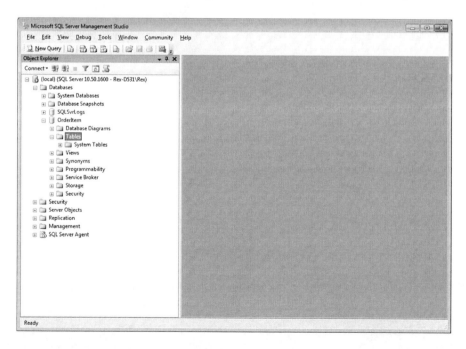

- Create tables

  To create a table in the database, right click on "Tables" and select "New Table" to open a window to define columns for that new table (in this example, the Customer table).

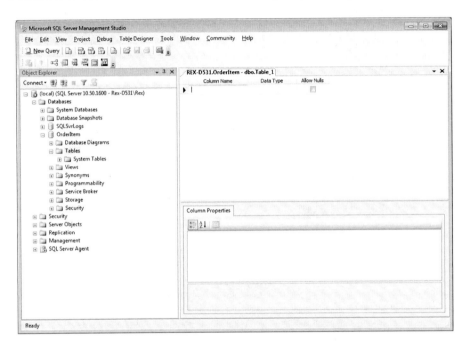

Referring to the physical data model, enter the name of the first column in Customer with an appropriate data type.

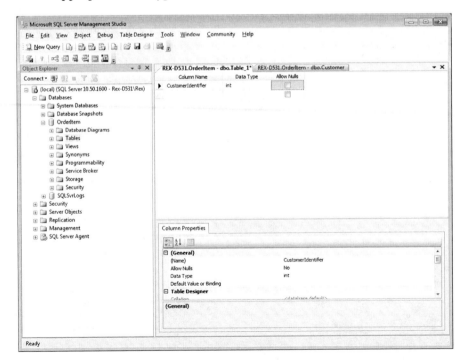

Click on the next row under Column Name to enter the next column and data type. Continue adding columns for Customer until all columns have been entered.

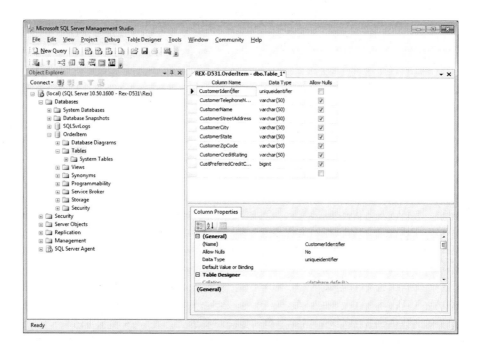

After all columns have been defined, modify the design to show the column(s) that define the table key. In this case, put the cursor on the box to the left of CustomerIdentifier, then right click and choose "Set Primary Key."

To save this design, click on the "x" at the top-right part of Table Design window.

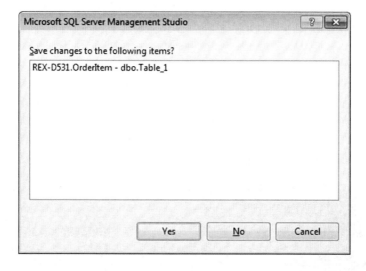

Clicking "Yes" brings up a display where the table name can be entered.

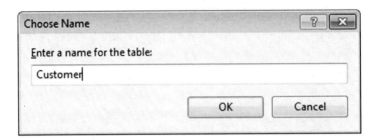

Repeat the above-mentioned sequence to create all tables shown in the physical data model.

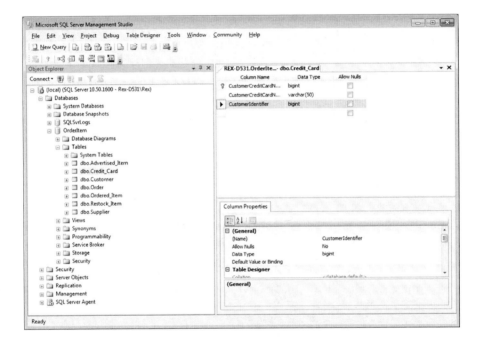

You are now ready to implement Referential Integrity constraints between tables in the database.

• Creating Referential Integrity Constraints

As was done with Microsoft Access, Referential Integrity constraints must now be created for all dependent tables in one-to-many relationships reflected in the physical data model.

Let us start with the relationship between Customer and Credit_Card. To create a Referential Integrity constraint in Credit_Card:

Under Tables, select Credit_Card and then Design to alter its definition.

Next, select the column involved with the one-to-many relationship; in this case, it is the CustomerIdentifer column (the key of Customer) that establishes/enables that relationship.

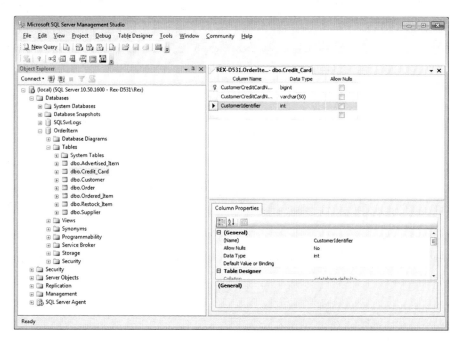

Next, click on the arrow at the left column of CustomerIdentifier, right-click, and select "Relationships" from the pop-up window, which generates the following:

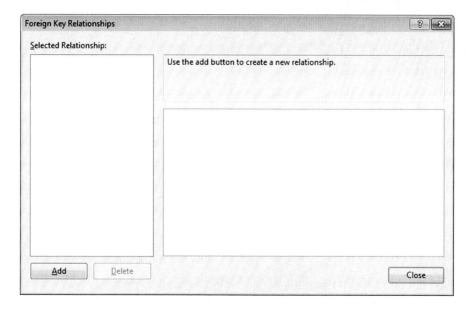

Click "Add" to create a new Referential Integrity Relationship.

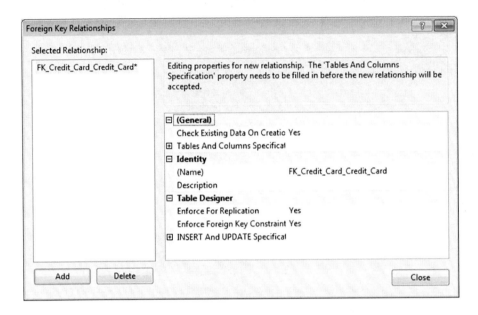

Click on "Tables and Columns Specifications" to open a window where the column relationships are specified.

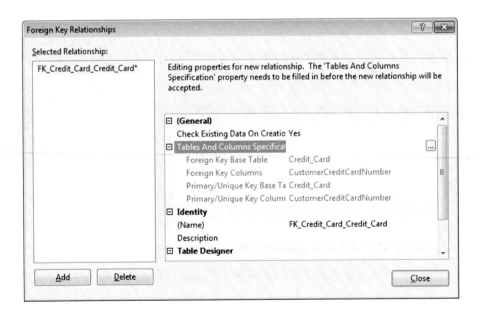

Click the box at the right side of the display containing "…" to open the following:

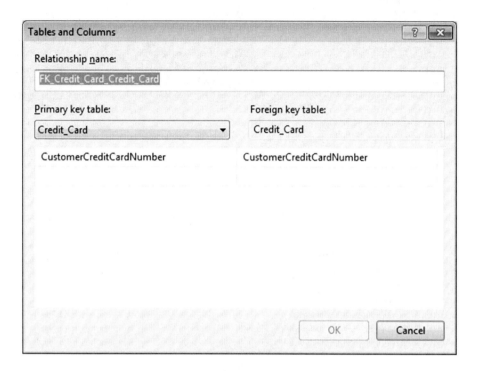

Using the pull-down arrows for "Primary key table," change the Primary key table to "Customer."

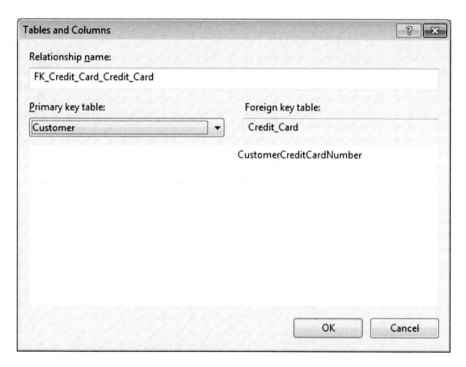

Clicking on the first open row under Customer generates a list of all columns in the Customer table.

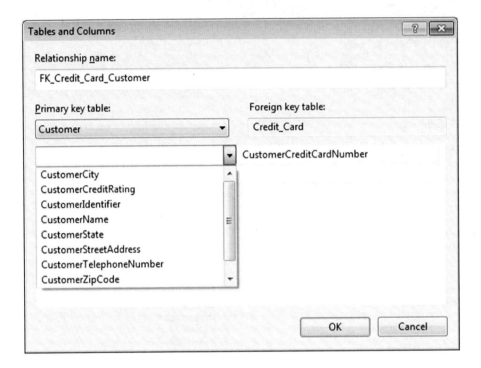

Select CustomerIdentifier to complete the primary key specification for this relationship.

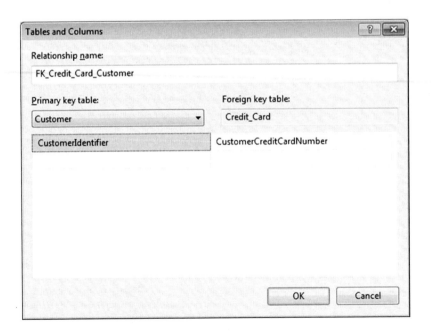

As this relationship is based on the Customer key appearing in the Credit_Card table, click on "CustomerCreditCardNumber" then select the arrow to the right to generate a list of all columns in that table. Select "CustomerIdentifier."

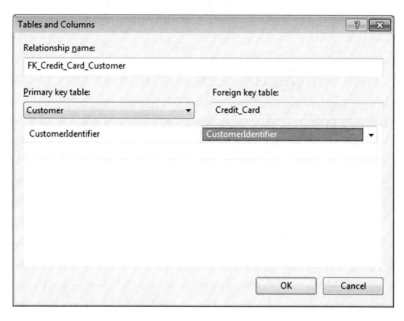

Review all selections and verify the table names and columns match what is shown in the physical design model. Click OK to create that Referential Integrity relationship in the database.

As part of saving these changes, you will be prompted that you want these changes to be saved.

Refer to the physical design model and continue making these adjustments for all tables having foreign key relationships.

When adding each new relationship, make sure the "Relationship name" assigned makes logical sense; each of mine include the name of the Primary key table.

To verify your results, in SQL Server Management Studio, select "Views," right click, and then select "New View." A list of all tables in OrderItem will be displayed. Do a "block select" to select all names displayed and then click "Add." The following display shows all one-to-many relationships currently defined in the database. Rearranging those gives the display shown on the next page.

Creating a View with this complexity does not make sense and is not practical, but the visual display serves as a visual aid to ensure all one-to-many relationships have been created.

After this verification, click on the "x" at the top right of the view display to close it and respond "No" when asked if you want to save the view.

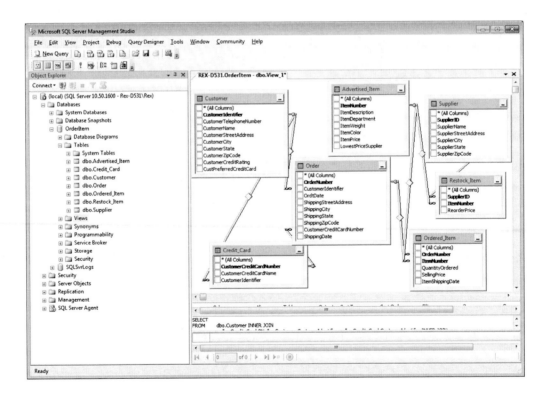

- Additional indexes

We now need to update our tables to create indexes where needed. First, check all tables involved with foreign key relationships to ensure that the column(s) with the foreign key have indexes. For example, in Credit_Card, CustomerIdentifier is a foreign key to Customer; therefore, we want to create an index on the CustomerIdentifier column in Credit_Card.

To create this index, first use SQL Server Studio Manager to navigate to the Credit_Card table and expand the Keys and Index sections as shown in the following.

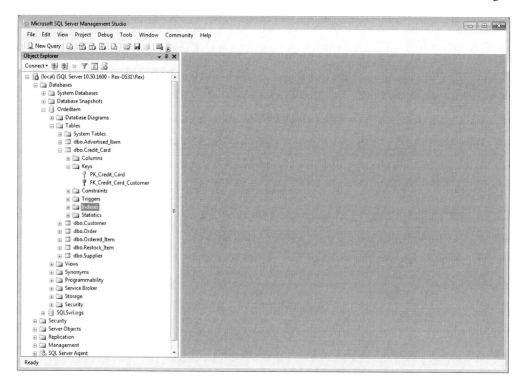

Note the name of the Referential Integrity constraint created earlier. SQL Server gives the user total flexibility for naming objects, but I recommend naming the index based on the name used for the Referential Integrity constraint to make it easier to cross-reference items as the design is completed. In this case, I will use FK_Credit_Card_Customer as the name of the index that will be created.

Next, select Index, right click and select the New Index option.

Enter the name for the new index (FK_Credit_Card_Customer) and complete the remaining items; that is, it will be NonClustered (rows in this table would not be ordered by the CustomerIdentifier) and it will not be unique (the Customer may have many credit cards on file).

Clicking "Add" now brings up a window to pick the column to be indexed.

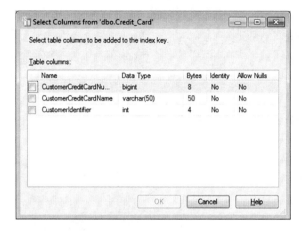

Select CustomerIdentifier as the column to be indexed.

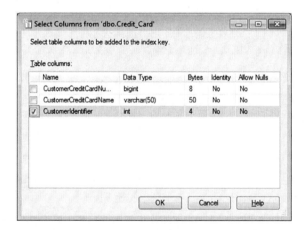

Clicking OK brings up a screen with specifications for the new index.

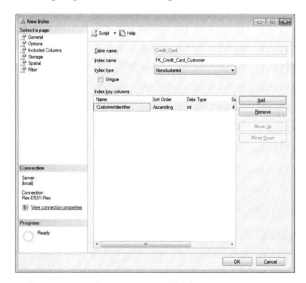

Clicking OK will create the new index.

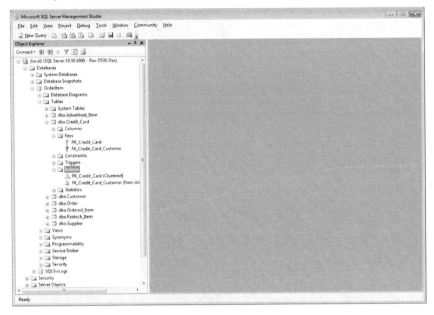

Referring to the physical design model, create new indexes for columns in all tables containing foreign keys.

As a final review for our first-cut physical solution, we need to review the anticipated call patterns for all significant user accesses to determine if any additional indexes are needed. For example, we might want to create an index on the Customer's CustomerTelephoneNumber to support immediate, direct retrieval of the Customer record using their phone number.

Once again, because we are using an RDBMS, indexes can be added or deleted as needed to maintain the highest possible performance for the application system.

3.5.3 Using Oracle

Oracle systems tend by their nature to be large and complex and use rigid change management processes to test and migrate SQL Data Definition Language change packages between development, test, and production environments. Those changes are best managed strictly using scripts to define all involved objects.

Fortunately, Computer Associate's erwin software provides a graphical tool that database administrators can use to create both logical and physical data models. When the model is complete, the database administrator can then generate the Data Definition Language statements needed to create or modify data objects. erwin is covered in detail in Chapter 5.

The next chapter contains a review/exercise in the creation of a 3NF data model for a university environment, as well as the physical design of the resulting tables for that environment using Microsoft Access and SQL Server. Chapters 6 and 7 then go into more detail on how to use Microsoft Access and SQL Server to design and support application systems for reviewing and updating data.

QUESTIONS

1. When creating a database table, what data type would you recommend for the various columns with zip codes? Why?

2. When creating a database table, what data type would you recommend for the various columns with telephone numbers?

3. If the physical data model is to be expanded to include information for individual stores associated with each customer, describe in detail what changes need to be made.

4. As part of the changes made for Question 3, are any changes to Referential Integrity constraints needed? Why or why not?

5. The Supplier table in Figure 3.2 has a minimal amount of information. What columns do you recommend be added?

6. Describe in detail what steps to be taken to add the new columns from Question 5 to the Supplier table. How much down time/maintenance time is required?

7. Using the physical data model in Figure 3.2, describe the sequence of tables to be accessed to show all information regarding a customer order and all items on that order.

8. Are any indexes needed to provide a higher level of performance for Question 7?

9. What must be changed in the physical data model to store information with customer ratings for items purchased from each supplier?

10. Using the Physical Data Model in Figure 3.2, describe the sequence of tables to be accessed in order to show, for an advertised item, the available suppliers for each that have a customer rating of "4" or better.

11. If the query described in Question 10 runs too slowly, what would you do?

12. Using the physical data model in Figure 3.2, for a specific Advertised_Item, describe the sequence of tables to find the Supplier having the lowest price for that item. Are any indexes necessary and why?

13. A database has been created based on the physical data model in Figure 3.2, and we find that we frequently need to find Customer records based on their telephone number. What changes need to be made to provide a higher level of performance?

14. When using Microsoft Access, what steps are necessary to create an Index for a column in a table?

15. When using SQL Server, what steps are necessary to create an Index for a column in a table?

Normalization and Physical Design Exercise

4.1 INTRODUCTION

The normalization process is an essential skill for business analysts participating in a database design project. Without an accurate understanding and definition of what data are needed, the design and implementation team simply cannot do their job.

As normalization will probably be new to most readers, this current chapter will help develop that skill by designing a database for a university. After reviewing data requirements, a third normal form data model will be developed. Physical design issues will also be reviewed, resulting in a physical design model. Implementation issues for these tables will also be reviewed.

4.2 CREATING THE ENTITY/ATTRIBUTE LIST

Let us begin by reviewing some of the information that is needed for a university's database. The subjects needed include

- Entries describing the various schools in the university.

- The departments that exist for each school and, for each, the various curriculums available and their associated degrees.

- Courses offered within each department and, where applicable, course prerequisites.

- Curriculum information must be cross-referenced on the school's website to map job classifications to applicable curriculum(s) available.

- Information for faculty members for each department.

- Information for students currently enrolled, and transcript records for each completed course.

- Finally, for each course, information on assignments for each course as well as grades recorded as they are completed.

Take a few minutes to create an initial list of the entities applicable to the university environment. When finished, compare your list to that shown below.

Entity	General Information
School	The name and description of each school in the university
Department	The name and description for each department within a school
Curriculum	Information about the various degree programs offered with a department
Degree	For each department, information about the various degrees that are offered
Faculty	Information for each faculty member
Course	Information describing what covered for each course
Course prerequisite	Course prerequisite(s) when applicable
Job classification	Job titles in the industry and their relationships to curriculum(s) supported by the university
Student	Information for each student currently enrolled
Student transcript	Grades for completed courses and the credit hours earned
Course offering	Information about the courses currently offered
Assignment	Information about each assignment given for a course

Compare your list to the above.

Next, create an entity/attribute list for this initial list of entities. When ready, compare your results to that shown in Figure 4.1.

There will, of course, be differences, for several reasons.

- The names chosen for entities and attributes will be different.

  This is only to be expected; in fact, each member of a design team would have their own personal interpretation of the data elements needed and what to name them. That is why it is important to work together as a team to develop a common set of terms as well as an explicit definition for each.

  And, of course, the documentation needs to be maintained as a reference for team members. Although this *could* be done by thinking of each entity as a table and documenting the details using the relational database management system to be used, this is problematic; it is too early to be making physical design decisions. The entity/attribute lists represent only *hypothetical* table definitions. It is much better to use a data modeling tool such as erwin (reviewed in Chapter 5) to document logical data structures as they develop, then modifying them as needed as the physical design decisions are made.

- Figure 4.1 results include some intentional issues as discussion items for the normalization exercise.

Attribute	Description
School	
SchoolID	A unique identifier for each School
SchoolName	The name of the School
SchoolDescription	A description for the scope of subjects offered by the School
SchoolCampusLocation	The campus address for the Dean's office
SchoolDeanID	The FacultyID for the Dean
Department	
DepartmentID	A unique identifier for the Department
DepartmentName	The name of the Department
DepartmentHeadID	The FacultyID for the Department head
DeptCampusLocation	
Degree	
DegreeID	A unique identifier for the Degree
DegreeName	The name of the Degree
Course	
CourseID	A unique identifier for the Course
CourseName	The name of the Course
CreditHours	The number of credit hours associated with the Course
CourseDescription	A general description for the subjects covered in the Course
CoursePrerequisite	
CourseID	A unique identifier for the Course with a prerequisite
PrerequisiteCseID	The CourseID for the prerequisite
CourseOffering	
CourseID	The course identifier associated with this class offering
SectionID	The section number associated with this class offering
FacultyID	The Faculty member teaching this class offering
Location	The building and room number where the class meets
ClassSchedule	The day(s) and time the class meets
StudentID	The Students enrolled in this class offering
Faculty	
FacultyID	A unique identifier for a Faculty member
DepartmentID	The Department to which the Faculty member is assigned
FacultyPrefix	The title associated with the Faculty member
FacultyLastName	The last name of the Faculty member
FacultyMiddleName	The middle name of the Faculty member
FacultyFirstName	The first name of the Faculty member
FacultyStreetAddr	The street address of the Faculty member
FacultyCity	The city associated with the Faculty member's mailing address
FacultyState	The state associated with the Faculty member's mailing address
FacultyZipCode	The ZipCode associated with the Faculty member's address

FIGURE 4.1 An initial entity/attribute list.   (*Continued*)

Attribute	Description
Curriculum	
CurriculumID	A unique identifier for the Curriculum
CurriculumName	The name for the Curriculum
DegreeID	The unique identifier for the Degree associated with this Curriculum
CurriculumDescription	A description of the scope of subjects associated with the Curriculum
CourseID	The Course numbers associated with this Curriculum
Job Classification	
ClassificationID	A unique identifier for this Job classification
ClassificationName	The name commonly used for jobs with this classification
ClassificationDescription	A description of the type of work associated with this job
CurriculumID	The unique identifiers for Curriculums related to this job
Student	
StudentID	A unique identifier for each student
DepartmentID	The Department identifier associated with a student
StudentLastName	The last name of the Student
StudentMiddleName	The middle name of the Student
StudentFirstName	The first name of the Student
StudentTelephoneNumber	The contact phone number for the Student
StudentStreetAddr	The street address for this Student
StudentCity	The city associated with the Student's mailing address
StudentState	The state associated with the Student's mailing address
StudentZipCode	The zip code associated with the Student's mailing address
ClassLevel	The current class level for the Student (e.g., Freshman)
Student Transcript	
StudentID	The Student identifier associated with this transcript grade
CourseID	The Course number associated with this transcript grade
Grade	The grade recorded for this Student and Course
DateCompleted	The date this grade was reported
CreditHoursEarned	The number of credit hours earned upon course completion
Assignment	
CourseID	The Course identifier associated with this Assignment
SectionID	The Section number associated with these class assignments
AssignmentNo	A unique sequential number assigned to each Assignment
AssignmentDescription	A description of the work to be done to complete the assignment
AssignmentGrade	The Student grades reported for each completed Assignment

FIGURE 4.1 (Continued)   An initial entity/attribute list.

4.3 MOVING TO THIRD NORMAL FORM

As the first step in normalization, review Figure 4.1 to identify changes needed to move to first normal form. If you recall, each entity must have a unique identifier, and there can be no repeating groups. Compare your results to Figure 4.2.

Attribute	Description
School	
*SchoolID	A unique identifier for each School
SchoolName	The name of the School
SchoolDescription	A description for the scope of subjects offered by the School
SchoolCampusLocation	The campus address for the Dean's office
SchoolDeanID	The FacultyID for the Dean
Department	
*DepartmentID	A unique identifier for the Department
DepartmentName	The name of the Department
DepartmentHeadID	The FacultyID for the Department head
DeptCampusLocation	The campus address for the Department
Degree	
*DegreeID	A unique identifier for the Degree
DegreeName	The name of the Degree
Course	
*CourseID	A unique identifier for the Course
CourseName	The name of the Course
CreditHours	The number of credit hours associated with the Course
CourseDescription	A general description for the subjects covered in the Course
CoursePrerequisite	
*CourseID	A unique identifier for the Course with a prerequisite
*PrerequisiteCseID	The CourseID for the prerequisite
CourseOffering	
*CourseID	The course identifier associated with this class offering
*SectionID	The section number associated with this class offering
FacultyID	The Faculty member teaching this class offering
Location	The building and room number where the class meets
ClassSchedule	The day(s) and time the class meets
StudentID	The Students enrolled in this class offering
Faculty	
*FacultyID	A unique identifier for a Faculty member
DepartmentID	The Department to which the Faculty member is assigned
FacultyPrefix	The title associated with the Faculty member
FacultyLastName	The last name of the Faculty member
FacultyMiddleName	The middle name of the Faculty member
FacultyFirstName	The first name of the Faculty member
FacultyStreetAddr	The street address of the Faculty member
FacultyCity	The city associated with the Faculty member's mailing address
FacultyState	The state associated with the Faculty member's mailing address
FacultyZipCode	The ZipCode associated with the Faculty member's address

FIGURE 4.2   The revised entity/attribute list. (Continued)

Attribute	Description
Curriculum	
*CurriculumID	A unique identifier for the Curriculum
CurriculumName	The name for the Curriculum
DegreeID	The unique identifier for the Degree associated with this Curriculum
CurriculumDescription	A description of the scope of subjects associated with the Curriculum
CourseID	The Course numbers associated with this Curriculum
Job Classification	
*ClassificationID	A unique identifier for this Job classification
ClassificationName	The name commonly used for jobs with this classification
ClassificationDescription	A description of the type of work associated with this job
CurriculumID	The unique identifiers for Curriculums related to this job
Student	
*StudentID	A unique identifier for each student
DepartmentID	The Department identifier associated with a student
StudentLastName	The last name of the Student
StudentMiddleName	The middle name of the Student
StudentFirstName	The first name of the Student
StudentTelephoneNumber	The contact phone number for the Student
StudentStreetAddr	The street address for this Student
StudentCity	The city associated with the Student's mailing address
StudentState	The state associated with the Student's mailing address
StudentZipCode	The zip code associated with the Student's mailing address
ClassLevel	The current class level for the Student (e.g., Freshman)
Student Transcript	
*StudentID	The Student identifier associated with this transcript grade
*CourseID	The Course number associated with this transcript grade
Grade	The grade recorded for this Student and Course
DateCompleted	The date this grade was reported
CreditHoursEarned	The number of credit hours earned upon course completion
Assignment	
*CourseID	The Course identifier associated with this Assignment
*SectionID	The Section number associated with these class assignments
*AssignmentNo	A unique sequential number assigned to each Assignment
AssignmentDescription	A description of the work to be done to complete the assignment
AssignmentGrade	The Student grades reported for each completed Assignment

FIGURE 4.2 (Continued)   The revised entity/attribute list.

In reviewing the above, note the following:

- An "*" denotes unique identifiers for each entity.

- Attributes shown in bold italics are *repeating groups*, that is, when associated with this entity, this value has more than one value.

Unique identifiers: In creating the information in Figure 4.1, unique identifiers were included and were simply flagged with an "*." Of course, for some entities, more than one attribute must be used to identify a unique occurrence of the entity.

Repeating groups: For each attribute that has more than one value, it must be removed and placed *where it belongs*. Next, we must check to see if the relationship between those two attributes is one-to-many or many-to-many. If that relationship is one-to-many, we are OK and simply continue, but if it is many-to-many, we must create a new entity to store the *intersection* data (the attributes common to both).

Let us look at each from Figure 4.2:

- StudentID in CourseOffering

Does StudentID appear where it belongs? (Yes, in Student).

Is the relationship between Student and CourseOffering one-to-many, or many-to-many? (Many-to-many; a student may be enrolled in multiple courses, and each course will have more than one student).

A new entity "Course Enrollment" is needed, along with attributes for a student enrollment:

```
Course Enrollment
  *CourseID
  *StudentID
  EnrollmentStatus
  DateEnrolled
  MidTermGrade
  FinalGrade
```

- CourseID in Curriculum

Does CourseID appear where it belongs? (Yes, in Course).

Is the relationship between Course and Curriculum one-to-many or many-to-many? (Many-to-many; a Course will be relevant to multiple Curriculums, and any Curriculum will be associated with multiple courses).

A new "Course Curriculum" entity is required along with relevant attributes:

```
Course Curriculum
  *CurriculumID
  *CourseID
  Opt-MandatoryFlag
  CurriculumCseInfo
```

- CurriculumID in "Job Classification"

  Does CurriculumID appear where it belongs? (Yes, in Curriculum).

  Is the relationship between Curriculum one-to-many or many-to-many? (Many-to-many; any particular job/job classification may be associated with more than one curriculum, and a curriculum will be associated with many jobs/job classifications).

  A new "Curriculum Job Classification" is needed, along with descriptive information about how they are associated.

  ```
  Curriculum Job Classification
    *CurriculumID
    *ClassificationID
    Job Relationship
  ```

- AssignmentGrade in Assignment

  Is AssignmentGrade where it belongs? (No, we need a new entity "Student Grade.")

  ```
  Student Grade
    *CourseID
    *SectionID
    *StudentID
    *AssignmentID
    AssignmentGrade
    DateGraded
  ```

  Is the relationship between "Student Grade" and "Assignment" one-to-many or many-to-many? (One-to-many; as defined earlier, an Assignment will have multiple grades (one for each student), but a "Student Grade" is associated with one Assignment).

With these adjustments, we have moved to a first normal form for the data model as shown in Figure 4.3.

Attribute	Description
School	
*SchoolID	A unique identifier for each School
SchoolName	The name of the School
SchoolDescription	A description for the scope of subjects offered by the School
SchoolCampusLocation	The campus address for the Dean's office
SchoolDeanID	The FacultyID for the Dean
Department	
*DepartmentID	A unique identifier for the Department
DepartmentName	The name of the Department

FIGURE 4.3   The first normal form entity/attribute list.   (*Continued*)

Attribute	Description
DepartmentHeadID	The FacultyID for the Department head
DeptCampusLocation	
Degree	
*DegreeID	A unique identifier for the Degree
DegreeName	The name of the Degree
Course	
*CourseID	A unique identifier for the Course
CourseName	The name of the Course
CreditHours	The number of credit hours associated with the Course
CourseDescription	A general description for the subjects covered in the Course
CoursePrerequisite	
*CourseID	A unique identifier for the Course with a prerequisite
*PrerequisiteCseID	The CourseID for the prerequisite
CourseOffering	
*CourseID	The course identifier associated with this class offering
*SectionID	The section number associated with this class offering
FacultyID	The Faculty member teaching this class offering
Location	The building and room number where the class meets
ClassSchedule	The day(s) and time the class meets
Faculty	
*FacultyID	A unique identifier for a Faculty member
DepartmentID	The Department to which the Faculty member is assigned
FacultyPrefix	The title associated with the Faculty member
FacultyLastName	The last name of the Faculty member
FacultyMiddleName	The middle name of the Faculty member
FacultyFirstName	The first name of the Faculty member
FacultyStreetAddr	The street address of the Faculty member
FacultyCity	The city associated with the Faculty member's mailing address
FacultyState	The state associated with the Faculty member's mailing address
FacultyZipCode	The ZipCode associated with the Faculty member's address
Curriculum	
*CurriculumID	A unique identifier for the Curriculum
CurriculumName	The name for the Curriculum
DegreeID	The unique identifier for the Degree associated with this Curriculum
CurriculumDescription	A description of the scope of subjects associated with the Curriculum
Job Classification	
*ClassificationID	A unique identifier for this Job classification
ClassificationName	The name commonly used for jobs with this classification
ClassificationDescription	A description of the type of work associated with this job
Student	
*StudentID	A unique identifier for each student
DepartmentID	The Department identifier associated with a student
StudentLastName	The last name of the Student

FIGURE 4.3 (Continued)   The first normal form entity/attribute list.

Attribute	Description
StudentMiddleName	The middle name of the Student
StudentFirstName	The first name of the Student
StudentTelephoneNumber	The contact phone number for the Student
StudentStreetAddr	The street address for this Student
StudentCity	The city associated with the Student's mailing address
StudentState	The state associated with the Student's mailing address
StudentZipCode	The zip code associated with the Student's mailing address
ClassLevel	The current class level for the Student (e.g., Freshman)
Student Transcript	
*StudentID	The Student identifier associated with this transcript grade
*CourseID	The Course number associated with this transcript grade
Grade	The grade recorded for this Student and Course
DateCompleted	The date this grade was reported
CreditHoursEarned	The number of credit hours earned upon course completion
Assignment	
*CourseID	The Course identifier associated with this Assignment
*SectionID	The Section number associated with these class assignments
*AssignmentNo	A unique sequential number assigned to each Assignment
AssignmentDescription	A description of the work to be done to complete the assignment
Course Enrollment	
*CourseID	The Course identifier for this enrollment record
*StudentID	The Student identifier for this enrollment record
EnrollmentStatus	A label giving the student's enrollment status in this course
DateEnrolled	The date the student enrolled in this course
MidTermGrade	The student's mid-term grade for this course
FinalGrade	The final grade given for this student in this course
Curriculum Course	
*CurriculumID	The Curriculum identifier associated with this course
*CourseID	The Course identifier for this course
Opt-MandatoryFlag	An Optional/Mandatory flag for this Course/Curriculum relationship
CurriculumCseInfo	Descriptive information on how this course is associated with this Curriculum
Curriculum Job Classification	
*CurriculumID	The Curriculum identifier for this Job relationship
*ClassificationID	The Classification identifier for this Curriculum relationship
Job Relationship	Descriptive information about how this job title maps to this Curriculum
Student Grade	
*CourseID	The Course identifier for this course/student/assignment
*SectionID	The Section identifier for this course/student/assignment
*StudentID	The Student identifier for this course/student/assignment
*AssignmentID	The Assignment number for this course/student/assignment
Assignment Grade	The grade given for this student/assignment
DateGraded	The date the grade was given

FIGURE 4.3 (Continued) The first normal form entity/attribute list.

Now that the data model is in first normal form, let us use this information to draw the data model and verify that it makes sense. Refer to Figure 4.3 and use this information to draw all one-to-many relationships in the data model. Be careful and only draw arrows when the key of one entity is embedded within another.

When you are finished, compare your results to that shown in Figure 4.4.

After drawing the logical data model, review the diagram to see if all one-to-many relationships are shown and that they make sense. Do you see any issues in the above-mentioned diagram?

There should be a one-to-many arrow between Department and Course, but it is not shown above because at this moment, the key of Department (DepartmentID) does not exist within Course.

> In my initial entity/attribute list, I (deliberately) neglected to add the DepartmentID attribute to the Course entity.
>
> In drawing the above-mentioned diagram, the design team should recognize that there should be a one-to-many arrow between these two entities, but that relationship is not supported by the current entity/attribute definitions. This is easy to resolve; just add the DepartmentID attribute to the Course entity and add the one-to-many arrow between Department and Course.

When drawing the logical data model, do not just draw one-to-many arrows where they intuitively belong. Draw them only where/when supported by the entity/attribute list, check the diagram for errors/omissions, and adjust the entity/attribute list and diagram accordingly.

Figure 4.5 shows a corrected logical data model based on the first normal form entity/attribute list.

Now let us continue with the Normalization process.

Let us review the requirement for second normal form. As stated in Chapter 2:

> For second normal form, each non-key attribute must depend on the key and all parts of the key.

Take a minute to review Figure 4.5 and see what, if any, changes need to be made for the data model to be in second normal form.

No changes are necessary; the data model is in second normal form.

Next, the requirement for third normal form is: "A non-key attribute must not depend on any other non-key attribute."

Review the data model once more to see if any changes are necessary for third normal form.

Once again, no changes are necessary for third normal form.

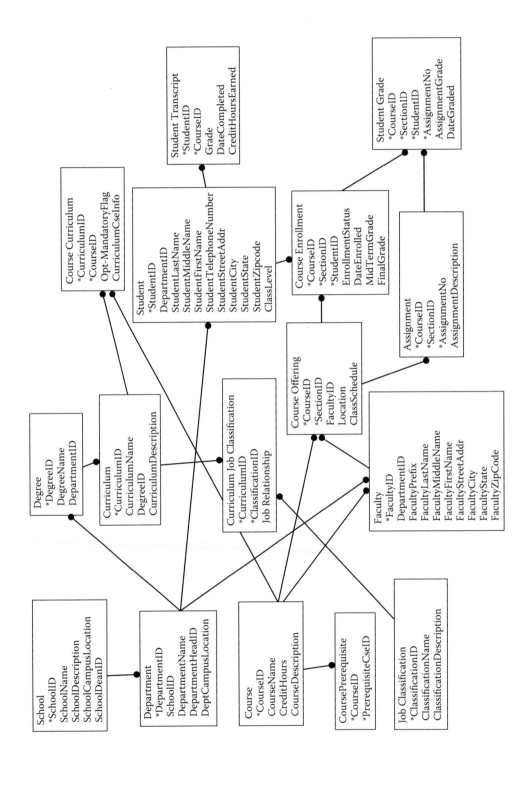

FIGURE 4.4 The logical data model (based on Figure 4.3).

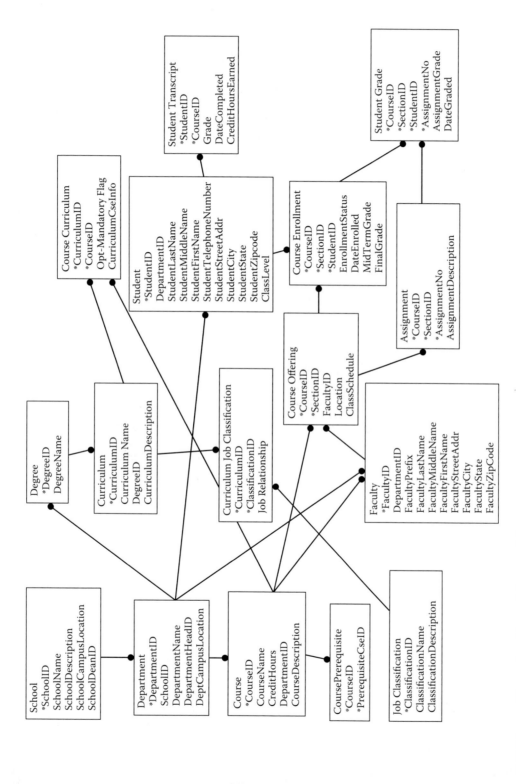

FIGURE 4.5   The updated logical data model.

4.4 THE PHYSICAL DATA MODEL

The data model developed earlier gives us a *clean* data model that could be implemented *as is*; we need to review how the data will be used before making physical design decisions.

With our university data model, most data elements are rather static. The most active area involves inserting new Student Grade entries for each assignment, and in viewing grades that have been posted. One approach would involve de-normalizing that entity and creating a table that has one column for each week's assignment. The following structure shows the table design for Student Grade for a 16-week semester.

```
Student Grade
  *CourseID
  *SectionID
  *StudentID
  Assignment1
  Assignment2
  Assignment3
  Assignment4
  Assignment5
  ...
  Assignment16
```

This implementation drastically reduces I/Os for inserting new grades and searching for grades.

After making this change, the initial physical design model is given in Figure 4.6.

Note, however, the one-to-one relationship between Course Enrollment and Student Grade. Why?

- The key of Course Enrollment appears within Student Grade.

- The key of Student Grade appears within Course Enrollment.

A one-to-one relationship should always raise a *warning flag*. If the two entities have identical keys, then why not combine all attributes into one entity?

There may be times when having two separate entities makes sense. For example, the two entities may be populated at different points in time. Having two separate entities may then make sense, using one to store active/current information and the second to store older, historic data.

In this case, however, I recommend combining Course Enrollment and Student Grade, moving all Student Grade attributes into Course Enrollment. The physical data model reflecting this change is shown in Figure 4.7.

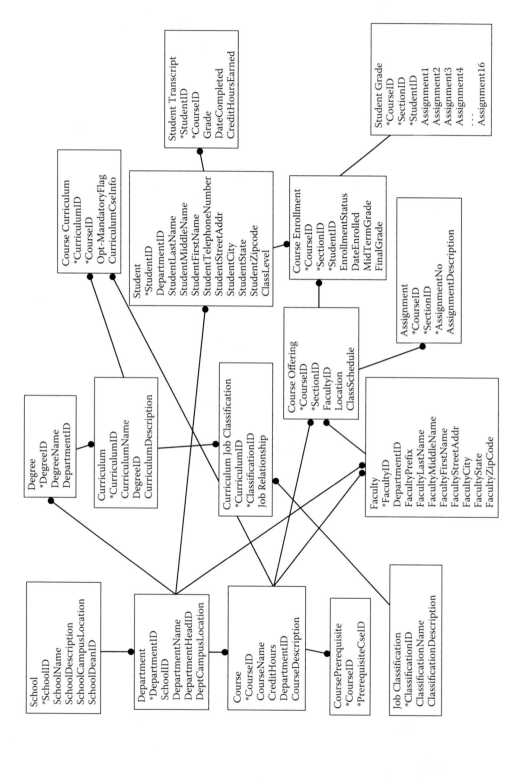

FIGURE 4.6   The initial physical data model.

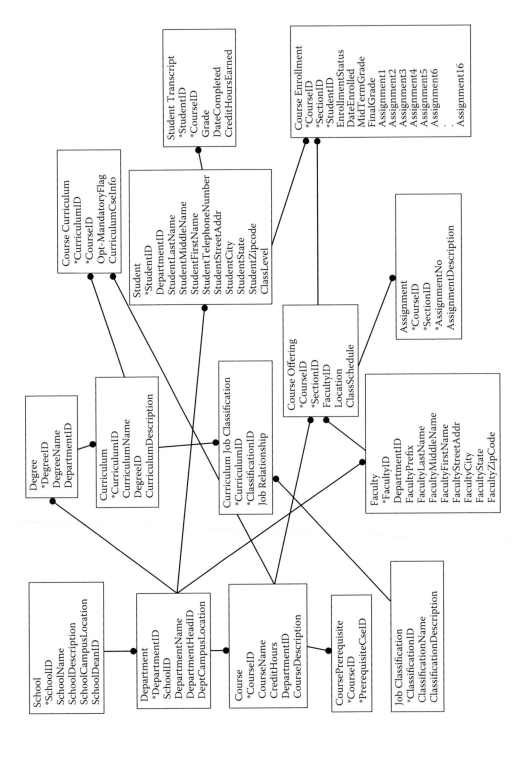

FIGURE 4.7 The physical data model.

When implementing the aforementioned physical data model, we would of course create indexes for columns that are unique identifiers. We would also create indexes on attributes in a table that serve as foreign keys to another table.

If our database implementation supports some sort of clustering of tables (e.g., Oracle Tablespaces), we would want to cluster this information by grouping tables on disk based on projected update activity and storing *like* data together.

School	Course	Student
Department	Course prerequisite	Student transcript
Degree	Course offering	
Curriculum	Course enrollment	
Job classification	Assignment	
Curriculum job classification	Student grade	
Course curriculum		
Faculty		

The normalization process may seem overwhelming at first. The good news is that it is really just *applied common sense*; entities are created for each unique object in the scope of the design, and attributes are associated with the entity it describes. With a little practice, normalization will become second nature, and new data models will need minimal adjustments to get to third normal form.

The next chapter reviews how the erwin data modeling tool can be used to create logical data models which, in turn, are used as input to physical data models.

QUESTIONS

1. Explain the difference between a Logical Data Model and a Physical Data Model.

2. When does a one-to-many relationship exist between two entities?

3. Can a Logical Data Model contain a many-to-many relationship? Why/why not?

4. Is a one-to-one relationship valid? Why/why not?

5. When describing a column in a table, what is the meaning of the Optional or Mandatory setting?

6. What information is considered when moving from a Logical Data Model to a Physical Data Model?

7. What changes would you make to the Physical Data Model to add a telephone number for faculty? Give an example. What Storage format would you use?

8. What changes would you make to the Physical Data Model to add minimal grade requirements for prerequisite courses? Would this be an Optional or Mandatory column?

9. What changes would you make to the Physical Data Model to add email address for students and faculty? What Storage format would you use?

10. What changes would you make to the Physical Data Model to add information on textbooks needed for each course?

11. In Course Curriculum, what storage format would you choose for the Opt-Mandatory column?

12. If this university had multiple campus locations, what changes would you make to the Physical Data Model to store information about faculty positions at each campus location?

13. If this university had multiple campus locations, what changes must be made to the Physical Data Model to track what courses are taught at each location?

14. What changes must be made to the Physical Data Model to store information regarding graduates?

15. Faculty members are optionally appointed as course developers. What changes to the Physical Data Model are necessary to track that information?

The erwin Data Modeling Tool

5.1 WHAT IS A DATA MODELING TOOL?

A data modeling tool is a software tool used by the design team developing a new business system that captures the information requirements for that system, documents the meaning and use of each data element, and supports the creation of the normalized data model for that system.

5.2 WHY DO I NEED A DATA MODELING TOOL?

As described in Chapter 2, designing a new business system involves the documentation, review, and refinement of all data requirements for the new system as the scope and details of that system evolve. A data modeling tool is essential in providing a central data repository for the team's use in reviewing and refining these data elements as the design develops and to support the generation of a normalized data model.

In addition, leading data modeling tools such as erwin[1] can also transform the logical data model into a physical data model. That physical data model would then be changed to reflect design changes resulting from anticipated access paths. Finally, Structured Query Language (SQL) Data Definition Language (DDL) commands can be generated to create tables in a relational database running under SQL Server or Oracle as well as others.

5.3 REVERSE ENGINEERING

One of the more significant features of erwin is that it also can *Reverse Engineer* a database, that is, connect to an existing database, analyze the table and columns it contains, and create a physical design model of that structure. This is a *wonderful* feature to have for a database administrator (DBA) who *inherits* a running system that has minimal, if any, documentation!

Similar to anything else, however, this feature has limitations. erwin will analyze the tables it finds and report on the columns found within each, then create the one-to-many relationships found. If column names within the system being analyzed were chosen wisely, then the physical data model created by erwin will be logically correct and make sense. If, however, the original designers were careless in their choice of names, the resulting physical data model would not make sense.

For example, if the key columns for several tables were all named "SEQUENCE_ NUMBER," the resulting display would show relationships between all of these tables and not make any sense from the business perspective.

When this happens, the confusing/incorrect physical data model is *not* the fault of erwin; rather, it is just the result of the design and naming conventions chosen when the system was first built.

5.4 CHANGE MANAGEMENT

Next, a word on the need for a Change Management process.

Database systems are typically large and require complex web-based user interfaces, as well as logic embedded within stored procedures and triggers in the database. Members of development teams have members with a wide range of skills, each supporting the evolution of a small piece of an intricate infrastructure. The design and implementation of changes for a system upgrade must be carefully managed to simultaneously migrate changes for all components, avoiding surprises and downtime for users when system updates are made.

Complex systems typically require three different types of environments.

- Development environment

  A development environment will be supported by a host computer and its associated disk arrays and database. This is where development team members code and test individual components for components being developed.

  All members of the development team will carefully record and track individual changes to software and interfaces as they are developed. DBAs apply updates using DDL statements and carefully record details of each individual change.

  When the development team has successfully completed testing a set of updates, change packages are prepared to migrate these changes to another environment. For DBAs on the team, their change package will consist of the DDL for all sequential changes made to the development database.

- Test environment

  A test environment will run on another host with its own set of disk arrays and database.

  The purpose of this environment is to test the accuracy and completeness of a change package with changes being migrated. If errors or omissions are found, changes are backed off, and the development team will research and resolve the issues found, preparing a new change package to be applied to the test environment.

  After a change package has been successfully tested, the team can now migrate those changes to the production environment.

- Production environment

  As the name suggests, this is the host environment for the real-time production environment. It of course runs on another host with its own set of disk arrays and database.

  These systems often run 24×7, and some high-availability systems have an acceptable downtime of a few hours per year. Migration testing of changes to a test environment is essential for the smooth migration of a change package to the production environment with no surprises.

DBAs have online graphical user interface tools that give them the capability to make quick and easy changes to tables, stored procedures, and triggers. However, using this type of tool makes it difficult to impossible to track *all* changes, then sequentially apply those changes to another environment.

For this reason, DBAs apply all changes using a sequence of DDL updates, recording each into a master set of changes to be applied when the change package is ready to be applied to another environment.

For licensed users of erwin, my recommendation is to use it to first create the tables in the initial physical data model (or reverse engineer a live system). After creating that initial baseline, manually create DDL change packages for subsequent updates to the database while keeping erwin up to date as changes are applied. Details on how to use erwin for tracking changes are beyond the scope of the current book.

Let us now see how to use erwin to create the logical and physical models for the University data model created in Chapter 4.

5.5 DOWNLOAD AND INSTALL ERWIN TRIAL SOFTWARE

There are two ways to download and install trial versions of the erwin data modeling tool.

- *Demo software trial*: Go to http://erwin.com/resources/software-trials and select "Request Demo"; fill out and submit the form and select "Submit Request." You will be sent a link and instructions on how to download and install a limited version of the software.

- *Academic software trial*: The vendor now supports another version of erwin that can be downloaded and used for one year. This version does, however, require the use of an email account associated with an educational institution.

  Go to http://erwin.com/education/erwin-academic-program/academic-edition and click on "Get erwin Data Modeler Academic Edition." After submitting the requested information, you will receive a link and instructions on how to download and install the trial software.

5.6 CREATE THE UNIVERSITY LOGICAL DATA MODEL

After downloading and installing erwin, use the Start sequence to find the "erwin/erwin Data Modeler" executable and double-click it.

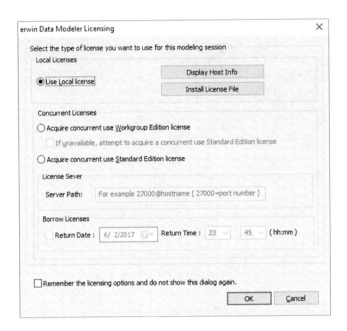

- Click OK to use the locally installed trial license to get this display.

- Next, click the File/New option to get the following:

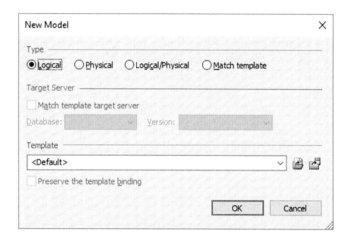

- Leave the Logical option selected and click OK.

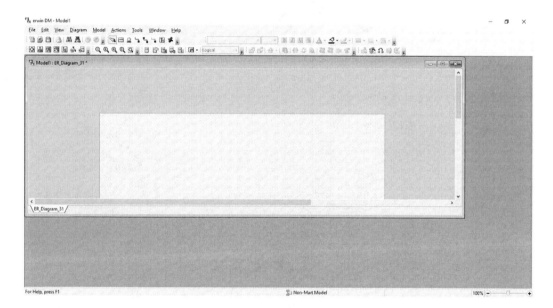

- Next, select the View/Windows/Explorer Pane option.

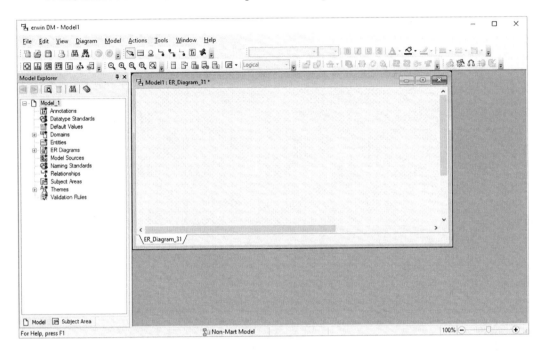

You are now ready to use this display to add the entities and attributes for the University logical data model.

To add new entities, select Entities/New to get the following.

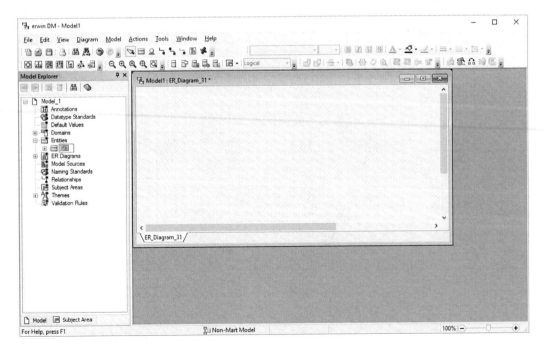

- Under Entities, change "E/1" to the name of the first entity to be defined (in this case, "School").

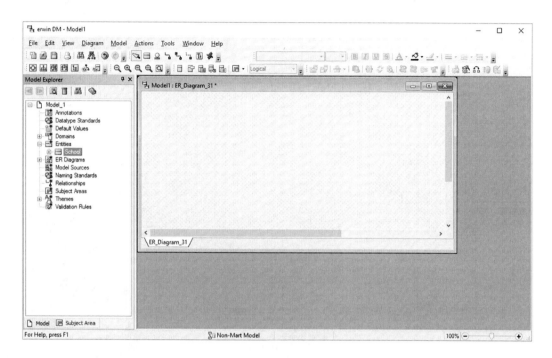

- Next, select School, then right-click and select "Properties."

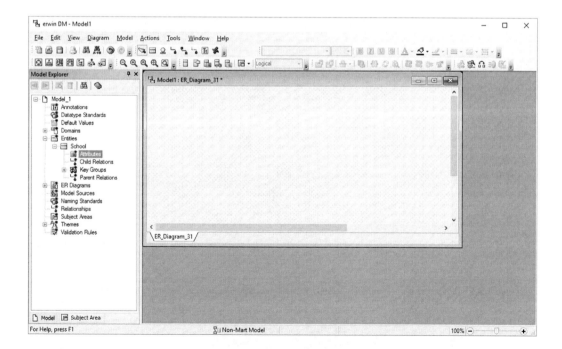

- Use this window to add attributes for School. Start by selecting the Attributes/New option to get the following:

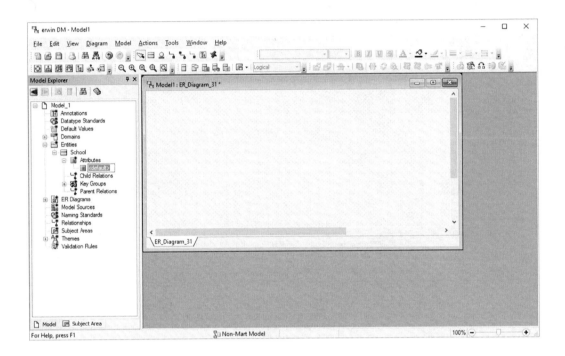

- Change "<default>" to the first attribute to be added, in this case SchoolID.

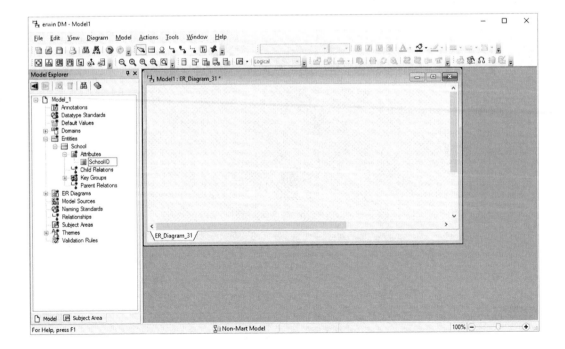

- Optionally, select SchoolID/Properties to open a window where a detailed definition for this attribute can be entered. This becomes the central information repository for the design team.

- Select the Attributes/New sequence to add another attribute.

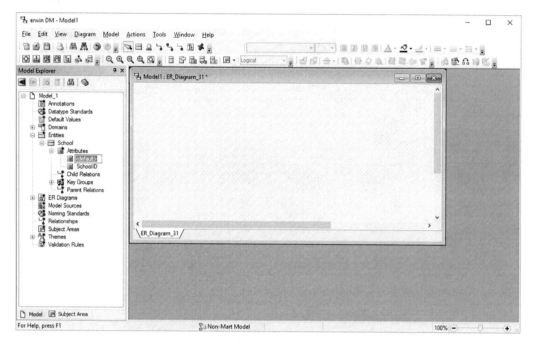

- Change "<default>" to the next attribute being added (in this case, SchoolName).

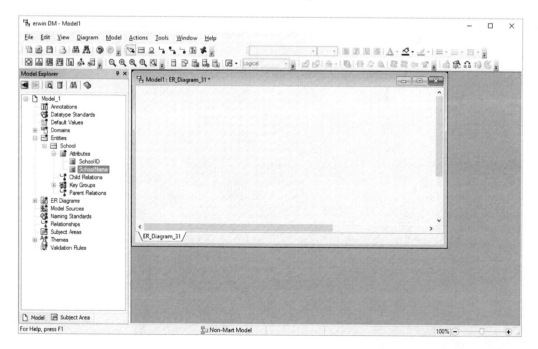

- Repeat this sequence to add the other attributes for the School entity.

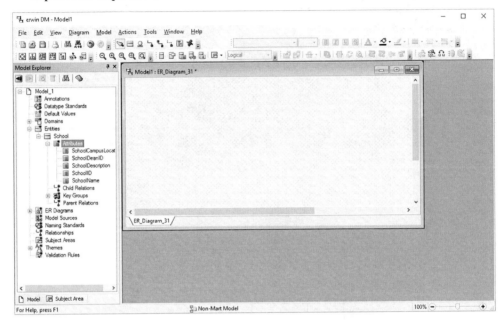

- Let us now set properties for these attributes. Select SchoolID, then Properties to get the following.

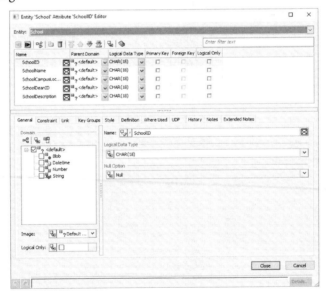

Use this screen to identify the key column for the entity (in this case, SchoolID) and to change the data type to the data type anticipated for the physical design model.

In this case, all were changed to varchar(50), where a value of SchoolID has

- A mixture characters and numbers.
- A maximum length of 50 bytes.

- The varchar option results in a SchoolID value of only 10 bytes to require 10 bytes of physical storage. Using varchar therefore supports flexible yet efficient implementations.

- Continue using this sequence of command to add the other entities and attributes in the University data model.

Note that at any time, the "File/Save As" feature can be used to save the logical data model. The following display shows all of the entities after being created in the logical data model.

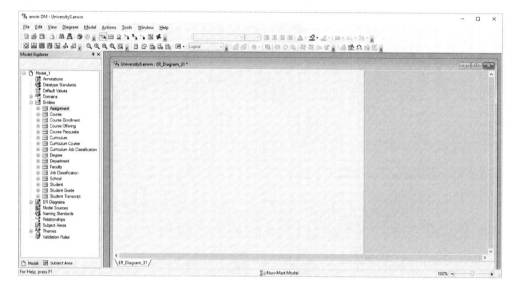

- To create the logical data model diagram, we will now add each entity to the diagram on the right. To add Assignment, select it in the left pane, then select "Add to Diagram."

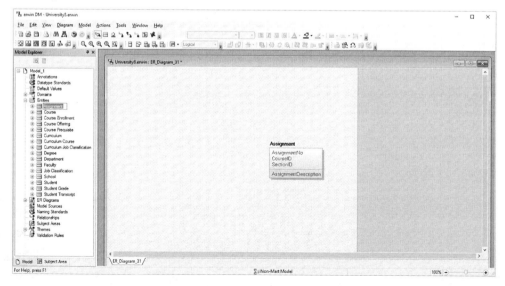

- Note the layout/arrangement of attributes in Assignment. The top section, with AssignmentNo, CourseID, SectionID, identifies the primary key for that entity (in this case, the concatenation of these attributes). The attributes below the line are the non-key attribute(s).

- To add Course to the diagram, first select Course and "Add to Diagram" to get the following:

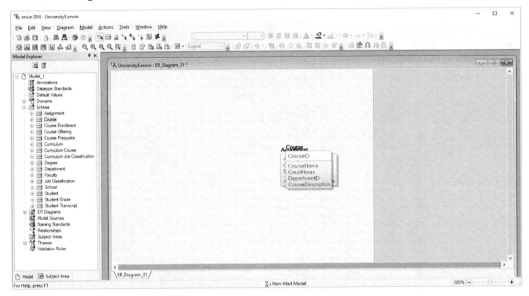

- Note how the CourseID attribute is shown as the primary key.

- When adding entities to the diagram, they will overlay each other as shown earlier. It is best to move each as it is added to make each visible in the diagram, just select an entity in the diagram, and drag it to a new position.

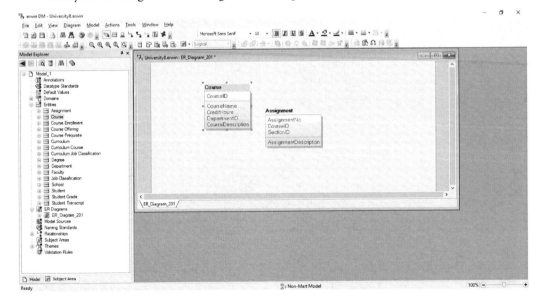

- Continue adding other entities, moving each in the display and arranging them close to associated entities.
- The next display shows the diagram with all entities; the Model Explorer window was closed to free up space in the display.

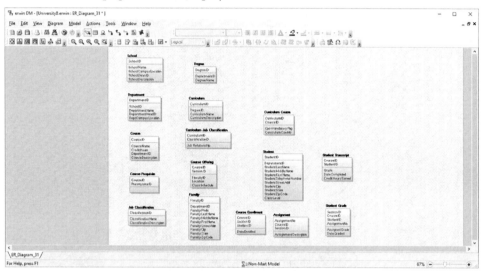

Now let us modify the diagram to add one-to-many relationships.

- To add a relationship between School and Department, first select the one-to-many icon (under the Tools label).
- Click on the key of School (SchoolID), hold the mouse button down, and drag the arrow to SchoolID in Department.
- Check to confirm the arrow drawn connects the SchoolID attribute between School and Department.
- Release the mouse button.

The following screen will be generated.

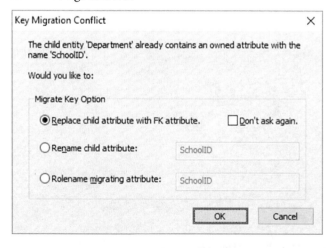

- Click OK to finish defining this relationship.

- In the following diagram, note the one-to-many relationship created between School and Department.

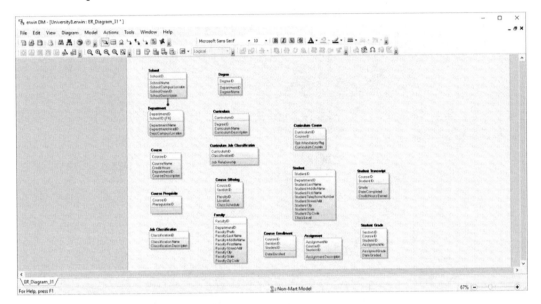

- Note, however, that the primary key for Department was changed to include the foreign key SchoolID. SchoolID is a foreign key but does not need to be part of the primary key.

- To make this change, select the Department entity, right-click, and select Attribute Properties; the following window will open.

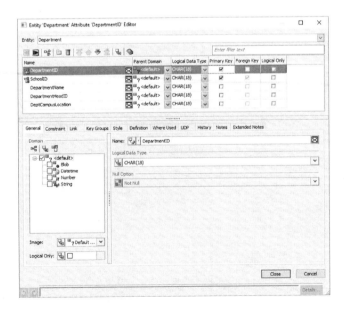

- On the SchoolID row, simply click on the check in the Primary Key column to deselect that specification.

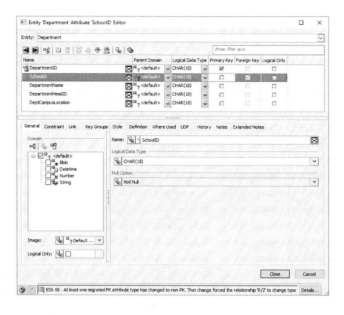

- Closing that window corrects the attribute specifications for Department. Note the change in the following window.

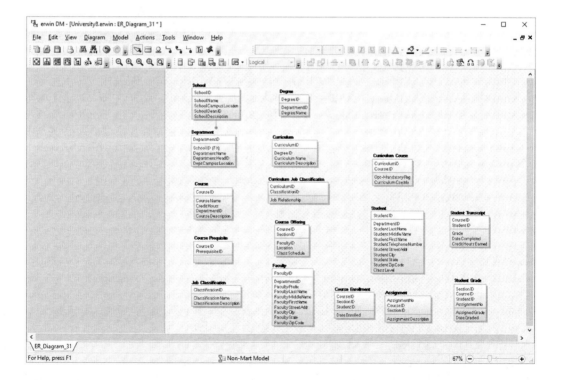

- Continue analyzing the logical diagram, adding all one-to-many relationships reflected in the logical model. When finished, compare your results to the one on the next page.

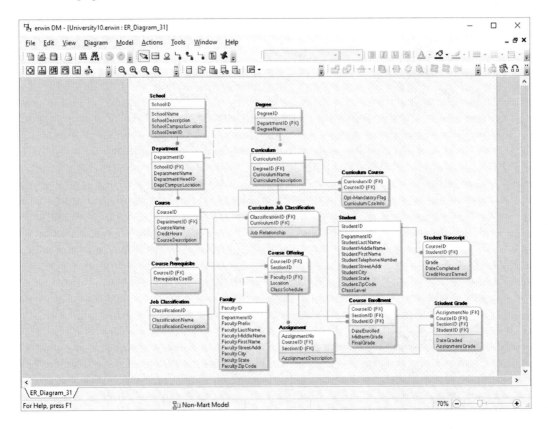

This is the third-normal form logical data model for the University database.

As with any logical model, one-to-many relationships can only exist when the primary key of an entity exists within another entity. In addition, the diagram must *make sense*; if your business sense suggests a one-to-many relationship exists between two entities, the primary key of the first should be added as a foreign key to the second entity.

5.7 CREATE THE UNIVERSITY PHYSICAL DATA MODEL

After completing (and saving) the logical model, it can be used to create a physical data model.

- Move the mouse cursor through the Actions/Design Layers sequence and click on Derive New Model.

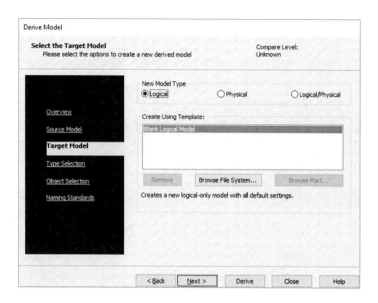

- Next, change the New Model Type to Physical.

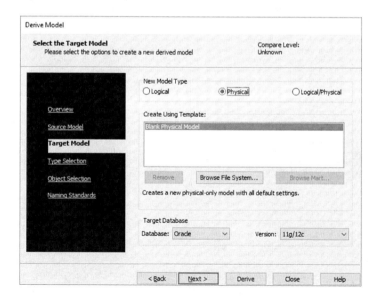

- Under Target Database, use the pull-down to select the type of RDBMS to be used (in this case, SQL Server).

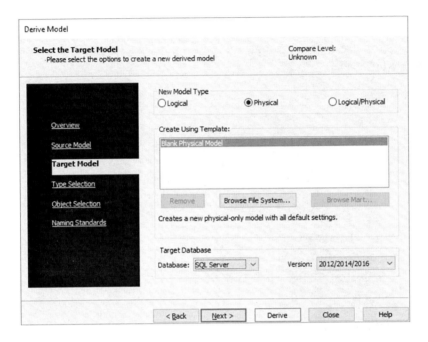

- Clicking Next takes you to a screen to specify how much of the logical model is to be used as input for the conversion.

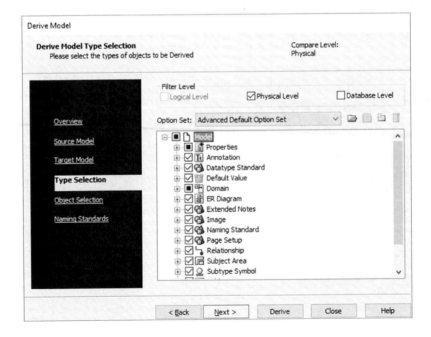

- Clicking Next allows you to specify the objects to be linked in the new model.

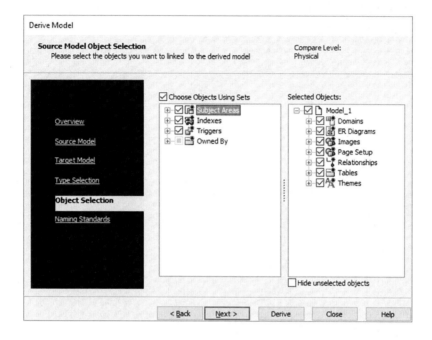

- Clicking Next opens another window with options for Naming Standards.

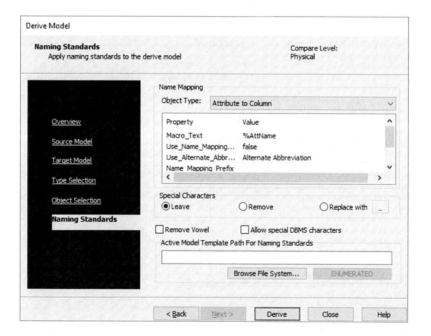

- Click Next to create the physical model.

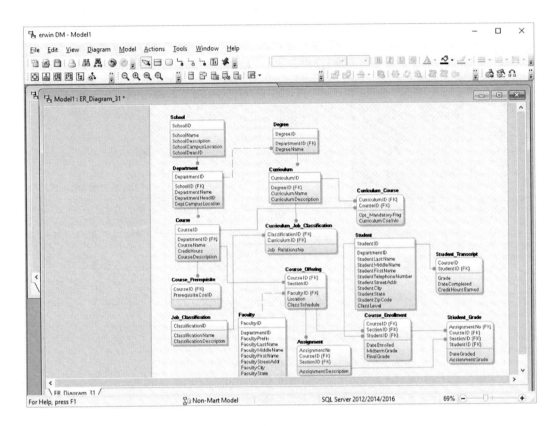

This diagram now represents tables and columns to be created in a new database. This physical model should be saved with an appropriate name.

Before we create physical tables, let us refer to the usage analysis for this model and note the insert activity required when new Student_Grade rows are entered, and the subsequent read activity to retrieve Student_Grade rows for review or updating.

To provide an implementation with a higher level of performance, let us de-normalize the Student_Grade table, removing AssignmentNo while adding a column for each week's grade. This design requires only one row in the table to hold all grades for each student and eliminates the I/O activity when new grades are added. The physical design model now looks that shown on the next page.

Remember that our third-normal form data model was deliberately kept *clean and simple* to give a good foundation for the original physical design. Now, however, we must review usage requirements, anticipate physical accesses to satisfy user requirements, and make changes to the physical design as needed to improve performance of the system.

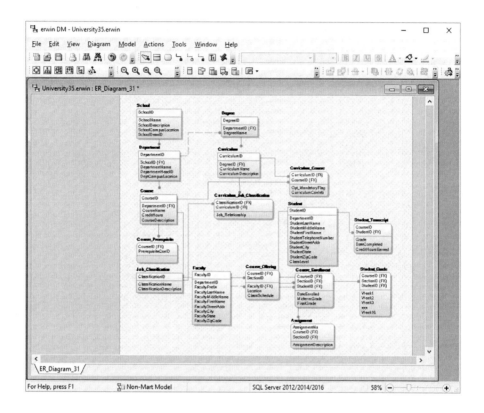

If there are no further changes based on initial performance predictions, we can now use erwin to create DDL statement to create a database containing these columns, attributes, and constraints.

5.8 CREATE AN SQL SERVER UNIVERSITY DATABASE

Finally, to generate DDL for the database:

- Use the cursor to follow the Actions/Forward Engineer menus and select Schema to get this window:

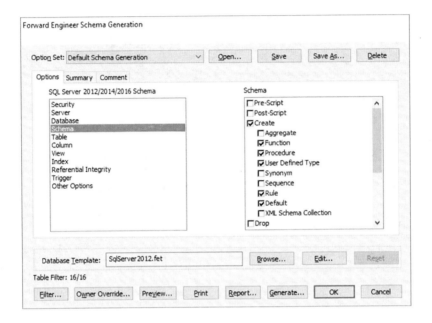

- Next, select Report to get the following:

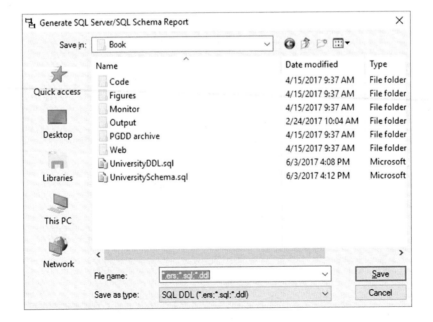

- Navigate to the directory in which you want to create the DDL file and name the file to be created:

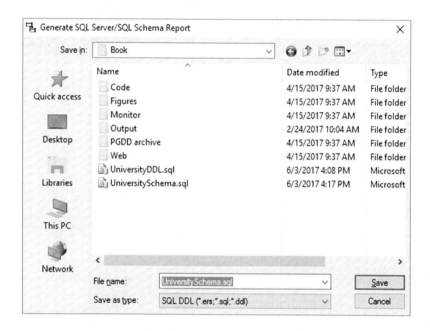

- Clicking Save will create a DDL file to define all tables, columns, and constraints shown in the physical design model.

erwin has the capability to directly connect to an Oracle or SQL Server instance to create and/or manage databases, but that is beyond the scope of the current book.

To see the SQL code generated by erwin to create the schema from this physical model, refer to Appendix C—University DDL.txt.

QUESTIONS

1. What is a data modeling tool? How does it help a design team when designing a new database?

2. What is the difference between a logical data model and a physical data model?

3. Name two RDBMS products supported by erwin's physical data modeling software.

4. What is reverse engineering, and when/how is it used?

5. What does the erwin reverse engineering file use as input, and what does it produce?

6. How accurate are the results of a reverse engineering process?

7. What is the change management process, and why is it important?

8. Describe the components of a change management system and describe what they do.

9. When using erwin for logical data modeling, where is the information entered that gives a full definition/description for each attribute?

10. When defining attributes in a logical data model, what is the purpose of defining/selecting logical data types?

11. When using erwin for logical data modeling and defining a new entity and its attributes, how is the key column identified?

12. After creating tables in a logical data model, how are one-to-many relationships identified?

13. After creating a logical data model, what needs to be done to create a matching physical data model?

14. When creating a physical data model, when/how are referential integrity constraints created?

15. When using erwin for physical data modeling, what needs to be done to create the DDL to create a new database?

REFERENCE

1. Erwin tutorial, learndatamodeling.com, https://learndatamodeling.com/blog/erwin-tutorial/ (accessed August 24, 2017).

Using Microsoft Access

6.1 OVERVIEW

Microsoft Access is a relational database management system (RDBMS) that is included as a component in the Professional and Enterprise versions of Microsoft Office. Although it lacks the depth of RDBMS features provided by SQL Server or Oracle, it has a number of features which make it ideal for developing applications for many desktop users.

- Users can design tables and views and can import data into tables.

- It includes tools to help the user to quickly create queries and view and update data.

- Microsoft Access includes a graphical user interface (GUI) allowing the user to quickly create reasonably complex interfaces.

- As it is embedded in higher end Microsoft Office packages, it is available for use by all users in the Department of Defense and Intelligence communities.

- Microsoft Access supports a somewhat limited version of SQL. However, a complex query can often be accomplished by combining multiple smaller, simpler views to create the more complex result.

Access can be used to develop and deploy database management system (DBMS) tools for a team of users. One database can be designed as the team GUI containing the query and update mechanisms needed. This database would contain a link to another Access database that contains the table(s) being viewed/updated. Deploying the Access GUI to each user's computer would allow each user to view and/or update the single database instance with the *data* shared by the user community.

- Access provides an ideal platform to rapidly develop a prototype of a new system, allowing users to *see* and provide quick feedback on features that are needed.

- Tables in Access can be defined as links to tables that reside in another RDBMS. Mechanisms created in Access can then be created to view and update data, for example, from an SQL Server table.

Let us begin by using the OrderItem database created in Chapter 3.

6.2 MODIFICATIONS TO THE DATABASE DESIGN

The physical design for the OrderItem database used in the current chapter is based on that developed in Section 3.5.1 with the following changes:

- In the Customer table, the DataType for the CustomerIdentifier was changed from AutoNumber (used in that chapter to illustrate that feature) to ShortText with a length of 50 bytes. This format is more realistic and flexible for that column and presents fewer issues when generating Forms and Reports.

- In the Advertised_Item table, the ItemWeight and ItemColor columns were removed.

With those changes, the OrderItem database now contains the following structure:

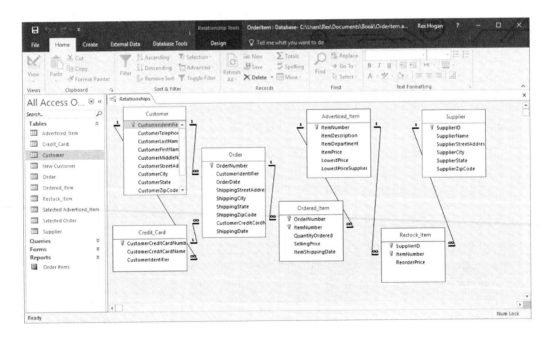

6.3 LOADING DATA INTO TABLES

Data can be loaded into tables in a number of ways.

- For quick development and testing, Access allows the user to open a table directly and enter new rows, or to modify data already loaded.

Note that when loading tables involved with one-to-many relationships, tables on the primary (*one*) side of the relationship must be added before rows on the *many* side. For example, a Customer record must be created before any Credit_Card rows with that CustomerIdentifier can be added.

- Tables are often loaded by importing data from an external file. To load Customer data, select Customer, then use the "External Data" tab to select the source type.

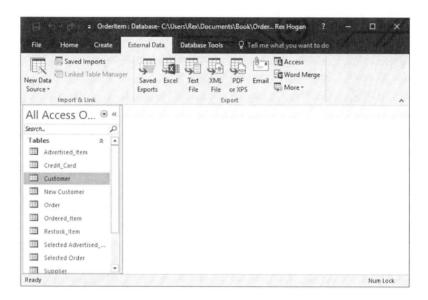

The most common sources for table imports are Excel files. Choosing the Excel file opens a window allowing you to navigate to and select the file to be imported.

The import mechanism will attempt to match the table design to the file content and gives the user the option to skip/ignore columns in the file being imported.

As an option, the user may import the file *as is* into a new table using column names found on the first line of the input file. After importing the file, the user can then run an SQL command using the "INSERT INTO <table1> VALUES (<column names>) SELECT <column names> FROM <table2>" syntax to take rows from the table just created and add them to the table to be updated.

The import wizard also makes it easy to import data from delimited flat files, where columns of information are separated by special characters (e.g., tab characters).

6.4 CREATING QUERIES

The Query wizard is an easy and powerful tool for use in building complex queries.

6.4.1 Create a Customer-Credit_Card Query

- To create a query showing Customer and Credit_Card rows, click on the Create tab, then find the Query Wizard.

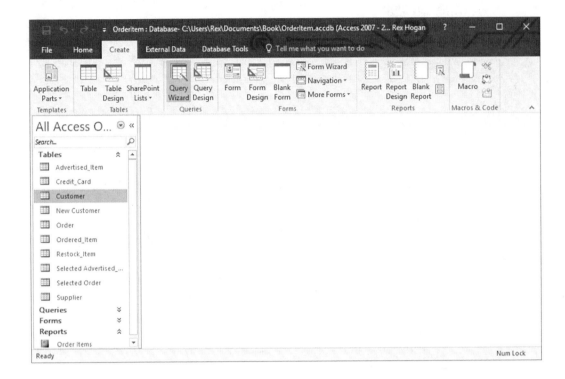

- Next, select "Simple Query Wizard" and click OK.

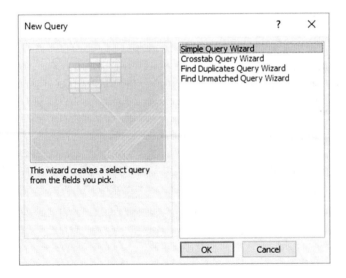

- By using the pull-down menu for Tables, select the primary table of interest (in this case, Customer).

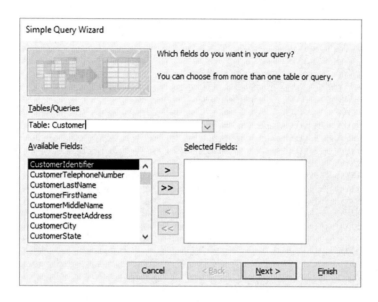

- Individual column names can be selected for use by selecting the column name and clicking ">"; clicking ">>" will add all columns to the query being build.

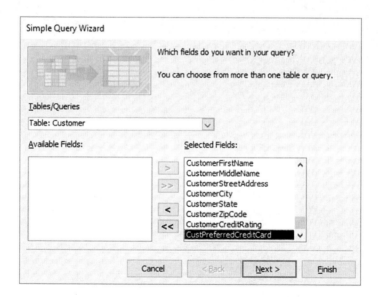

- Clicking Next brings up a screen allowing you to see the results of the query being developed, or you can choose the Modify option to continue developing the query.

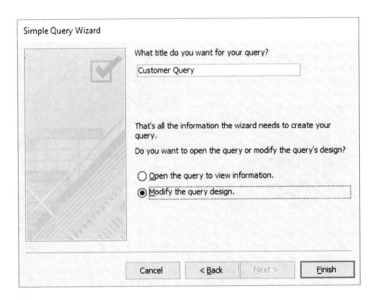

- Clicking Finish opens the query in design mode.

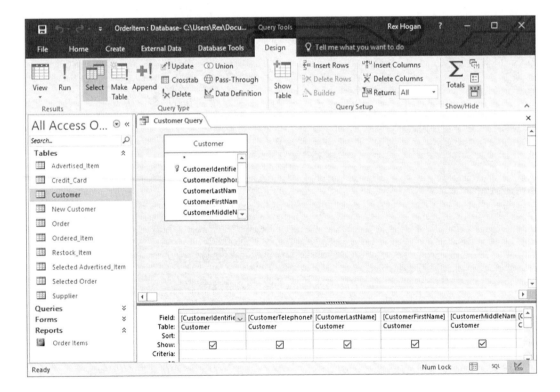

- To add the Credit_Card table to the query, click in the design pane, then right-click and select the "Show Table" option to bring up the following.

- Select the table to be added to the query design (Credit_Card) and click Add. The "Show Table" menu will remain open to add other tables; click "Close" to close that panel.

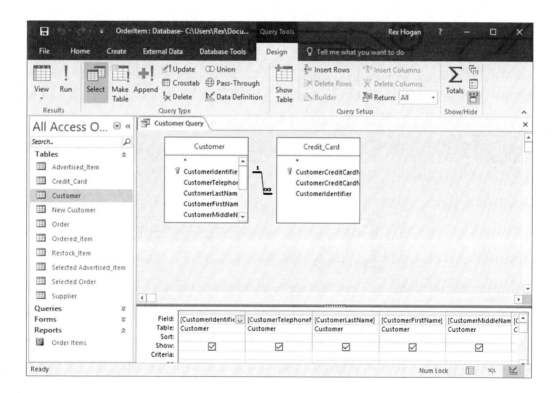

- The query now will show all Customers and their associated Credit_Card rows. Click the View option to see the data returned by the query as it stands.

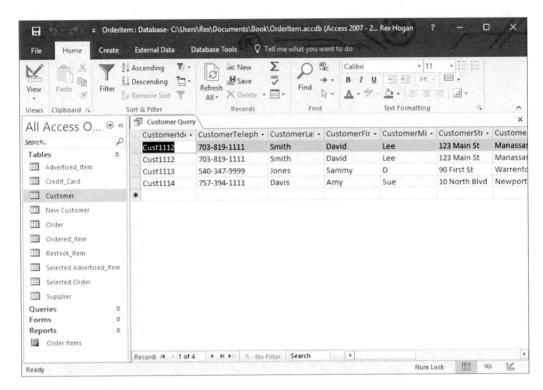

Optionally, you can also select "SQL View" to see the SQL statement that will be used to run the query.

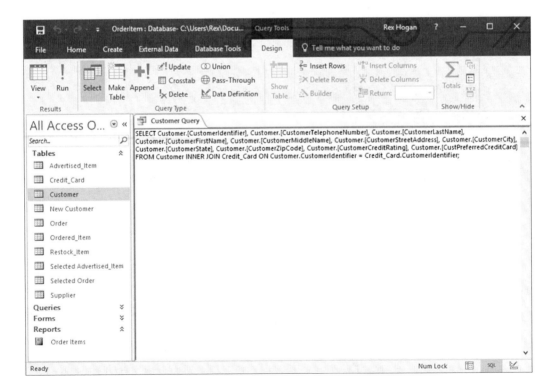

Delete or rearrange the order of columns if desired; when finished, clicking x on the Customer Query line will close the query, giving you the option to rename it.

6.4.2 Create a Query Using SQL Commands

In some cases, it will be simpler to simply enter the SQL for a query directly in the Design Panel. Assume one Supplier with the SupplierID "Supp1234" has raised the price of each of the items they sell by 10%.

- Use the Query wizard to start building a query on the Restock_Item table, and when the panel opens, switch to SQL View. Next, replace the code displayed with the following SQL command:

```
UPDATE Restock_Item SET Restock_Item.reorderprice =
reorderprice*1.1
WHERE (((Restock_Item.[SupplierID])='Supp1234'));
```

- At the top of the pane, select the "Update" button, then close the query and give it an appropriate name.

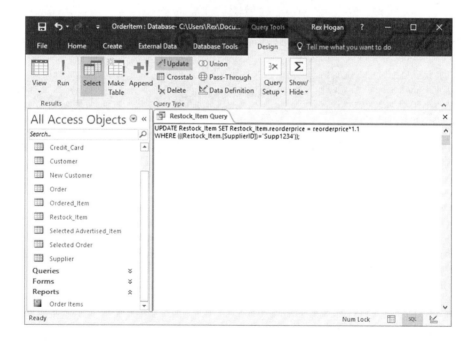

6.4.3 Filtering Query Results

In viewing Query results, Access provides pull-down options for each column to allow the user to filter results as needed.

Let us see how a query can be created and used to view and filter prices from Suppliers for an Advertised_Item.

- By using the Query wizard, start building a query for the Advertised_Item table.

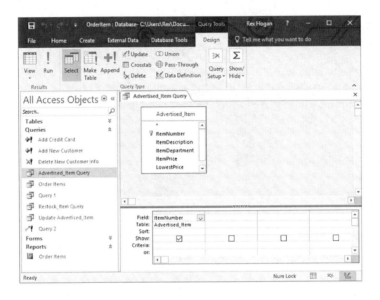

- Next, click in the design pane and add the Restock_Item and Supplier tables.

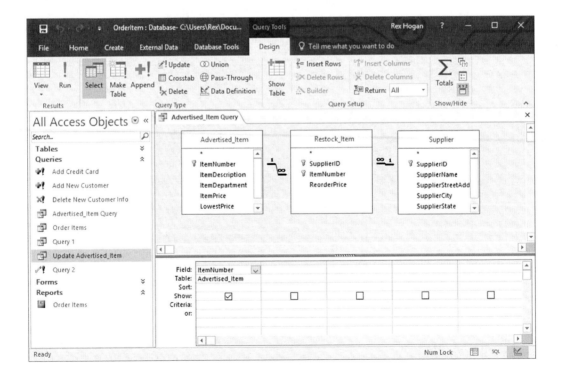

- Update the query to display the Supplier name and the ReorderPrice.

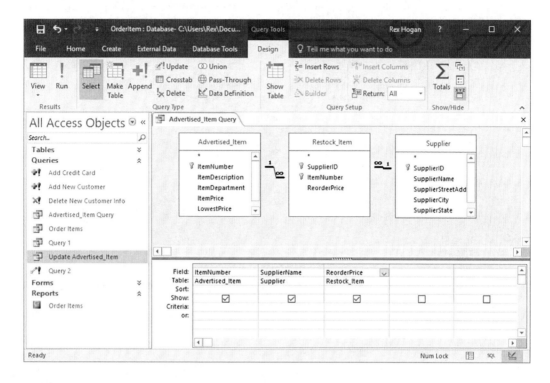

- Finally, save and open the query to view the results.

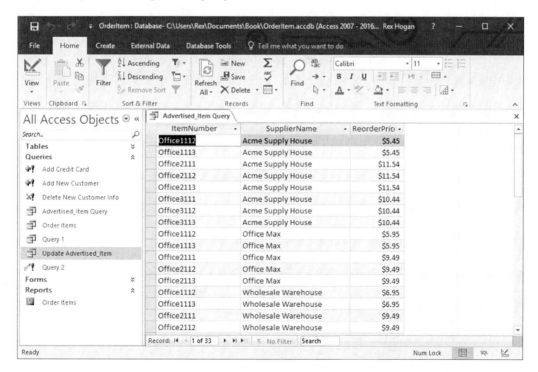

- To see prices for one item (e.g., ItemNumber Office1111), click on the pull-down for ItemNumber to see a list of all values for that column; deselect all values and select only Office1111.

- Alternatively, select the Text Filters/Equals sequence:

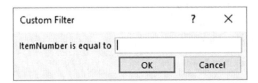

- Entering Office1111 filters the output display to show the prices offered by the four Suppliers in the database.

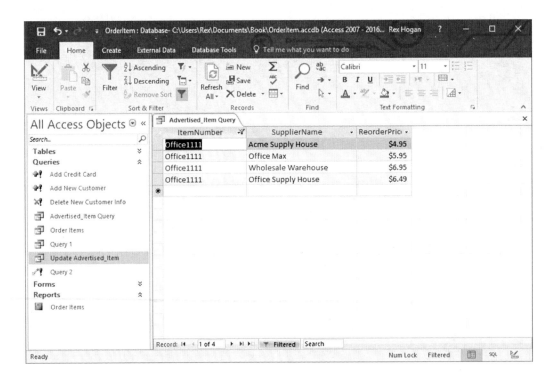

The ad-hoc use of query results can be very effective.

- For example, if a Supplier was discontinuing selling three specific items, the above-mentioned query could be filtered to show all prices for items from that supplier and then sort results by ItemNumber. Next, select an ItemNumber being discontinued.

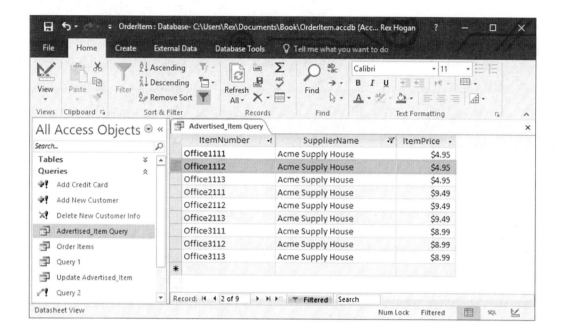

- Right-clicking on this row opens a pop-up menu containing the "Delete Record" option; click that option to delete the row selected.

6.5 USING FORMS

The Query wizard is a powerful tool used to view and update data in tables. Typical users, however, need a better user interface to view and update data of interest.

The Forms wizard is a fundamental tool used to create displays to select and update data in tables. Although they are relatively easy to create and use, they are normally built using queries to make it easy to filter and/or update subsets of data of interest to the user.

6.5.1 Create a Form to Update Advertised_Items

As a first example, let us create a form to select and update information about an Advertised_Item. We will first need a mechanism to select a unique Advertised_Item row of interest.

- Create a table that will be used to hold the key for the Advertised_Item of interest. I have named this table beginning with the word "Selected" to set it apart from a typical application data tables ("Selected Advertised_Item"). This table will have one column with the same storage format as Advertised_Item's ItemNumber.

- Next, we will create a form that can look up ItemNumber values from Advertised_Item and store the selected value in this table.

- After that value is stored, we will then open another form to display and edit the columns in the selected Advertised_Item row.

Let us begin by creating a form to set the value in the "Selected Advertised_Item" table.

- Click on the "Selected Advertised_Item" table name, then click the Create/Form icon.

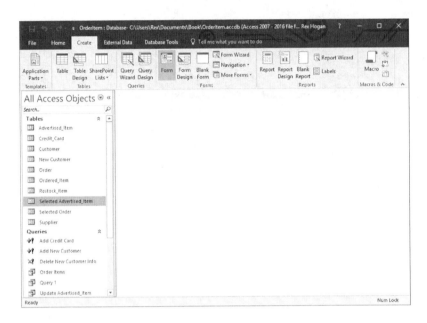

- Clicking "Form" creates a form with an empty ItemNumber data element.

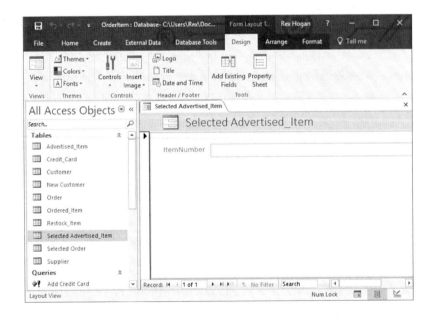

- At the top left, click on View and Design View to switch to a design view of this form.

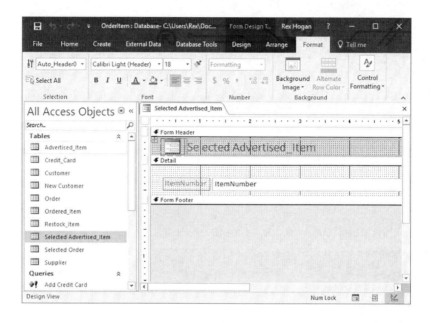

Now we will change the ItemNumber to a Combo box.

- Select the ItemNumber element, then delete it.

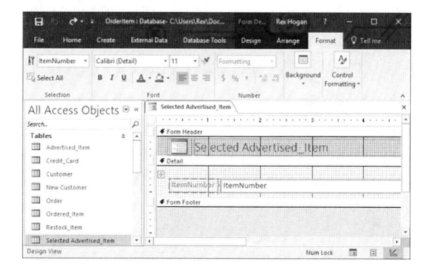

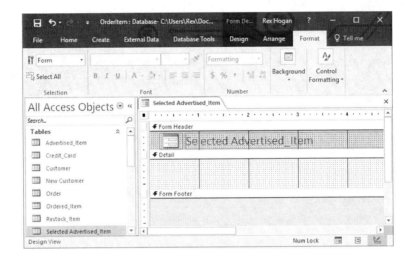

- Next, choose the Combo box icon from the Design tab.

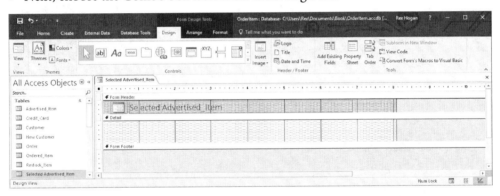

- Click on the location where ItemNumber originally was located starts a wizard for the drop-down function for the Combo box.

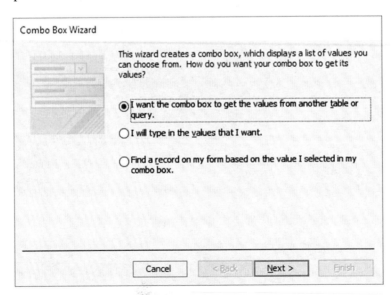

- Click Next to see a list of data sources for the lookup. Choose the Advertised_Item table.

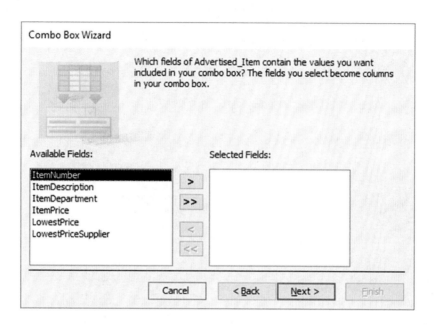

- Next, move the column to be retrieved (ItemNumber) to the right pane by clicking ">."

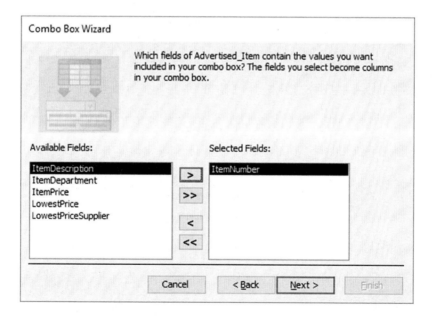

- Click Next through the next series of results.

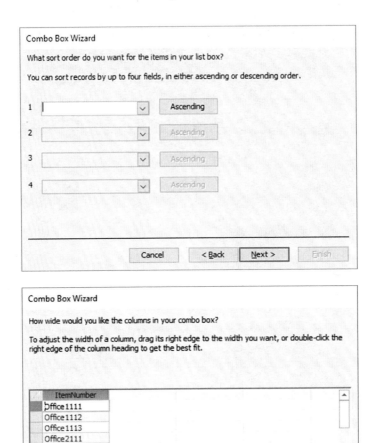

• Next, choose the option to store the results as ItemNumber.

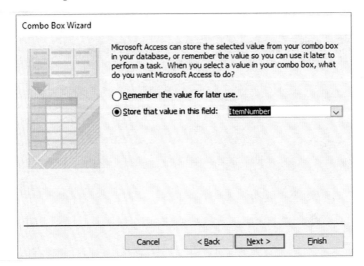

- Clicking Next allows you to store the data retrieved with a name.

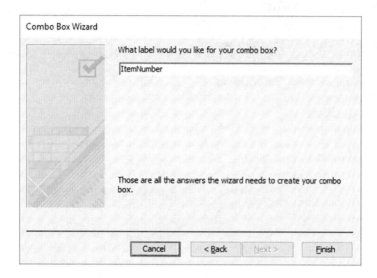

- Clicking Finish shows the completed form in design mode.

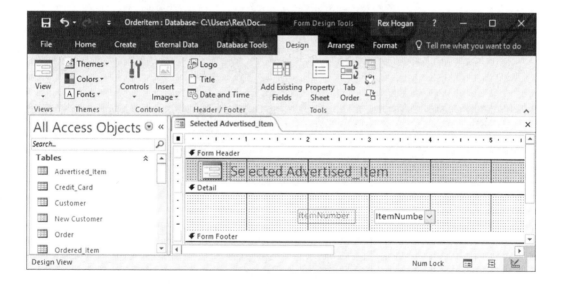

- Rearrange and resize the placement of the element as desired. Leave enough space above Form Footer to add a "Save" button later.

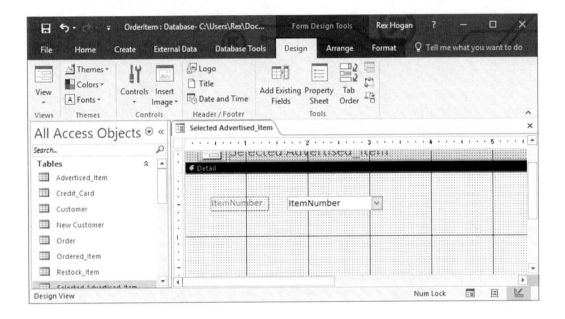

- Save the form with the current design, then click the View/Form View option to see how it works.

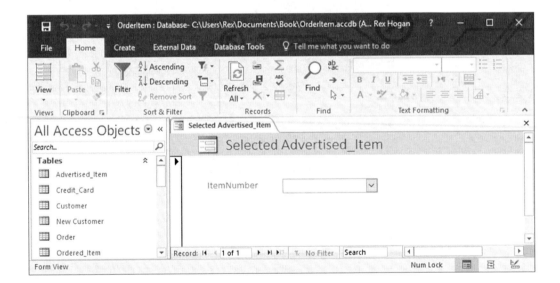

- Click the pull-down to see a list of ItemNumber values from Advertised_Item.

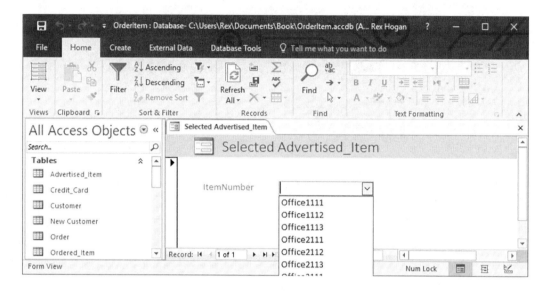

- Selecting a value and closing the form will store that value in the "Selected Advertised_ Item" table.

- Next, create a query linking this table (once populated) to Advertised_Item and save it with an appropriate name (in this case, "Update Advertised_Item" as that is the intended use of the query and associated form).

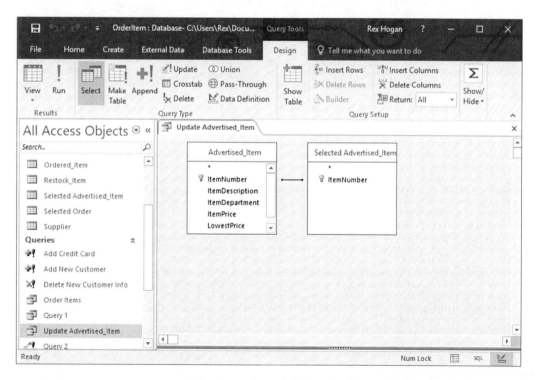

- After saving the query, select it as a source in the left pane, then click on Create/Form Wizard.

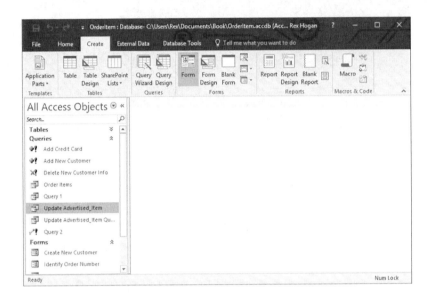

- Clicking on Form opens a display of the data returned by the query.

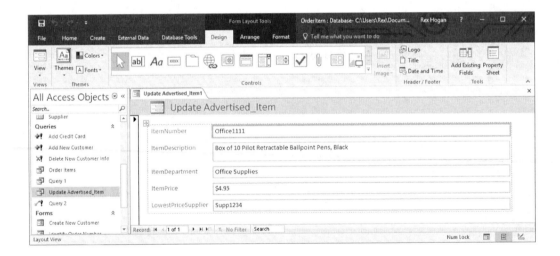

- Click View/Design View to edit the layout or size of the data elements displayed. Expand the display over the Form Footer label to leave room for a button/command to be added.

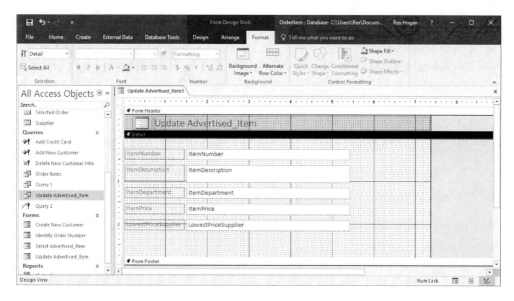

- Save the form with the current design.

Note that this form allows for all Advertised_Item columns to be edited. However, the ItemNumber column is the key field for this table and should not be changed. If the item advertised changes significantly, a new Advertised_Item should be created and an older, now obsolete item should be deleted.

To prevent alteration of the ItemNumber column:

- Put the form in Design mode, right-click ItemNumber, and click Properties. Scroll down the "All" tab until the *Locked* entry is found.

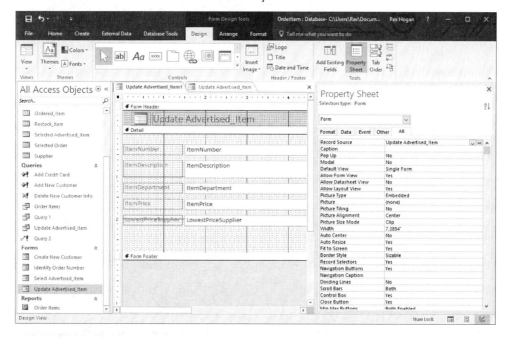

- Change *No* to *Yes* to prevent this column from being updated.

- The two forms needed to select an Advertised_Item and then to change the data found have now been created. The only remaining tasks are to link these forms together by adding buttons to each, invoking commands to close that form and open the other.

- Open the "Select Advertised_Item" form in Design mode.

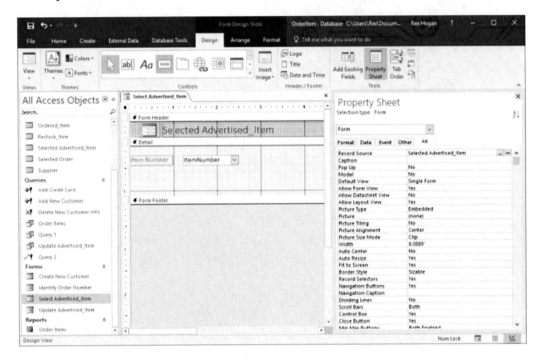

- Next, select the "Button" box and click in the Design panel slightly above Form Footer. Immediately cancel the wizard that opens and save the change giving the box the name "Select."

- Next, click on the newly created "Select" box, right-click on the surrounding orange perimeter, and select "Build Event."

- Enter commands to first close this form (and thereby saving the ItemNumber selected), then to open the "Update Advertised Item" form to view/edit that information.

```
DoCmd.Close acForm, "Select Advertised_Item", acSaveYes
DoCmd.OpenForm "Update Advertised_Item"
```

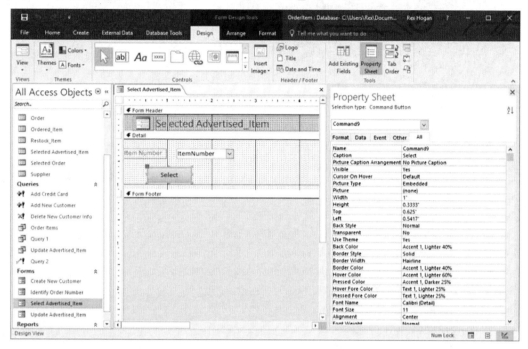

- Now repeat this process with the "Update Advertised Item" form to add a button closing this form (after edits have been made) and to open the "Select Advertised_Item" form to perform more edits.

6.5.2 Create a Form to Add a New Customer

Creating a Form to add a new Customer row is fairly simple but once again involves the use of several Access objects to capture the data and add it to the Customer table. The following steps create the objects needed for the Form.

- First, create a work table ("New Customer") to hold/capture data elements for the new Customer.

- Open the Customer table in Design mode and do a "File/Save As" to create a table named "New Customer."

- Next, create a query to add the row from "New Customer" into "Customer."

- Use the Query wizard to create a new query, switch to SQL View, and enter the following command:

```
INSERT INTO Customer
SELECT *
FROM [New Customer];
```

- Save this as an Append query as "Add New Customer."

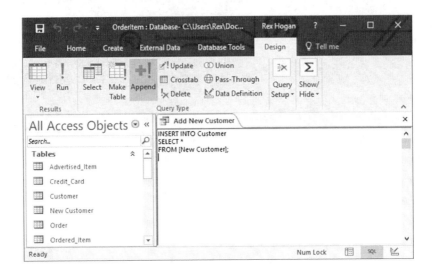

After adding a Customer, we will also need to add a row to the Credit_Card table to record the credit card number included in the Customer table.

- Use the Query wizard to create a query, switch to SQL View mode, and enter the following command.

```
INSERT INTO Credit_Card ( CustomerCreditCardNumber,
CustomerIdentifier )
SELECT [New Customer].CustPreferredCreditCard, [New Customer].
CustomerIdentifier
FROM [New Customer];
```

- Save this query as "Add Credit Card."

We will also need a query to delete the contents of "New Customer" after the updates are run.

- Use the Query wizard again to create another query, switch to SQL View, and enter the following command:

```
DELETE *
FROM [New Customer];
```

- Save this query as "Delete New Customer Info" and save it as a Delete query.

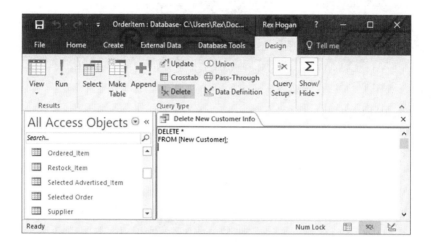

Next, create a Form based on "New Customer."

- Select the "New Customer" table and click on Create/Form to open a form with the New Customer data elements.

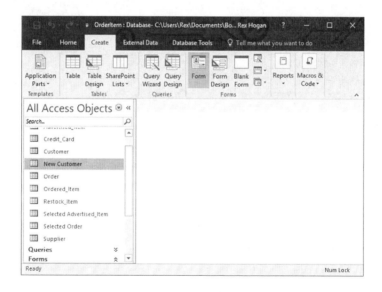

- Put the form in Design mode and adjust the length of the data elements. In addition, increase the space above the Form Footer to allow space for a button.

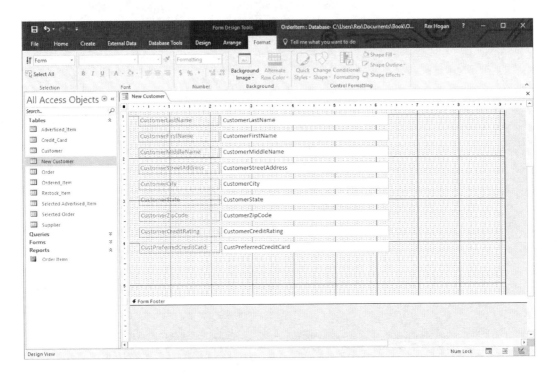

- Click on Design/Button, then click in the blank space above Form Footer where you want to add the button to open the Create Button Wizard.

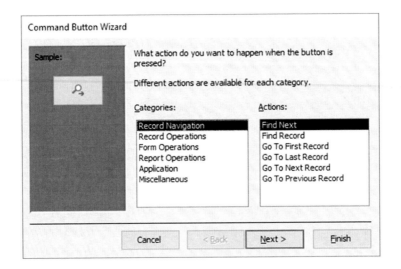

- Select "Cancel" to stop the wizard, creating a black button on the form.

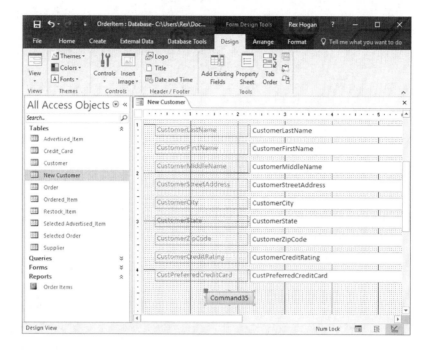

- Next, put the cursor on the yellow box around the button, right-click, and select "Build Event."

- Pick "Code Builder" and click OK. When the window opens, add commands to

  - Close the form (saving data that was entered).

  - Turn automatic warning off (pending update queries about to the run).

  - Execute the query to insert the new Customer using the "New Customer" table.

  - Execute the query to add the customer's credit card.

  - Execute the query to delete information in the "New Customer" table.

  - Turn warnings back on.

- Re-open the "Create New Customer" form to add more Customers.

```
DoCmd.Close acForm, "Create New Customer", acSaveYes
DoCmd.SetWarnings False
CurrentDb.Execute "Add New Customer", dbFailOnError
CurrentDb.Execute "Add Credit Card", dbFailOnError
DoCmd.OpenQuery "Delete New Customer Info", acViewNormal,
acEdit
DoCmd.SetWarnings True
DoCmd.OpenForm "Create New Customer"
```

- Save the form with an appropriate name; it is now ready for use.

6.5.3 Generating a *Master* Screen for Users

Forms and queries generate powerful and useful tools for users in reviewing, analyzing, and processing data. However, as more user tools are developed, the number of tools and their relationship can easily become lost or muddled from the user perspective.

To group and find like items, a *Master* display is often created and used to identify and classify the tools available. If appropriate, additional Forms can be used to group functional buttons at a lower level of detail, and those Forms shown on the Master "dashboard" to create a hierarchical ordering of subject areas and the tools available for each.

6.6 GENERATING REPORTS

Forms work well when dealing with a single row of data retrieved from a table or query but have limitations in dealing with display multiple rows of data. The Query browser, of course, displays multiple rows of data but has limited options for customizing the output display. Reports bridge these elements to produce a customized display showing multiple rows of data.

6.6.1 Using Reports to View a Customer Order

Building a Report to display data requires, as with Forms, a few minutes of thought and analysis to determine the various items necessary in generating the report.

In order to display all items associated with a Customer order, we need to

- Identify the Order number involved. Preferably, this can be selected by a drop-down list rather than entering the Order number manually.

- Use a Query to find the Customer information and all items on the order.

- Generate a customized Report using that query to display the columns of information desired.

Let us start by creating a table to hold the value of the order number of interest.

- Open the Order number in design mode and note the format for the OrderNumber column; in this case, it is a text column 50 bytes long.

- You can do a "Save As" to create a "Selected Order" table and then remove all columns but OrderNumber, or close the Order table and use the Create Table wizard to create a new "Selected Order" table having one column, OrderNumber, with a data format of 50 text bytes.

Next, create a query to display the information needed.

- The query will include "Selected Order" (to link to Order), Order, Customer (to get the Customer name), Ordered_Item (to get the quantity ordered), and Advertised_ Item (to get the item name). Study the following diagram and note the columns from each table that are selected to be displayed.

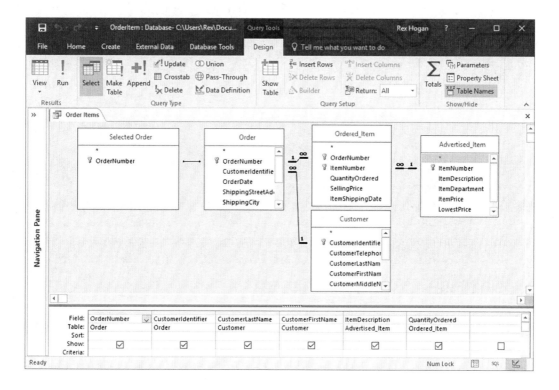

- Save the query with an appropriate name; here, the name "Order Items" was used.

We need a way to specify the OrderNumber of interest; we will do that with a Form.

- Select the "Selected Order" table name, then click on Create/Form to open the Form wizard.

- Save the Form wizard and reopen it in Design mode.

- Select and delete the OrderNumber row.

- Go to the Design tab and select the Combo box icon, then click in the form where OrderNumber appeared.

- Use the wizard to select the Order table, then OrderNumber to retrieve those values, storing them in this location in the Form.

- Next, add a Button with the name "Select" at the bottom of the form. Cancel the Button wizard when it opens; we will update the button later with actions to be taken after the OrderNumber is selected.

- Save the Form with an appropriate name (e.g., "Identify Order Number").

Finally, let us create a Report to display the relevant information.

- Select the Order Items query, then click on the Create/Report to open the Report wizard. Note that the display opens showing all columns in one line.

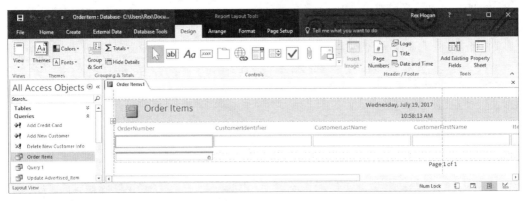

We need to modify this output to add a drop-down box to save a value in "Selected Order" and rearrange the column display into something more readable.

- Save the Report, then reopen it in Design Mode.

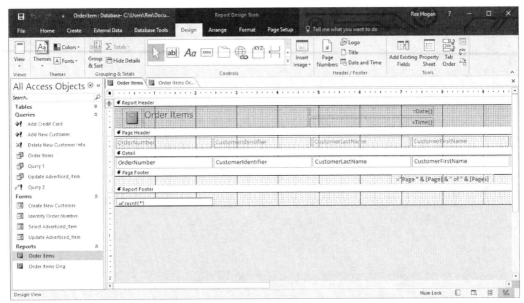

- Note that the report has column names in the Header section, with all column values in the Detail portion.

  We want to rearrange the format to display order-specific information (the Order number and Customer information) in the Header, leaving in the Detail portion those data elements with more than one row (ItemDescripton and QuantityOrdered).

- With the Report in Design mode, carefully move the cursor over the portion for the Page Header until the "+"-like symbol appears. Click the mouse and drag the symbol down to enlarge the Header portion.

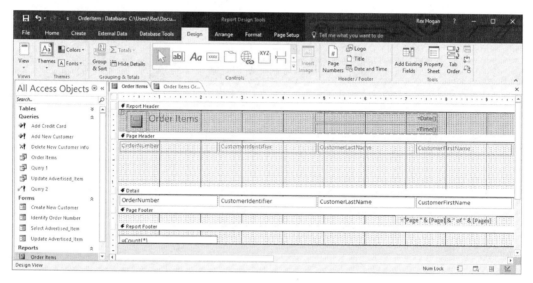

- In the Detail portion, pick an item to be moved to the Header. Click on it, *copy* that item, then move the mouse and click in the Header, and do a *paste* to add the item to that section. Finally, delete the item from the Detail section.

  The following display shows OrderNumber after being moved.

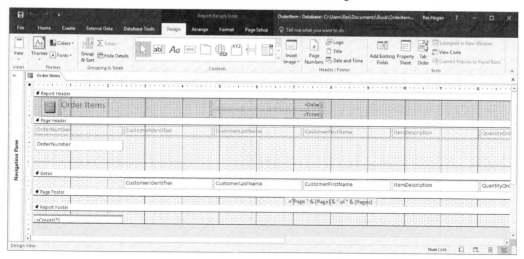

- Repeat the copy/paste operation on the Customer elements to move then all to the Header. Resize each as appropriate.

  In addition, delete the ItemDescription and QuantityOrdered labels from the Header.

- Finally, select the Detail section and enlarge it slightly. Then move the ItemDescription and QuantityOrdered elements to the left and resize them accordingly.

  Note that the Header now includes information about the order as a whole, and the Detail section contains information about the individual items on the order. "View" the report to check the display of the items it contains, and Save and close the report when you are finished.

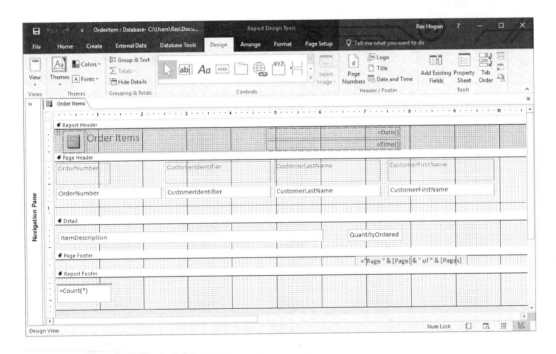

We now have to make one final modification to tie all of this together.

- Go back to the Form just created ("Identify Order Number") and put it in "Design View" mode.

- Select the "Save" button added at the bottom, right-click on the orange box, and select "Build Event."

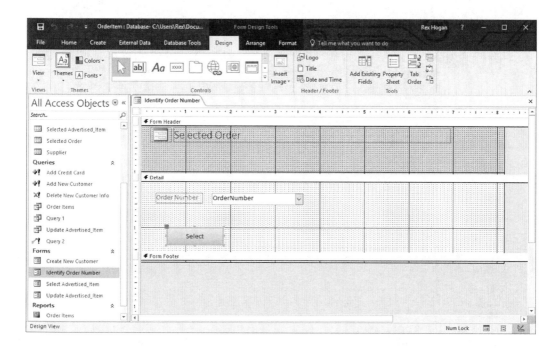

- Choose "Code Builder" to open a window to enter commands.

- When this Form is initially opened, we will use the drop-down menu from the Combo box to select an OrderNumber. After that number is selected, we just need to close this form (and thereby update the Query results) and open the Report to see the results.

  To perform these functions, enter the following commands in the code section of the above-mentioned window:

  ```
  DoCmd.Close acForm, "Identify Order Number", acSaveYes
  DoCmd.OpenReport "Order Items", acViewPreview
  ```

- Save these changes and close the Form.

The following screens give an example of how the Query/Form/Report elements work together.

Alternatively, after the "Selected Order Number" table has been updated, the Report can be opened manually.

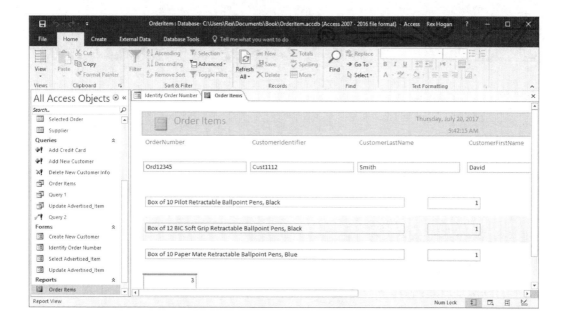

Hopefully, you now see how Microsoft Access can be used to create a reasonably sophisticated GUI for users. It just takes a bit of thought and analysis to identify and design all of the individual components and queries required.

- Access does not support complex queries, but often several small, simple queries can be created that together produce the desired result.

- When building multiple tools to achieve a result, naming conventions can help identify associated items in Queries, Forms, and Reports and make the overall system more understandable and easier to maintain.

6.7 DEPLOYING ACCESS FOR A TEAM OF USERS

As shown earlier, a Microsoft Access Database uses Table objects to define database tables, and other object types to support Queries, Forms, and Reports to sort or analyze data in those tables.

To deploy that Database to a team of users, it needs to be divided into two different data bases.

- The first database would host (contain) only the Table objects (the core data tables shared by the user community).

- The second database would serve as a team GUI and contain all of the objects and code used to access or analyze the data.

- The Tables section of the GUI database would initially be empty when initially created. The External Data/New Data Source icons would be selected.

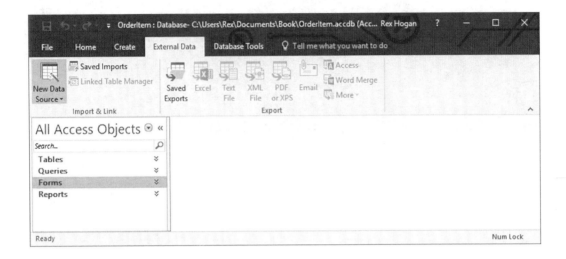

- A connection wizard will open; select "From Database" and Access.

- Select the "Link" option as shown and click OK. Next, browse the network shared by users to find and select the *data* portion of the database. Select all tables in that database.

- Linked tables will now appear in the Tables section of the GUI database.

- That GUI database can now be given to each user who needs access to the database.

6.7.1 Linking to an SQL Server or Oracle Database

Important note: The above-mentioned instructions can also be used to link to tables residing in SQL Server or Oracle. When starting the connection wizard, use the New Data Source/From Other Sources/ODBC (Microsoft's "Open Database Connectivity" interface) database option.

- The wizard needs a DSN name to identify the type of ODBC driver needed to access the data.

- If one has not already been created, clicking "New" presents a pull-down list of DBMSs that are supported. "ODBC for Oracle" and "SQL Server" are both on the list.

- Select the appropriate ODBC driver and navigate on the user network to the location where the database is installed. You will be asked to log on to that database.

- When finished, the tables selected will appear as linked objects in the Table section of the GUI database.

As a result, the GUI database now provides all of the Windows-based functions for users with the data component running in SQL Server or Oracle.

6.8 THE ROLE OF PASS-THROUGH QUERIES

Microsoft Access supports a reasonable degree of queries to view or modify data. Complex queries can often be created by combining the results of multiple simple queries to achieve a more complex query requirement.

If the source data resides in SQL Server or Oracle, the Query wizard can be used in "SQL View" mode to enter, for example, a complex SQL Server query to run against the linked table. In the Design tab, "Pass-Through" would then be selected as the query is saved. When executed, this classification instructs Access to not attempt to execute the logic but to simply pass the query logic directly to the host RDBMS for execution on that server.

This allows the GUI to be designed and developed using much more complex queries than those supported by Microsoft Access.

In summary, Microsoft Access provides a platform to rapidly develop and deploy data and user interfaces to view and/or update the data and has these advantages:

- Microsoft Access is deployed as part of the desktop environment for all users in Department of Defense and in the Intelligence community. It therefore is a common, *free* software environment for use by analytical teams.

- The linked table and Pass-Through options for queries support an environment where complex queries can be run against *industrial strength* database platforms such as SQL Server and Oracle.

- Users often have difficulty describing what functionality is needed in a new system. A design team can rapidly design and develop both tables and user interface mechanisms in a prototype that users can see and react to, in order to determine core user requirements.

It is amazing how much can be done with such a simple tool.

QUESTIONS

1. What software product(s) are required to install and use Microsoft Access? Is a Microsoft Access database a logical or physical database?

2. Where is a Microsoft Access database stored?

3. How do you assign the DataType for a column in a table?

4. When creating a table, how are key column(s) identified?

5. When defining a column in a table, how can an index be created on that column?

6. When defining an index on a column, does that index have to be unique?

7. Can a table be created that does not have a unique key?

8. When creating a table whose key column is an ever-increasing numeric value, what DataType should be used for that column?

9. What steps are taken to import data into a table?

10. What steps must be taken to create a Query for three linked tables in the database?

11. Can columns in a table be updated using a Query?

12. What steps are followed to create an Update query?

13. How can you use Microsoft Access to view data in a table in an SQL Server database?

14. How can you run a query against a table in an SQL Server database using SQL Server-specific SQL?

15. How can a table be manually browsed or filtered?

Using SQL Server

7.1 OVERVIEW

SQL Server is a relational database management system (RDBMS) developed by Microsoft and runs on Windows platforms ranging from a laptop to a dedicated database server. It comes with a graphical user interface (GUI—the SQL Server Management Studio) that makes it easy to create and manage individual databases running on that platform. Although primarily aimed at small-to-mid-range applications, it is suitable for large, complex Internet applications with multiple concurrent users.

7.1.1 Advantages

- SQL Server is relatively inexpensive and is easy to install. Trial versions are available to download and install, as well as a free entry-level "Express" version.

- The SQL Server Management Studio provides a central tool to define tables, indexes, views, and referential integrity constraints within a database.

- SQL Server handles complex queries and supports functions and stored procedures.

- SQL Server does not require the *care and feeding* from database administrators (DBAs) typically required with Oracle.

- SQL Server supports full-text search against character-based columns, allowing the user to search for a word embedded in a column.

- SQL Server also supports the ability to replicate a database on a remote host and supports failover to that host should the primary host fails.

7.1.2 Change Management for SQL Server

I have used SQL Server for years in doing rapid prototyping of database applications. The fact that SQL Server is so easy to use is both *good* and *bad* news. The development team must pay additional attention in documenting and migrating design changes as they are developed and deployed to minimize downtime for the upgrade and to avoid surprises in the upgrade process.

- Changes often include table modifications as well as to code (stored procedures, functions, views, or to the web interface).

- Individual changes using the Management Studio must be carefully documented to capture the sequence and details involved with each change.

- To properly develop and test design changes, you need additional computer platforms to host development and test versions of the database.

  - The development platform is used to test individual changes as they take place. Later, all planned changes are combined together in a *change package* to upgrade the application from one level of functionality to the next.

  - The test platform is where the change package is applied and tested. If the change package is applied successfully, it is ready for use in upgrading the production platform with minimal downtime for production users. If errors *are* found on the test platform, the change package must be corrected and retested.

  - After successfully testing a change package, that package is ready for use in updating the production platform.

In the current chapter, we will review key factors in the creation and use of an SQL Server database.

7.2 DATABASE CREATION/INSTALLATION

7.2.1 Installation Planning

- *Preinstallation considerations*: Before installing SQL Server, decisions need to be made on what features are needed. In addition, early planning must be done on how to map the different type of files across the disk drives that are available.

  - Will redundant array of inexpensive disk (RAID) drives be used? If not, how many drives are available and how will they be used? (This is covered in more detail in the following.)

  - Does the Full-Text Search feature need to be installed?

  - Is Database Failover needed? If so, the SQL Server Replication feature must be installed.

  - Logons to SQL Server can be done using Windows accounts or accounts internal to SQL Server ("Mixed Mode"). Which are to be used to control access to the database?

I recommend using SQL Server accounts to control all database access. This gives DBAs total control of accounts and how they are used.

- *Installing SQL Server on a laptop*: As mentioned earlier, SQL Server can be installed on a laptop or desktop. Although these platforms have limitations in terms of performance and protection against hardware failures, they provide a database platform at minimal hardware expense.

   After installation, periodic database backups must be taken. If possible, they should be stored on a different drive from the database itself to protect against device failure.

   - If only one drive is available, consider using a zip drive to store a backup of the database.

   - If two drives are available, install the database and all its files on one drive and the log files and periodic backups on the second.

- *Installing SQL Server on a server*: If the server is configured with multiple drives, we want to separate as much as possible the RDBMS system software, data files, indexes, database log files, and files created from database backups.

   Fortunately, systems today are more commonly built using RAID technology.

   - RAID 5 configurations using a combination of striping (for performance) and parity checking (for recoverability), and protect against single-device failure. As data are striped, performance is not as much of an issue, and device separation for files is not important; the system will continue to run after failure of one drive.

   - RAID 10 configurations combine disk mirroring and disk striping and support a higher level of performance while providing against single device failures. They require twice as many drives as a non-RAID installation but avoid the overhead required for the RAID 5 parity when updates are made.

   When using RAID arrays, all files for the RDBMS and its databases can be placed on the same RAID array.

- *Prerequisites*: As you might guess, SQL Server has specific hardware and software prerequisites for each version. These can be found by using the Internet to request a download, then reading the "System Requirements" section from the download page.

   The next section describes the steps necessary to install a trial version of the SQL Server 2008 R2 "Enterprise Edition" on a laptop. After downloading and extracting the software, the installer displays a number of options in the left pane; the planning options are shown on the next page. *Hardware and Software Requirements* will use the Internet as a resource to download and display this information. Clicking on "System Configuration Checker" will check the computer being used to see if all requirements have been met. If the computer is connected to the Internet and some software is needed, in most cases, that software will automatically be downloaded and installed.

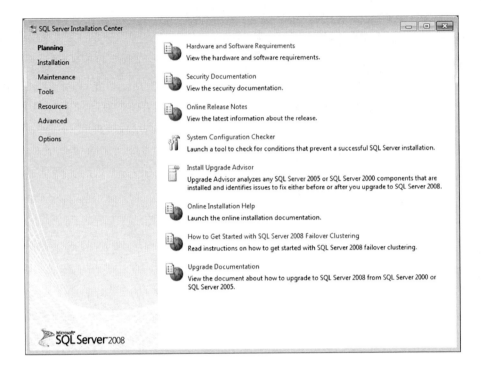

7.2.2 Software Installation

Continuing with the installation of SQL Server 2008 R2, the Installation tab displays the following options.

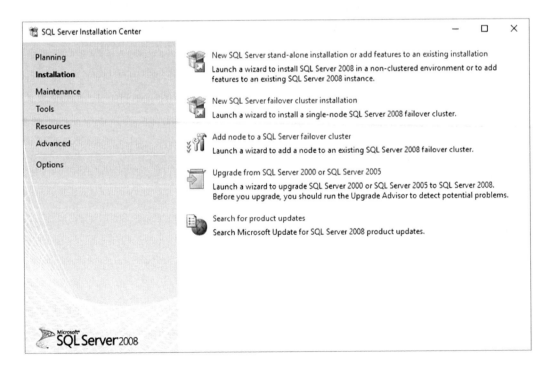

Clicking on the first link to install a "New SQL Server stand-alone installation…" starts the installation wizard, showing features available.

The following options were chosen to install a relatively simple database without the Full-Text Search or Replication features.

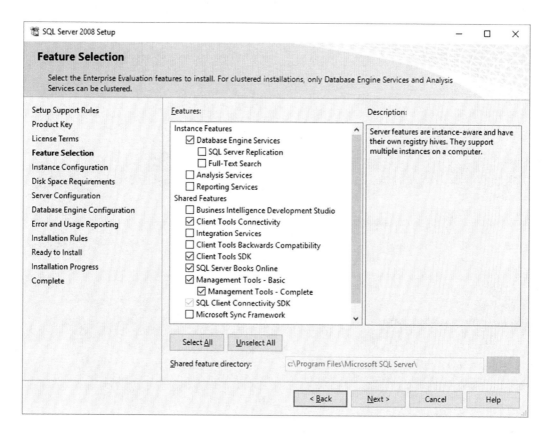

Selecting Next gives the user the option of changing the name of the SQL Server Instance being installed; I have chosen the default option of MSSQLSERVER.

Note that for security reasons, the user may choose to change the default name to make it more difficult for a hacker/intruder to identify any database instance running on the host.

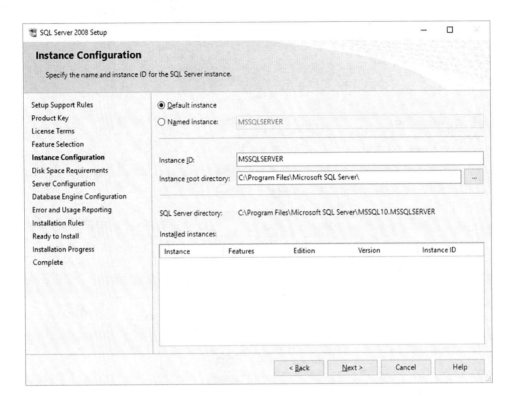

Clicking Next gives a summary of disk space found on that computer.

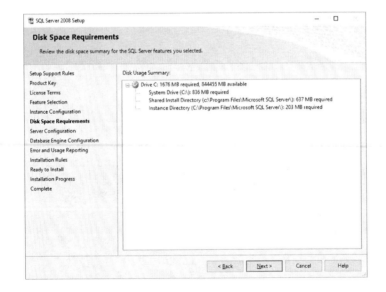

Clicking Next runs a check searching for installation issues.

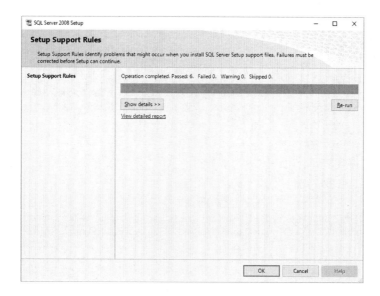

Click OK to display a screen to enter a product key, if available. Click Next to install a trial version.

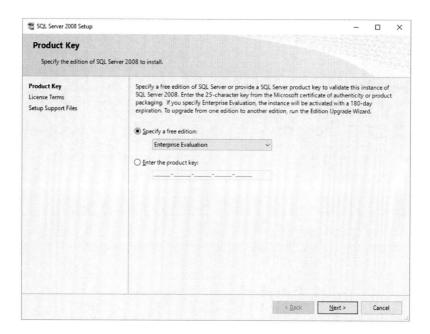

Click Next to display a screen of software license terms.

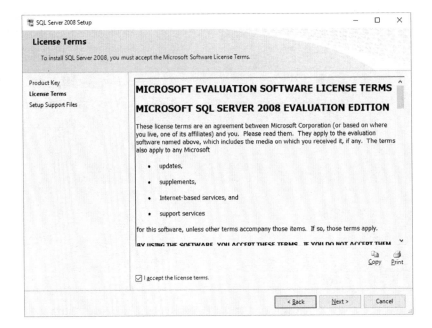

Accept the terms and click Next to advance to the next screen.

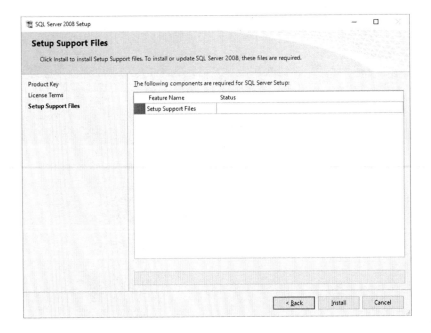

Click Install to begin the installation process. The next screen displays the results of a system check before installing the software.

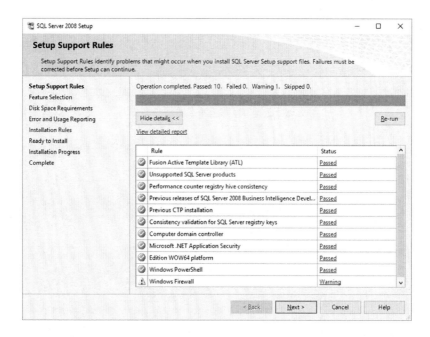

Click Next to see a display asking for the names of accounts used to manage SQL Server. Click the button to "Use the same account for all SQL Server services."

I have chosen the option shown in the following.

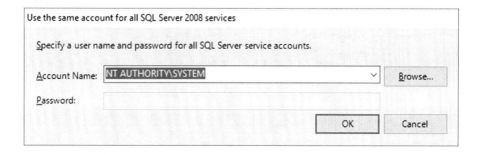

Clicking OK displays my choices for accounts.

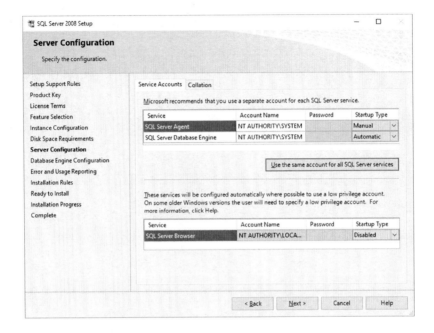

Clicking Next now displays options for accounts to be used. I recommend "Mixed Mode," preferring to control all data access using SQL Server account names for users.

Note also a section to enter the password for the SQL Server default Administrator account "sa."

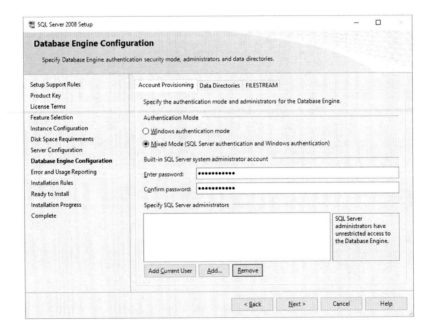

In addition, I want to register my Windows account as an Administrator; click Add Current User to make that change.

Click Next to display options for error reporting.

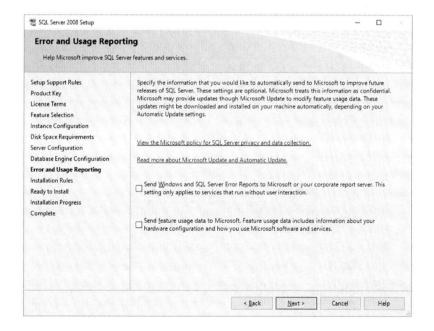

Click Next to continue with another installation check.

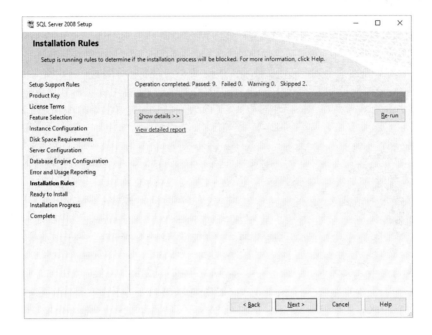

Click Next again for a preinstallation status screen.

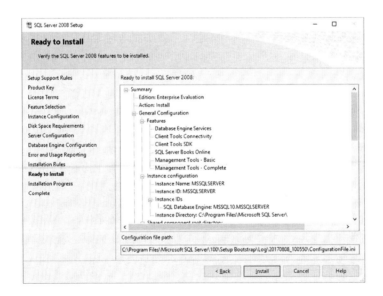

Click Install to begin the software installation.

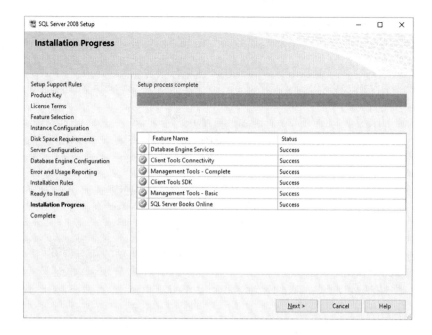

Click Next again to move to the final screen.

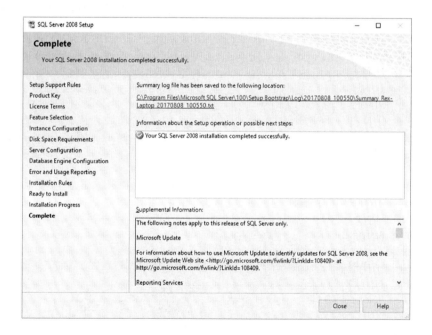

SQL Server is now ready for use.

7.3 CREATING DATABASES

At this point, the SQL Server instance/system software has been installed, but no databases have been created; that is done using SQL Server Management Studio. In the following, two databases will be created, SQLSvrLogs and the University database.

SQLSvrLogs: The SQLSvrLogs database has two tables storing information about warning messages and error messages from an SQL Server instance. Here is how this database is updated and used:

- Chapter 8 contains a Perl script designed to run continuously to extract warning and error messages from an SQL Server log file. It also describes how the *bcp* utility is used to load the contents of these files into tables.

- Chapter 11 describes how to use PHP to develop a web-based interface allowing a DBA or administrator to review warning and error messages. When reviewing new messages, status flags are set appropriately to keep track of records that have been reviewed, those that are being researched to see if corrective action is necessary, and those where the underlying problem/issue has been resolved.

Section 7.3.1 shows how to create a database with the WarningRecords and ErrorRecords tables. Although very simple in nature, these tables are interesting in several respects.

- Each table has one long varchar column storing the information found in the log record. Nothing in the log format is suitable for use as a unique identifier. As such, the "RecordKey" column was defined with an "int" data format to support ever-increasing numeric values automatically incremented as rows are inserted into the table.

- Users will use the web interface to review all Warning and Error log records and set flags for each row to label/classify the row as follows:

  - Reviewed (and can be ignored).

  - Pending (need to be researched further to determine if any corrective action is needed).

  - Resolved (and can subsequently be ignored from future reviews).

- The table design must include columns for each of these status flags using a "bit" data format. In addition, as part of the process when loading new rows, a Stored Procedure is needed to reset the *null* values for new rows to "0" (off).

The University Database: Chapter 4 describes the design of a University database to store information about courses offered, students enrolled, and student grades. Section 7.3.2 describes how to create a database in SQL Server to manage this information based on the physical data model shown in Figure 4.7.

7.3.1 Create an SQLSvrLogs Database

In this section, we will create an SQLSvrLogs database with tables to store WarningRecords and ErrorRecords. To understand the design and operational use of this database, let us review how it would be used in the field.

- In practice, new records for each table would be obtained by running a PERL script 24 × 7 modeled after the one shown in Section 8.5. New files are moved to the input directory referenced in the next paragraph.

- A script is needed on the database host to continually monitor an input directory for new files. When new files are found, they would be imported into the respective table, and a Stored Procedure run to initialize the Reviewed/Pending/Resolved flags described earlier.

Here are the steps required to create an SQLSvrLogs database with these two tables.

- Start SQL Server Management Studio, select Databases, right-click and chose New Database.

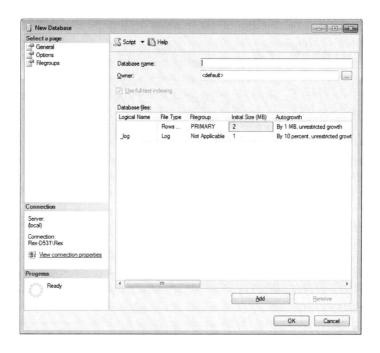

Enter the Database Name in the block shown.

If multiple drives are available, the location of the new database can be changed by scrolling to the right of this screen.

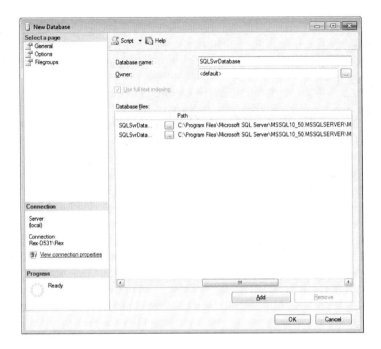

Click OK to create the database on the designated disk drive.

To create tables, first click on SQLSvrLogs to expand the options, click Tables, right-click, and select New Table.

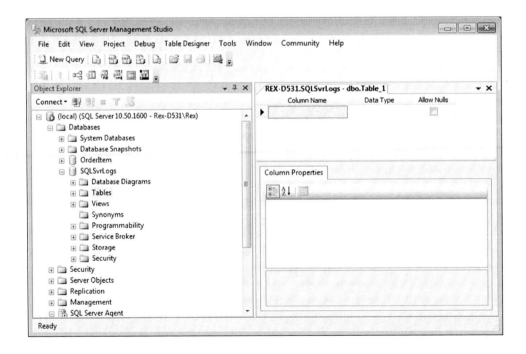

Use this window to define the following columns for the WarningRecords table:

Column Name	Format	Usage/Purpose
RecordKey	int	An ever-increasing value used as the key column
Message	Varchar(MAX)	The content of the log record
Reviewed	bit	Set after record has been reviewed
Pending	bit	Set for records to be researched
Resolved	bit	Set when issue has been resolved

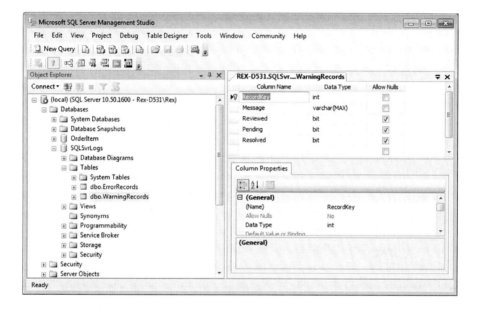

Note the "Allow Nulls" settings; this permits new rows to be added to the table with no (*null*) values for these columns.

After defining each column, click the x at the top right of the table definition window to close the window. You will be asked if you want to Save the table; choose Yes, then enter a name for the table being saved (WarningRecords).

Repeat this sequence to define the ErrorRecords table.

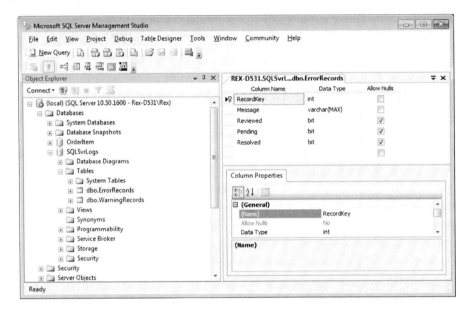

For this application, the web interface executes queries directly against each table. There are no subordinate/linked tables; therefore, no Referential Integrity constraints are required.

The only additional item needed is the Stored Procedure used to initialize the three status flags after new rows are added to the two tables.

It will identify all newly imported rows (having status flags of "null"), and reset each to zero. Section 7.10 shows how to create this Stored Procedure.

7.3.2 Create the University Database

This section describes the steps necessary to create the University database based on the physical data model shown in Figure 4.7.

First, using SQL Server Management Studio, right-click on Databases and select "New Database." Repeat the steps followed earlier to define the University database.

7.3.2.1 Table Definitions

Now create tables for each entity shown in Figure 4.7. For each, right-click on Tables and select "New Table." Create entries for each column using the following guidelines.

- In general, most columns should be defined using a Data Type of varchar(50). This results in using a variable number of bytes per column to store a character string up to 50 bytes long.

- Where appropriate, pick an appropriate Data Type of Integer or Date/Time.

- Click the "Allow Nulls" box for columns where information may not be available when the tables are initially loaded.

For example, here are the column definitions for the School table.

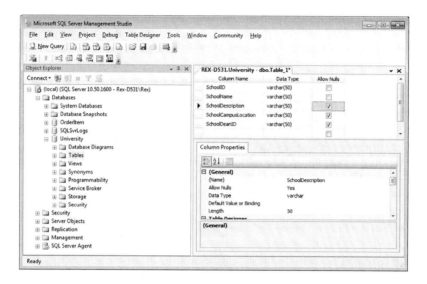

- After entering all column names for a table, identify the column(s) used as a key for the table. If the key is only one column, click on the line with that column, right-click, and select "Set Primary Key."

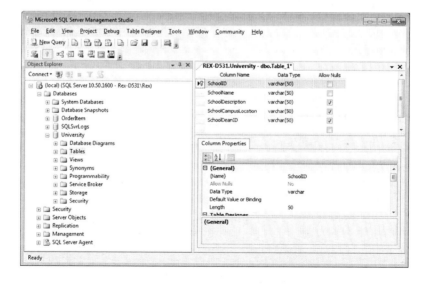

After all columns and the primary key are defined, select the x at the top right of the design window to close and save the definition, entering a table name when prompted.

If the table requires more than one column for the key (e.g., the Assignment table), select the first column in the key, hold the shift key down, and select the last column. In Assignment, the first three columns are used in combination to identify a unique assignment.

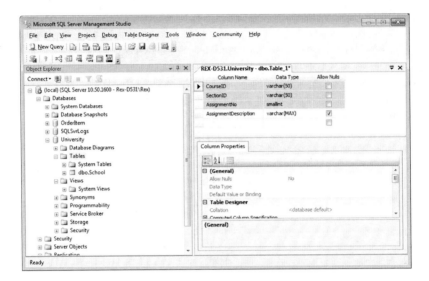

After doing the group select shown earlier, right-click, and select the "Set Primary Key" option.

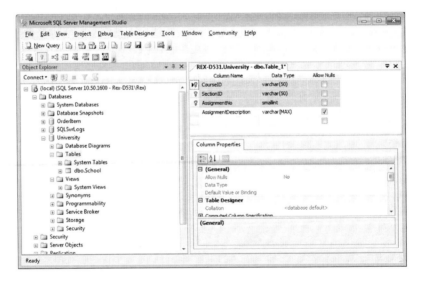

Finally, click on the x at the top right of the design window to close the table design; enter the table name when prompted.

Continue adding table definitions for all tables shown in Figure 4.7 and compare your results to the following.

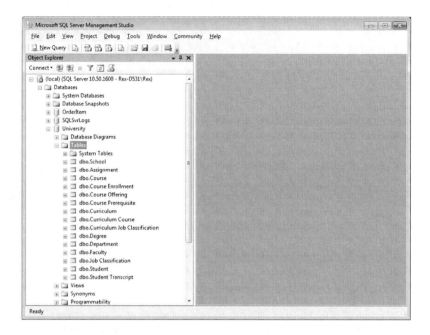

7.3.2.2 Creating Indexes

Next, we will create the indexes needed for these tables.

- As with Microsoft Access, indexes are automatically created for primary keys for tables.

- Indexes are also needed to support frequently used access paths anticipated by the design team. As one example, school administrators frequently need to see all students enrolled in a specific department.

  - If a query were executed specifying all students for a specific department and the Student table had no index on the DepartmentID column, the Student table would be scanned and only rows matching the DepartmentID qualifier would be returned. This would require a significant amount of I/O activity.

  - If the same query were executed after an index was created on the DepartmentID column in Student, then the RDBMS would use the index to retrieve only students within the specified department, requiring significantly fewer I/Os.

    To create an index on the DepartmentID column in Student, double-click on the Student table to show all options, click on Indexes, right-click, and select New Index from the pop-up menu. This opens the following window.

Fill in the Index Name entry.

- Next, select an Index type from the pull down.

  Indexes are Clustered if the rows in the table are in the sequence of the column specified. If not, they are NonClustered.

- Note the *unique* box, chosen when each value in the index will apply to only one row in the table. In this case, there will be many students with the same DepartmentID, so the box is not checked.

- Next, click the Add button to see a list of column names available. Click on DepartmentID.

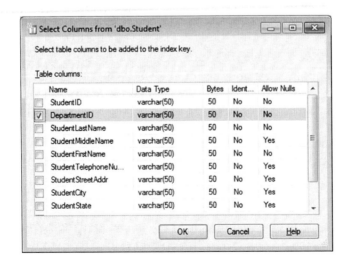

- Click OK to see details of the index being created.

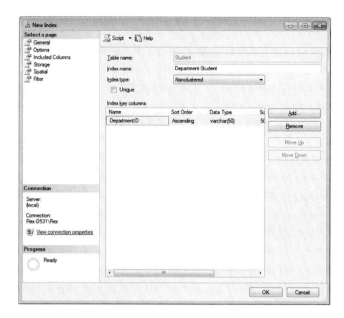

- Click OK again to create the index.

  Note the details of the new index on the Student table.

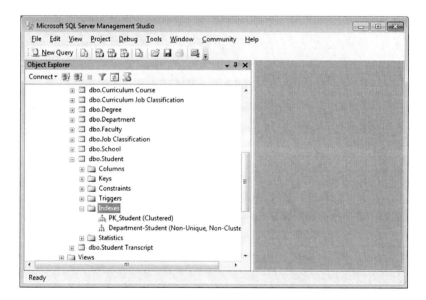

- In addition, administrators also frequently want to see all courses taught by a particular Faculty member. This will require an index be built on the FacultyID column in Course Offering.

Follow the above-mentioned steps to modify the Course Offering table.

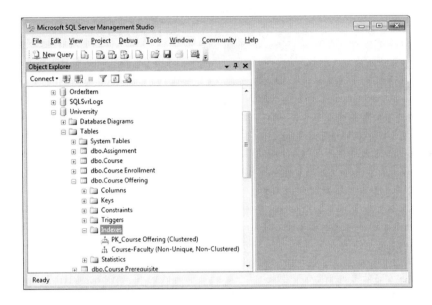

7.3.2.3 Index Maintenance
After the database is placed in operation, inserts and deletes of rows in tables will cause indexes to grow in size to allow room for new entries. Index maintenance must be periodically performed to condense all current entries and reclaim free space.

7.3.2.4 Referential Integrity Constraints
Referential Integrity constraints must now be created for all one-to-many relationships in Figure 4.7.

To create a constraint for the School–Department relationship:

- Select the table on the *many* side of the relationship (Department) and put it in Design mode.

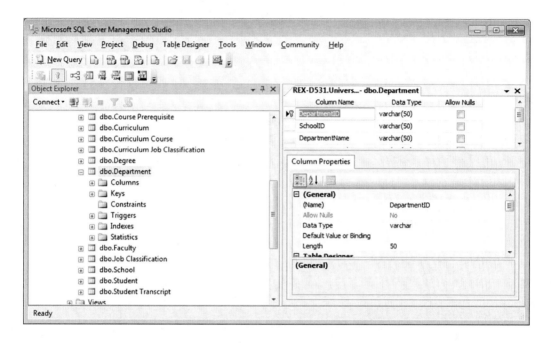

- Click on the SchoolID column, right-click, and choose Relationships.

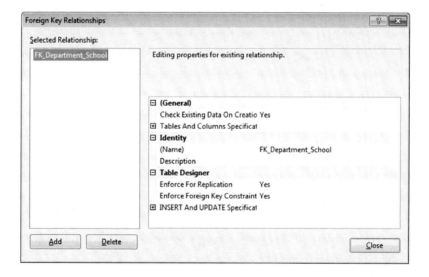

- Select "Tables and Columns Specifications," then click on the "…" button.

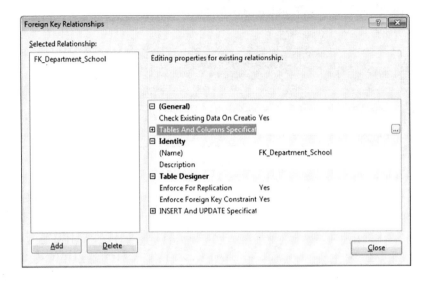

- In the next window, change the table name and columns within each to reflect the tables and columns associated with the one-to-many relationship.

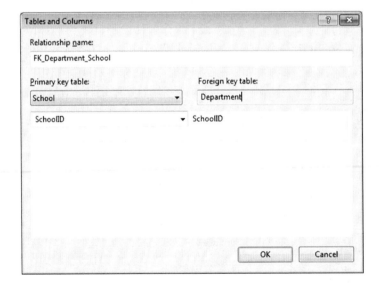

- Take a minute to review the table and columns identified for this relationship. If they are correct, click OK.

- Next, select Insert and Update Specifications.

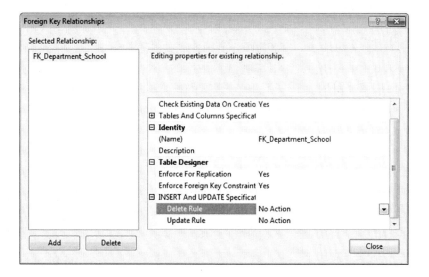

- Use the pull downs for the Update and Delete rules and change both to Cascade. This tells the RDBMS to enforce the RI constraint between School and Department.

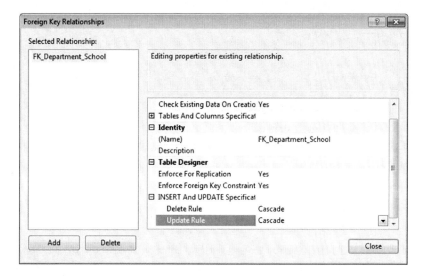

- Click Close to end the RI constraint specifications. Next, click the top right x on the Design window, and click Yes on the window to save these changes.

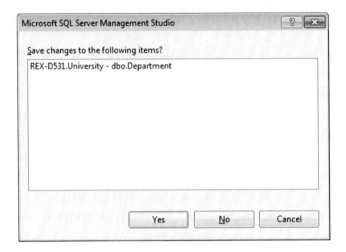

- Repeat this sequence to create RI constraints for each of the remaining one-to-many relationships.

At this point, the database is ready for use. As a first step, user accounts will be created.

7.4 USER ROLES

When creating user accounts for database users, you can set permissions for table-level read or update authority, or add administrative permissions for each user. This is very tedious and error prone. It is much easier to define Roles for users and grant detailed privileges at the Role level. Later, when creating an account for a new user, simply assign that role to the user to grant those permissions.

The SQL Server Management Studio can be used to create roles at a broad level. For example, for a University database, the following Roles would typically be used.

- *Read*: Read-only access to all tables, typically granted to students or administrative tasks that have no update authority.

- *Update*: Read and write access to all tables, but no authority to alter table definitions.

- *Developer*: A user with read and write access to all changes and can change table definitions.

To create one of these roles, use Management Studio to select the University database, click on Security and then Roles. Next, select Database Roles, right-click, and select New Database Role.

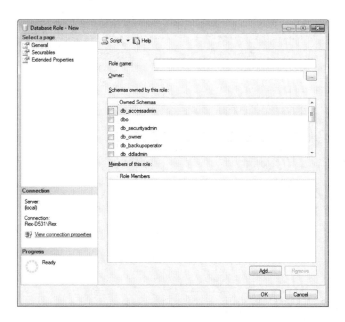

- Give the role a name (e.g., Developer), enter "dbo" for owner, then select the appropriate entry from the pull-down items. See the following to show read, update, and Data Definition Language authority for the Developer role.

- Click OK to create that role.

- Now repeat this process to create the "Read" role for read-only access and "Update" for users with table update authority.

For more precise permission control, use Transact-SQL (the command line interface) to define a schema and associate role to manage read and write permission at the Table level.

7.5 AUTHORIZED USERS

If you recall, we chose "Mixed Mode" when the database was created, which allows the use of both Windows accounts as well as internal SQL Server user accounts to control user permissions.

SQL Server accounts should be used to manage user accounts and permissions.

- In classified environments, SQL Server DBAs are not allowed to have system administrator accounts and privileges as a security measure. They therefore have no control over creation of Windows accounts.

- Having all user accounts in a single location makes them easier to manage.

User accounts on an SQL Server instance can be managed in two ways.

- To create an account for any/all databases running on that instance, select the primary Security tab, click on Logins, and right-click on the New Login pop up.

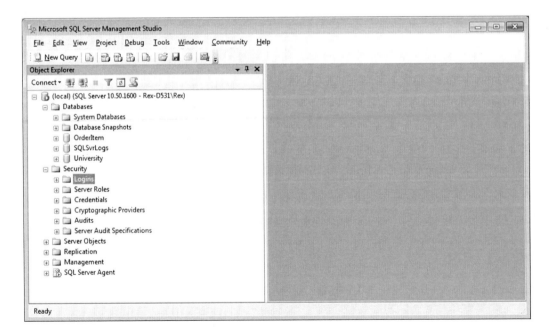

The following screen will open.

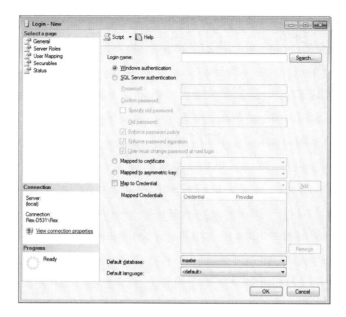

- Next, click on SQL Server authentication.

- Fill in the account name for the user and enter a password. Note the checks to force the user to change the password on the first logon and to enforce password policy (strength of the password and periodic changes).

- Click the Default database arrow and select the default database for this user.

- Click OK to create this account.

To grant Read access to this user, select the user name in the Security tab.

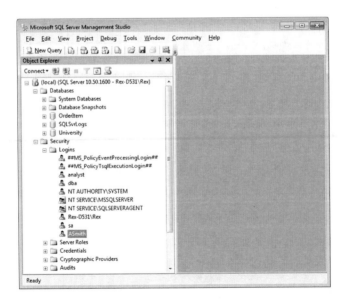

- Next, right-click on the name and select Properties.

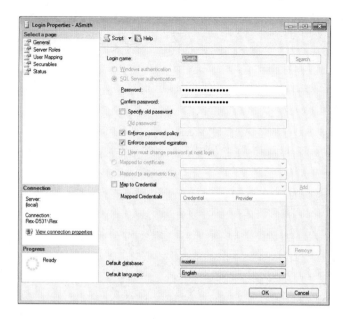

- Use the pull down to change the Default database to University. Next, click the User Mapping label.

- Click the box for University, then at the bottom select Read, Update, or Developer to assign that role to this user.

Remember to always use the primary Security tab to add users, then modify that user account to map it to the appropriate database and assign permissions as appropriate.

7.6 BACKUP/RECOVERY

Database Backup/Recovery services give the user the capability to restore a database to a point before a database failure occurred.

To take a copy of the database, first select the database in question.

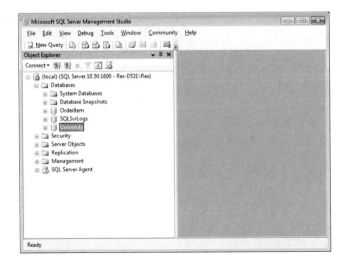

- Next, right-click and choose Tasks/Backup.

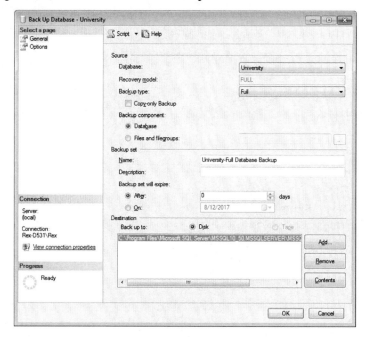

- Review the settings. Note that the Backup type gives options for Full, Differential, and Transaction Log.

  If desired, change the backup location to a different drive or directory. Click OK to take the backup file.

- Also note the Options tab.

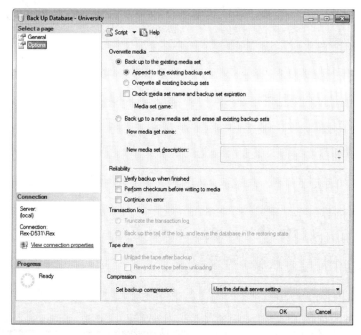

- Note by default, the output file is appended when a backup is taken. The Append provides more options for recovery in the future to deal with any user errors or application updates, but of course results in more disk space being used.

- Click OK to create the backup file.

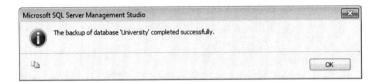

- To create a job to automatically take a backup on a scheduled basis, repeat the above-mentioned steps but click Scripts in the following window.

- After selecting Scripts, choose Script Action to Job.

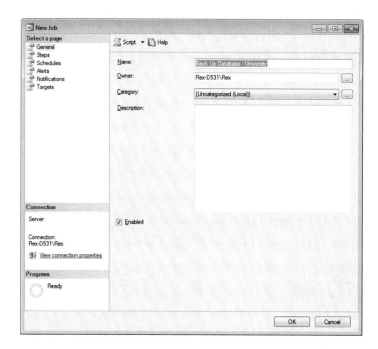

- From this window select Steps, then click Edit to see the details of the job being created.

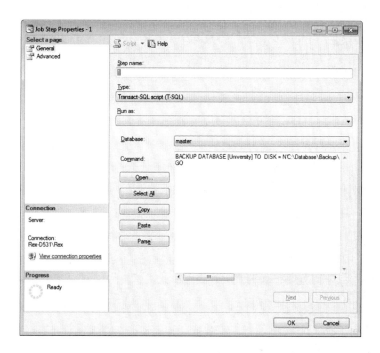

- From the prior window, click Schedule and then New.

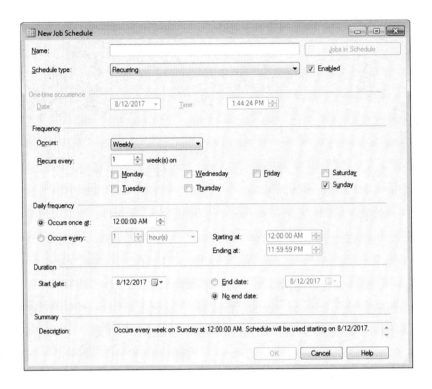

- Specify date and time settings, then click OK.

A job has now been created to automatically run the job per the settings recorded. See the Jobs entry in SQL Server Agent to monitor the status of the automated backup job.

7.7 LOADING DATA INTO TABLES

As with Microsoft Access, SQL Server has wizards which make it easy to import data from an external source into a table.

To start the process, select the name of the database to be updated.

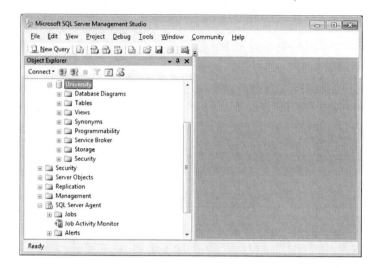

- Next, right-click and choose Tasks/Import data to start the import wizard.

- Click Next to move to the window where the source and destination are designated. Click the pull down on Data source to select the origin of the input. In the following, a flat file has been selected.

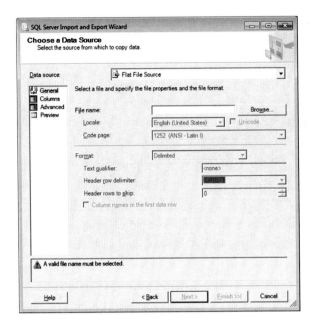

- Use the Browse button to navigate to the file to be imported.

    Note the entries under Format.

    - Text in the input file may have delimiters (e.g., "); enter that delimiter, if used.

    - If the file is originated from a UNIX platform, the Header row delimiter must be changed to line feed.

    - The input file may, or may not, have headers. Set the Header rows to skip accordingly.

- Clicking Next previews the data being imported.

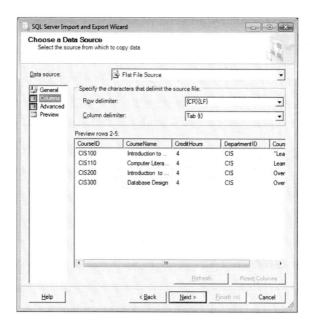

- Clicking Next moves to the Destination options.

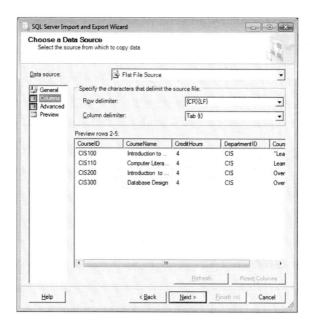

- Click Next to show a mapping between source and destination.

- Note that the Destination is populated using the name of the input file. Click the Destination column, then use the pull-down list to select the table being updated.

- Select Edit Mappings to verity the mapping on input and output column operations; change when appropriate. Click the Enable identity, insert if the target table has an ever-increasing integer value as its key column.

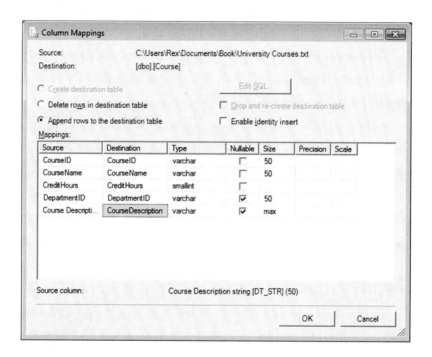

- Click OK, then select Preview to see anticipated results of the import.

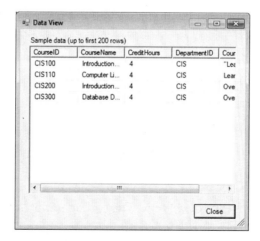

- Click Close, then Next to see one final check.

- Click Next, then Run immediately to start the import.

Note the option to save the details of the import operation to repeat the process in the future.

- Click Next, then Finish to start the import.

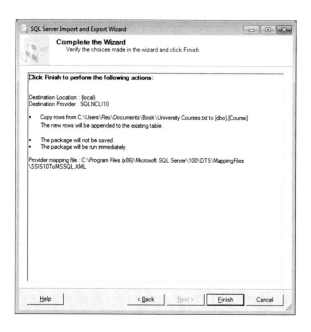

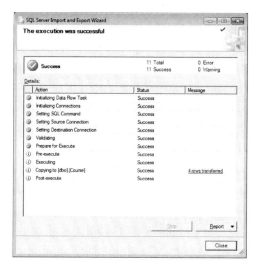

The Import/Export wizard can also be used to move table data between two different databases.

When loading data into tables with Referential Integrity constraints, the table on the *one* side of a relationship must be updated before the table on the *many* side.

7.8 CREATING VIEWS

Now let us see how to create a View to support queries against the database.

In Section 7.3.2, we saw how to create an index in the University database to more rapidly support a query to see all courses taught by a specific instructor. Let us now create a View to display the results of such a query.

- Expand the University database and click on View.

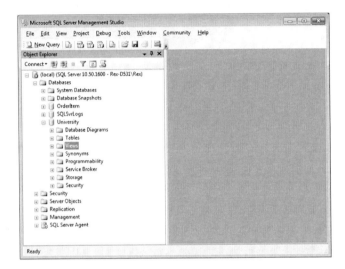

- Right-click on View and select "New view" from the pull down; the following window opens showing all tables available for the view.

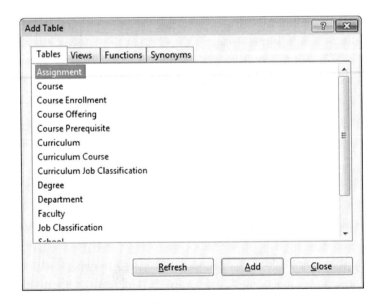

- For each table needed, select the table name then click Add. For this query, we will need information from the Faculty, Course Offering, and Course tables. The following display shows the design pane after adding these tables.

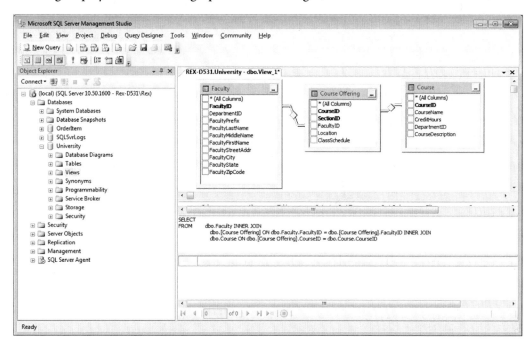

- Next, click on the column names to be displayed. For Faculty, we want the instructor's ID and name; for Course Offering, the ClassSchedule showing when it meets; and for Course, the Course ID and name.

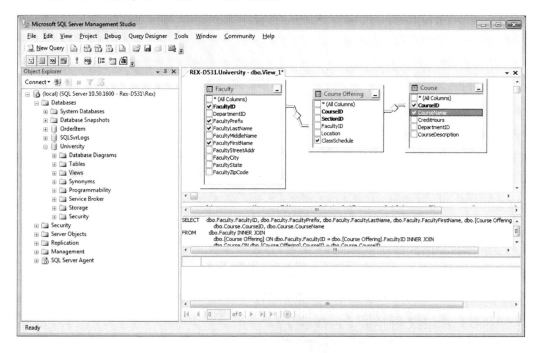

- Click the x at the top right of the design window to close the view, click Yes to save it, typing in a name on the next window.

The view has now been saved.

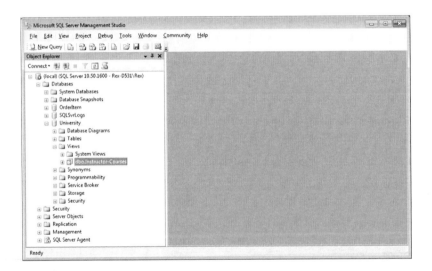

To run the query, open the Views tab in the University database and double-click the view to be used to run the query.

7.9 MANUAL QUERIES AND EDITS

SQL Server Management Studio makes it easy to manually view or update rows in a table.

- To manually see rows in the Course Enrollment table, expand the Tables option in the University database, right-click Course Enrollment, and click on "Select top 1000 rows."

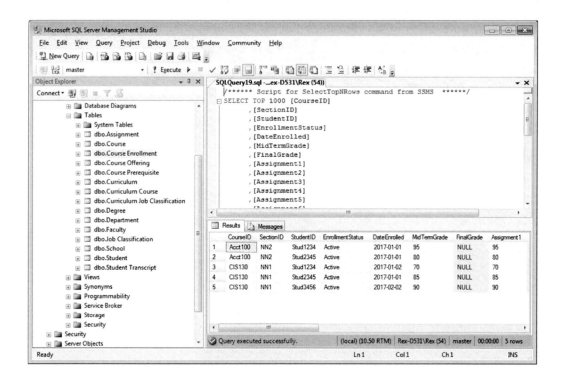

- To further qualify the query, scroll down the top-right pane to see all of the SQL code for the query.

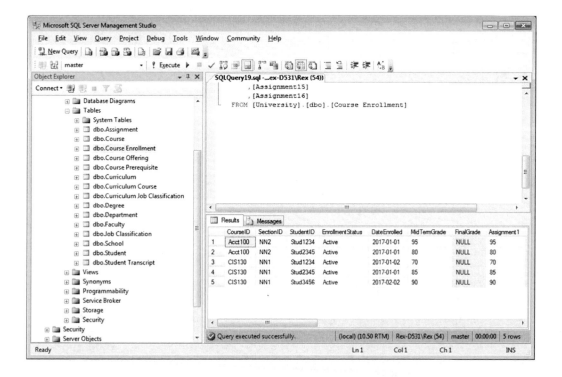

- To see only student for CIS130, add "where CourseID = 'CIS130'" to the SQL code, then click the "! Execute" button at the top of the window.

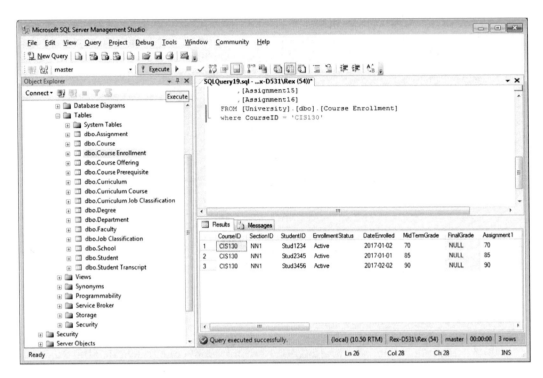

To do simple edits, select the table name, right-click, and select "Edit top 200 rows."

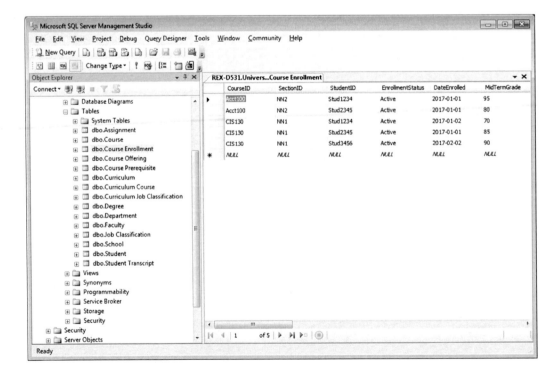

All of the columns in the display are editable. Change individual entries as needed, and click the x at the top right of the pane to close the table.

For more complex edits, create a view of the target table selecting columns of interest and qualifying the view if necessary to select rows of interest. Save the view, then select it by name, right-click, and select "Edit top 200 rows."

7.10 USING STORED PROCEDURES

A Stored Procedure is a collection of SQL statements that are compiled and stored in the RDBMS. When executed, it will typically perform a predefined set of updates to the database.

Stored Procedures are an ideal place to store repeatable application logic. Developers are removed from having to deal with the logic or rules embedded within the procedure and simply call/invoke it by name when needed.

As one example, in the SQLSvrLogs database, when new WarningRecords and ErrorRecords rows are imported, the tracking flags in each are *null* (have no value). A Stored Procedure is needed to initialize those flags to "0."

To create this Stored Procedure, expand the database and Programmability options, select Stored Procedure, and right-click on New Stored Procedure.

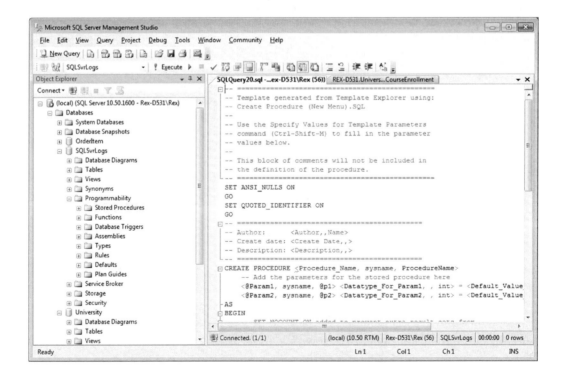

A template opens to enter the code for the Stored Procedure. Note the green blocks for comments and blue lines for SQL statements.

SQL code to initialize the tracking flags appears in the next window. Note the *where* qualifiers which limit the updates to only new rows which have *null* values by default.

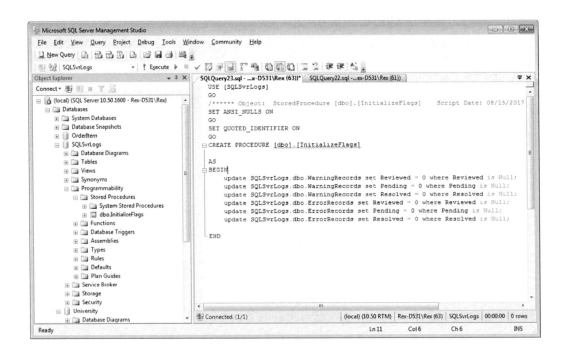

After adding the SQL code, click the "! Execute" button to run the code and create the Stored Procedure.

To make changes to a Stored Procedure, use the database/Programmability/Stored Procedure sequence to show a list of all Stored Procedures, select the one to be updated, right-click, and choose Modify.

A window will open showing the original code in a "Modify Procedure" block. Make changes as needed, then click "! Execute" to run the code to modify the logic.

7.11 USING SQL SERVER AGENT

SQL Server Agent is a component of SQL Server that allows DBAs to create and schedule jobs, including the details of each step within a job. To add a job, start (if necessary) open SQL Server Agent, select Jobs, right-click, and click on New Job.

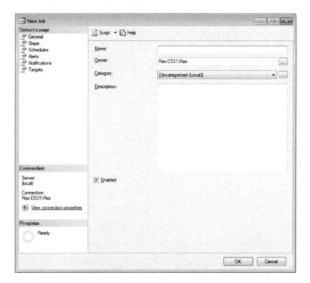

- Enter the job name and select a Category, then select Steps to add details of specific actions to take.

Note the buttons to move the sequence of tasks within a job. There are also options to specify the action to take when the step completes successfully or if it fails.

Jobs are often used to

- Schedule a backup of the database.

- Automatically import new files into tables.

- Generate daily reports.

- If connected to the Internet, run maintenance checks and send alerts to DBAs when appropriate.

- Rebuild indexes to conserve on space.

- As an example, at one point in time I had the responsibility of monitoring an SQL Server instance at a remote location. To verify SQL Server was continually running, I created a task that periodically did an export of a small table to a file, which in turn was ftp'ed to a server used to monitor the status of system components. The date/time of the exported file was used to verify SQL Server was running at that day and time.

The SQL Server Agent has a manual interface to Error Logs to view the current log or older logs that have archived.

Note also that the system services for SQL Server and for SQL Server Agent are independently managed, although of course the SQL Server service must be started first.

Although the SQL Server Management Studio gives the DBA a powerful, easy-to-use interface for defining and managing databases and for performing maintenance tasks, additional software tools are needed to provide user interfaces needed by users.

- Chapter 9 shows how Microsoft Access can be used as a GUI to provide application functionality, using links to SQL Server tables.

- For more sophisticated applications, Chapter 11 shows how to use PHP to create a web-based interface to an SQL Server database.

QUESTIONS

1. Explain the difference between a RDMS and a relational database.

2. When doing hardware planning for an SQL Server database, what type of files must be planned for and mapped to disk drives(s)?

3. If you installed SQL Server on a laptop, how would you configure the database files mentioned in #2?

4. If you installed SQL Server on a desktop computer with two disk drives, how would you configure/store the database files mentioned in #2?

5. If you installed SQL Server on a server with RAID 5 disk drives, how would you configure/store the database files mentioned in #2?

6. When configuring an SQL Server Database Backup, you can choose to overwrite or append the new backup to the output file. Which would you choose and why? What are the ramifications of this decision regarding recoverability options?

7. When creating a new table, how is the primary key identified?

8. When creating a table, when is the "Allow null" option selected for a column?

9. When creating a table whose key column is an ever-increasing numeric value, how is that column defined when it is created?

10. When defining a column in a table, how can an index be created on that column?

11. When creating tables for a new database, when are indexes automatically created?

12. What steps must be taken to create a View of three linked tables in a database?

13. When defining an index on a column, does that index have to be unique?

14. What is the significance of a "Clustered Index"?

15. What does it mean to *rebuild* an index? When is that done?

Using Perl to Extract and Load Data

8.1 WHY PERL?

After moving into the Intelligence Community and beginning to support Intelligence Analysts, it did not take long before users needed to find and extract specific types of data strings that were embedded within a collection of files or documents.

This began with finding and extracting phone numbers found within each file. By using Perl, you can, for example, search for data strings such as "nnn-nnnn" (three digits, followed by a dash, followed by four more digits) by specifying a pattern search "s/(\d\d\d-\d\d\d\d)/." In this pattern, the "\d" specification calls for a match of any numeric character. If the phone numbers include area codes, the search pattern would be "s/(\d\d\d-\d\d\d-\d\d\d\d)/."

Date strings were also important and can appear in various ways. Perl can be used to find and modify them when necessary to conform to a local standard. For example, a date string with the format "yyyy-mm-dd" can be changed to "mm/dd/yyyy" using the following search string:

```
"s/(\d{4})-(\d{1,2})-(\d{1,2})/$2\/$3\/$1/"
```

Let us analyze each element in detail.

- The "(" and ")" characters bound/identify a single search element.

- The (\d{4}) string specifies exactly four numerical digits.

- The (\d{1,2}) strings specify numeric strings either one or two digits long.

- So, the above-mentioned specifications within the first two "/" delimiters can be read as "four numeric digits followed by a '-' followed by one or two digits followed by a dash followed by one or two more digits."

- The "()" pairs delimit unique string variables. In the above, the first ($1) represents the year, the second ($2) the month, and the third ($3). Used in this context, it allows changing the order of the string variables found between the original and the modified output.

- This "s" syntax can be read as "change yyyy-mm-dd to mm/dd/yyyy."

In general, then, Perl scripts are used to search files and identify records that have character strings that match specific patterns. When found, that record is typically broken down into substrings, and records are written to an output file using the character strings found.

A typical application would be to analyze log records for a computer or database. Search patterns are created to identify/classify log records with *information*, *warnings*, or *errors*, decomposing those records, and writing these records to informational, warning, or error output files. When finished, those output files can then be reviewed by an administrator or database administrator (DBA) to determine the *general health* of the system being monitored and to identify any corrective action necessary.

Search patterns can also be used to identify:

- Variations of date and time expressions.

- Phone numbers and zip codes.

- Records that contain any of a number of search terms of interest.

When a record is found that matches some search pattern, Perl has numerous functions that support decomposing records/input strings and analyzing its contents.[1] The more useful include:

- split—to decompose a string into subfields based on a common field delimiter (often tabs, commas, or spaces).

- substr—to create a substring of a record beginning at a specified offset and length.

- length—find the length of a character string.

- index—find the location in a string where a substring begins.

- chomp—remove line separators between records in an input file.

- while—identifies the start of a series of commands. Used after opening a file, it identifies the start of logic on how to treat/process records in the file.

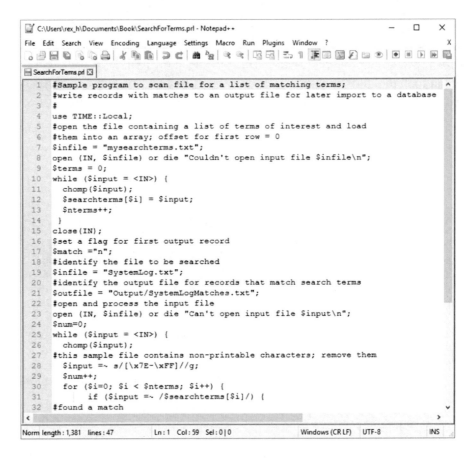

```
C:\Users\rex_h\Documents\Book\SearchForTerms.prl - Notepad++                    —    □    ×
File  Edit  Search  View  Encoding  Language  Settings  Macro  Run  Plugins  Window  ?          X

SearchForTerms.prl
  1  #Sample program to scan file for a list of matching terms;
  2  #write records with matches to an output file for later import to a database
  3  #
  4  use TIME::Local;
  5  #open the file containing a list of terms of interest and load
  6  #them into an array; offset for first row = 0
  7  $infile = "mysearchterms.txt";
  8  open (IN, $infile) or die "Couldn't open input file $infile\n";
  9  $terms = 0;
 10  while ($input = <IN>) {
 11    chomp($input);
 12    $searchterms[$i] = $input;
 13    $nterms++;
 14    }
 15  close(IN);
 16  #set a flag for first output record
 17  $match ="n";
 18  #identify the file to be searched
 19  $infile = "SystemLog.txt";
 20  #identify the output file for records that match search terms
 21  $outfile = "Output/SystemLogMatches.txt";
 22  #open and process the input file
 23  open (IN, $infile) or die "Can't open input file $input\n";
 24  $num=0;
 25  while ($input = <IN>) {
 26    chomp($input);
 27  #this sample file contains non-printable characters; remove them
 28    $input =~ s/[\x7E-\xFF]//g;
 29    $num++;
 30    for ($i=0; $i < $nterms; $i++) {
 31        if ($input =~ /$searchterms[$i]/) {
 32  #found a match

Norm length : 1,381  lines : 47      Ln : 1  Col : 59  Sel : 0 | 0      Windows (CR LF)   UTF-8        INS
```

FIGURE 8.1   First part of script to search file based on search terms.

See lines 10–14 in Figure 8.1 to see how a while loop is used to read all records in a file.

- if/then/else constructs to group logic to be used when specific search patterns are found.

- s—the general *substitute* operator, for example, "s/aaa/bbb/g," specifies changing the string "aaa" to "bbb" whenever found.

- system—execute an operating system command. For example, it is frequently used to execute a directory command to find the names of all files in a directory and write those names to a file. That file in turn can then be opened in the Perl script to identify and open files that need to be processed.

- sleep—pause the execution of a script for a specified time. This does not use any CPU time and is used in a script that runs continuously to wait for a specified time before continuing with the next cycle of checks/operations performed by the script.

- Arrays—a simple list accessed by index number.

Arrays are simple but extremely useful. In the following example, an array is used to store the contents of a file of search terms of interest to the user community associated with a specific subject area. Those terms then form the basis for a scan of a collection of log files, in which records containing any of these terms are written to an output file. This output file would then be imported into a database for further review and analysis.

As one possible application, users of Department of Defense computer systems are prohibited from using government systems for illegal purposes/acts, for example, to search the internet for pornography. By using this approach, system administrators can create a file of terms typically associated with pornography and use that file as input to scan new proxy log files to identify users doing internet searches using those terms. The script can be set up to run every hour, with the files for search results imported into a database for further review and analysis by system analysts.

Figure 8.1 shows the first part of a script to perform these operations, which is shown in Appendix D.

- Lines 7–15 open the input file of search terms and load each line as one element of the array.

- Next, lines 16–23 open the input file to be searched (in this case, a system log file).

- Lines 25–43 in Figure 8.2 show the logic for searching each record for a match of a search term.

- Line 26 removes the record separator at the end of the first record.

- The file being analyzed is a log file containing nonprintable characters. Line 28 removes those characters from the input record.

- Lines 20–42 show how, for each record, the record is scanned for a matching term. If a match is found, a record is written to an output file. Note the logic in lines 35–42 that opens the output file the first time a match is found.

  In practice, the output file would then be imported into a database. Analysts would then review what was found to see what, if any, further actions are necessary.

  As another example, Oracle Database Administrators can use this approach to constantly monitor Oracle database logs for informational, warning, and error conditions that are of interest.

- First, they would create three different files of search terms, each containing the Oracle message number/label of interest for that condition/state.

- When started, the script would read each set of search terms into different arrays.

- Next, the script would open and read the Oracle log file, searching for log records with a date–time stamp that is more current from the last time the script was run.

```
     C:\Users\rex_h\Documents\Book\SearchForTerms.prl - Notepad++          –  □  ×
 File  Edit  Search  View  Encoding  Language  Settings  Macro  Run  Plugins  Window  ?          X

 SearchForTerms.prl
 16   $set a flag for first output record
 17   $match ="n";
 18   #identify the file to be searched
 19   $infile = "SystemLog.txt";
 20   #identify the output file for records that match search terms
 21   $outfile = "Output/SystemLogMatches.txt";
 22   #open and process the input file
 23   open (IN, $infile) or die "Can't open input file $input\n";
 24   $num=0;
 25   while ($input = <IN>) {
 26     chomp($input);
 27   #this sample file contains non-printable characters; remove them
 28     $input =~ s/[\x7E-\xFF]//g;
 29     $num++;
 30     for ($i=0; $i < $nterms; $i++) {
 31         if ($input =~ /$searchterms[$i]/) {
 32   #found a match
 33           print "Match on $searchterms[$i] in $input\n";
 34   #open output file on first match
 35           if ($match eq "n") {
 36             open (OUT, ">$outfile") or die "Can't open output file $outfile\n
 37             $match = "y";
 38             }
 39           $message = "Found $searchterms[$i] in $input";
 40           print (OUT "$message\n");
 41           }
 42         }
 43     }
 44   close(IN);
 45   close(OUT);
 46
 47

 Norm length : 1,381  lines : 47    Ln : 12  Col : 29  Sel : 0 | 0    Windows (CR LF)  UTF-8    INS
```

FIGURE 8.2   Second part of script to search file based on search terms.

- When a new log record is found, it would be checked against each of the three arrays of search terms, with any matches written to an associated output file. Note that the name of the output file would contain an element identifying when the file was created.

- The script would save the most recent date–time stamp from the log file for use on the next cycle.

- The script would then *sleep* for a designated time frame (e.g., 30 min) before running again.

This script would run continuously, and at the end of each cycle, the files of search results would be moved to a directory to be reviewed by DBAs monitoring the database system's overall health.

- Hashes (associative arrays)—a hash is an array using an index to store a value. Hash variables provide extremely fast access in searching the array for values associated with the key term.

They are extremely useful when searching files for records that contain a match for some term in a predefined list. Terms of interest are first loaded into a hash when the script starts. Next, when a new record is read and broken into substrings, each substring can be compared to the indexed hash to one if there is a match.

- time, localtime—get the current date and time.

- A "." is used to concatenate two character strings, for example, $newstring = $string1. $string2.

- int—a function used to return the integer portion of a variable or calculation.

- %—a modulus operator to find the difference between to integers. I have often used this to make decisions on the basis of the current time stamp when an operation begins.

For example, assume an environment where one server acts as a file collection system that receives files and then pass them off to one of three servers for detailed analysis/processing. Let us also assume Server1 and Server2 have half the processing capability of Server3. Let us look at how % can be used to evenly distribute the workload across these three servers.

- First, get the current time and set a variable to the current value of the minute, $min.

- Next, compute the value of a variable based on a modulus of four by computing "$val = $min % 4;". As a result, the value of $val will vary from 0 to 3, that is,

```
if $min = 1, $min % 4 will equal 1;
if $min = 2, $min % 4 will equal 2;
if $min = 3, $min % 4 will equal 3;
if $min = 4, $min % 4 will equal 0;
if $min = 5, $min % 5 will equal 1; and so on.
```

Note that by using a modulus of 4, each value of $val will occur 25% of the time. The value of $val, therefore, can be used to invoke logic blocks that will be activated 25% of the time, based on the clock time when the logic starts. By using this approach, files can be forwarded using this logic:

```
$val = $min % 4;
if ($val == 1) {
 <commands to ftp/sftp files to Server1>
}
elseif ($val == 2) {
 <commands to ftp/sftp files to Server2>
}
elseif ($val == 3) {
 <commands to ftp/sftp files to Server3>
}
```

```
elseif ($val == 0) {
 <commands to ftp/sftp files to Server3>
}
```

Note also that because Server3 is twice as powerful as the other two, it will receive files 50% of the time, and each of the other servers receives files 25% of the time.

8.2 PERL VERSUS PYTHON

As much as I love Perl, Python has recently evolved as an equivalent software product. I have experimented with Python and see some advantages, but the two products have the same general functionality and capabilities.

Python uses and recognizes tabs as part of the logic to identify and manage the beginning and end of logical operations.

Perl takes roughly twice as much code to produce the same result, but a Perl script is *totally readable*; "what you see is what you get." Not having to worry about tab indentations make Perl scripts so much more readable and manageable, especially when you have inherited scripts written by someone else.

8.3 WINDOWS VERSUS UNIX

Perl software is free and runs on both Windows and Unix platforms.

For Windows, the ActivePerl project provides a commercial-grade community distribution which can be downloaded for both 32- and 64-bit computers. For Unix, Perl comes preinstalled on essentially all Unix operating systems.

Scripts written in Perl can run somewhat transparently between Windows and Unix computers.

- Scripts often must invoke *system* (operating system) commands. Those are of course different between Windows and Unix.

- If the script interrogates directories to find and process files, the most significant changes involve dealing with the separator variables when interrogating/using a directory path. Unix directory paths use "/" separators, whereas Windows uses "\" characters.

As an example, assume the user *Analyst* has a *Documents* directory that in turn contains an "InputFiles" directory. Our script needs to identify all files within the InputFiles directory and open and process each. Let us look at the code necessary to find and open each file.

For Unix, the script would first issue a command to create a file that contains the names of all files found there. The Perl commands would be

```
#create a variable identifying the directory to be checked
$chkdir = "/home/Analyst/Documents/InputFiles";
#create a file containing a list of all files in that directory
# and write the files found to a file named "filelist"
#..first, create the command to be executed
```

```
$cmd = "ls $chkdir > filelist";
#next, invoke that command to create filenames
system ($cmd);
#now open the list of files to be processed
$inputfile = filelist;
open (LIST, $inputfile) or die "Can't open file list
$inputfile\n";
while ($files = <LIST>) {
 chomp ($files);
#create a variable with the name of the file to be opened
# by concatenating the directory name and the file name
 $filenames = "$chkdir" . "$files";
#open and process that file
 open (IN, $filenames) or die "Can't open input file
$filenames\n";
 while ($input = <IN>) {
  chomp($input);
  .
  .
  .

 }
 close (IN);
}
close (LIST);
```

This script can be modified to run in Windows with minimal changes.

- First, the details of the directory path must be modified using "\" separators. Using the Unix naming convention shown earlier, the directory would be "\home\Analyst\ Documents\InputFiles;" using Windows naming conventions modifies the directory name to "\Users\Analyst\Documents\InputFiles."

- Next, a Perl variable set to "\Users\Analyst\Documents\InputFiles" would not work *as is* because the "\" character has a special meaning in Perl and is ignored as an input character/value. The "\" tells Perl to treat the next character in the string *as is* and to ignore any special meaning associated with it.

  For example, to use a "?" as part of a search pattern, we would use "\$" in that pattern to specify the use of the $ as a character. Otherwise, Perl treats the $ as a *metacharacter* specifying the end of a string.[1]

  To tell Perl we want to treat the "\" as a character value and not as a meta-character, we change the string to include two "\\" characters:

  "\\Users\\Analyst\\Documents\\InputFiles."

- In addition, the command to list files in a directory must be changed from the Unix "ls" to the DOS equivant "dir".

As a result, the Windows version of this script is

```
#create a variable identifying the directory to be checked
$chkdir = "\\Users\\Analyst\\Documents\\InputFiles";
#create a file containing a list of all files in that directory
# and write the files found to a file named "filelist"
#..first, create the command to be executed
$cmd = "dir $chkdir > filelist";
#next, invoke that command to create filenames
system ($cmd);
#now open the list of files to be processed
$inputfile = filelist;
open (LIST, $inputfile) or die "Can't open file list $inputfile\n";
while ($files = <LIST>) {
 chomp ($files);
#create a variable with the name of the file to be opened
# by concatenating the directory name and the file name
 $filenames = "$chkdir" . "$files";
#open and process that file
 open (IN, $filenames) or die "Can't open input file $filenames\n";
 while ($input = <IN>) {
  chomp($input);

  .

  .

  .

}
 close (IN);
}
close (LIST);
```

I have rarely had to move/migrate scripts between Unix and Windows. However, the fact that Perl scripts are 98% portable made it much easier and faster to develop new applications or services by reusing sophisticated logic regardless of the computer platform.

8.4 REVIEW KEY MATCHING FEATURES

In the previous sections, we have seen examples of Perl scripts to identify and open files in a directory that are ready for processing as well as scripts to search the contents of these files for a specific set of terms. Now, let us review some of the more advanced search patterns that can be used. In each case, assume the script has opened and is processing an input file read as $record.

To search log records for records beginning with "Error":

```
#read "if record begins with "Error"
if ($record =~ /^Error/) {
#additional logic on what to do
}
```

To search records for a phone number using a pattern of "nnn-nnn-nnnn":

Option 1:

```
#note multiple patterns of [0-9] (specifies any character from
0 to 9)
#with - delimiters
if ($record =~ /[0-9][0-9][0-9]-[0-9][0-9][0-9]-[0-9][0-9][0-9]
[0-9]/) {
#additional logic on what to do
}
```

Option 2:

```
#note (\d{3}) calls for 3 consecutive digits
if ($record =~ /(\d{3})-(\d{3})-(\d{4})/) {
#additional logic on what to do
}
```

To search records for a time pattern of "nn:nn AM":

```
#note the first pattern calls for either one or two digits
if ($record =~ /(\d{1,2}):(\d{2}) AM/) {
#additional logic on what to do
}
```

8.5 MONITOR SQL SERVER LOGS

Now let us take a look at a Perl script that can be used to continually monitor Structured Query Language (SQL) Server log files. First, let us review some basic information about the SQL Server log files.

- Note that SQL Server error messages are much simpler than Oracle log files, classifying each message as informational, warning, or error messages.

- SQL Server logs are installation specific. In this example, they were installed by default in the C:\Windows\Program Files\Microsoft SQL Server\MSSQL\Log directory.

- The simplest way to monitor the system is to continually monitor changes in the SQLAGENT.OUT file in SQL Server's Log directory. In this file, informational messages contain a "?" character, warning messages contain a "?", and error messages contain an "!".

  The following Perl script (shown in Appendix E) opens the SQLAGENT file and scans for informational, warning, and error messages. When found, they are written to a corresponding output file. At the end of the check cycle, the script pauses for 30 min and repeats the checks. Note that each output file includes a date/time stamp as part of the name to separate the information being generated from each cycle. At some appropriate time interval, all output files would be moved to a directory used by DBA's to monitor the database's status. Typically, another Perl script would run continuously in parallel to check for new files associated with error messages and display a *white on red* status message to alert DBA's to review new files for the latest error messages/updates.

Let us analyze this script in detail, starting with Figure 8.3.

- Line 5 defines a variable for the location of the SQL Server SQLAGENT file.

- Line 7 sets a user variable for the time delay between log checks. Here, it is set to 30 min, with the associated number of seconds computed in line 9.

- Line 9 determines the point at which the logic repeats with the next cycle.

- Lines 10–12 set flags for each class of output file; these flags control the opening of each class of file when the first record for each is found.

- Line 13 gets the current date and time information. A date–time variable is extracted in line 15 to make them usable as part of a file name; spaces and ":" characters are altered in lines 17 and 18.

- The log file is opened in line 20, and the cyclical check of the log records begins with line 21.

- Line 22 removes the line separators in the record.

- Line 23 removes all unprintable characters.

- Lines 23–27 extract the date–time string from the last non-blank record.

- In line 29, the date–time string is compared with the last date–time string from the previous check. If the current record has a date–time string with a lower value, it has already been checked and can be ignored.

- Lines 31–41 show the logic for handling informational records (i.e., those containing the "?" character).

- Lines 32–37 show the logic executed the first time an informational record is found in this check cycle. The file name is created embedding the date–time variable set in lines 14–19, the file is opened, and the log record written to it.

- In lines 38–40, if the output file is already open, the log record is written to it.

Figure 8.3 shows the remaining part of the script with logic for warning and error log records.

- Lines 42–52 duplicate the logic for lines 31–41 modified as needed to handle warning records identified with a "+" character. Note the use of the $warn variable to control the warning output file.

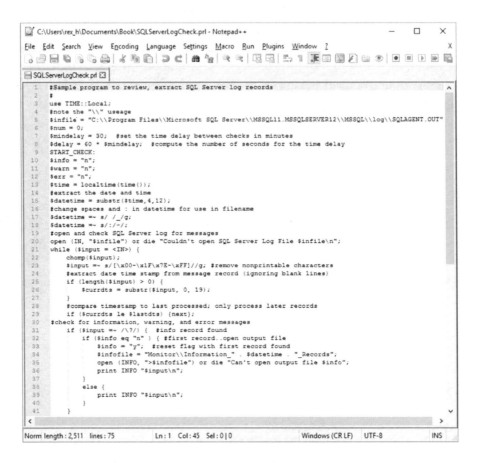

FIGURE 8.3   First part of script to monitor SQL Server logs.

- Lines 53–63 duplicate the logic for lines 31–41 modified as needed to handle error records identified with an "!" character. As was done earlier, the $err variable controls the error output file.

- After the file is checked, the last date–time string is saved in line 66. All files are then closed in lines 67–70.

- The local time is obtained in line 71 and used in the message generated by line 72.

- The *sleep* function invoked in line 73 temporarily halts all processing, and the process sleeps until the specified time delay ends.

- At that point, the logic is redirected by line 74 to resume processing at the START_ CHECK label at line 9.

Note that this process will loop/continuously process until manually interrupted/ canceled.

8.6 MONITORING WINDOWS LOGS

To monitor Windows logs, use the Windows Event Viewer to review the application, security, and system log collections. In each, errors are labeled using "Information," "Warning," and "Error" labels for each record. In most cases, simply reviewing the logs will provide sufficient information regarding the system's *health*.

To provide more of an in-depth analysis, Perl scripts can help by sifting through each file and consolidating message for each type. To perform this type of analysis,

- Open the Event Viewer and open the "Windows Logs" label to display the types of logs available for analysis. Note the Application, Security, and System labels.

- Select either the Application, Security, or System labels and note the list of log records that have been created. In the right-most pane, select "Save all events as" to create an external file containing these log records.

- Use the "Save as" browser window to navigate to the working directory in which these logs are to be stored for analysis.

- Next, change the "Save as type" to Text to create a tab-delimited text file using a file name indicating the type of log records being used.

- The script shown in Figures 8.3 and 8.4 can be modified to review and summarize these log records. These changes are fairly straight forward:

  - Change line 5 to indicate the directory path and name of the input file created earlier.

  - This script will be used once after each log record extraction and not run continuously. As such, the date–time information is not needed, so the code in lines 25–29 and 71–74 can be commented out or deleted. Note that the $datetime variable is still set for use when creating the name of the output file of log records.

  - In line 31, change the specification for information records from "/\?/" to "/Information/."

  - Similarly, in line 42, change "/\+/" to "/Warning/," and in line 53, change "/\!/" to "/Error/."

  - Finally, modify the $infofile, $warnfile, and $errfile variables to include the names "Application," "Security," or "System" based on the type of log file being analyzed.

- Repeat this process, changing the name of the input file and the $infofile, $warnfile, and $errfile variables as appropriate.

  These scripts are now ready for use. To analyze one or all of the Windows logs, use Event Viewer to extract and save the records to be reviewed in a tab-delimited file, then run the appropriate extraction script.

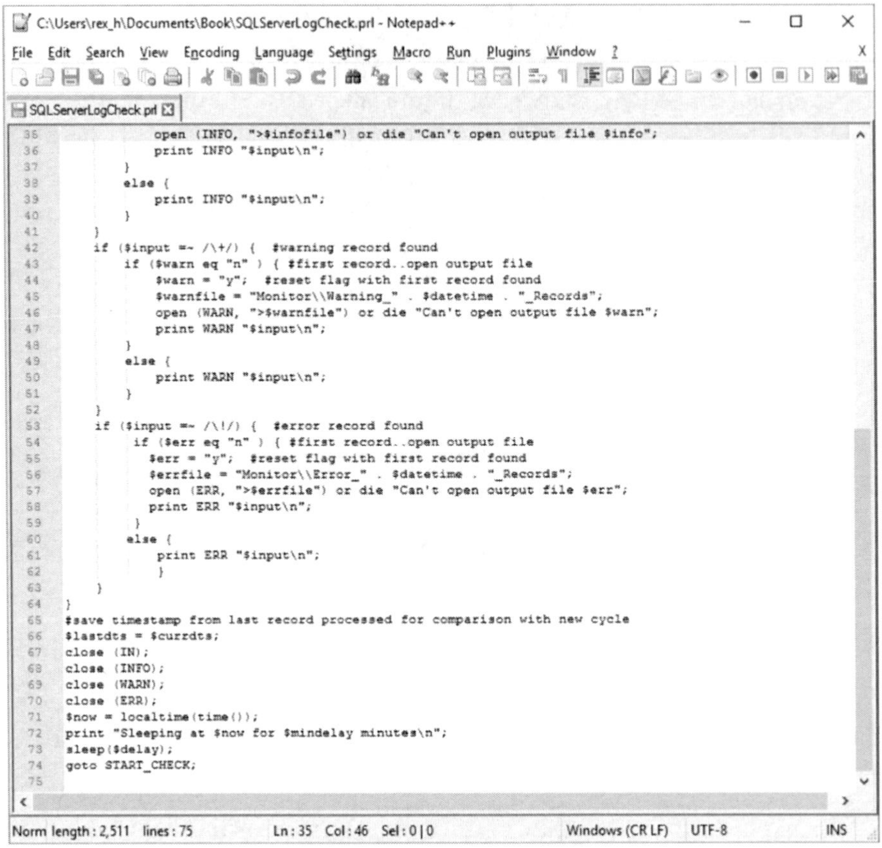

FIGURE 8.4   Second part of script to monitor SQL Server logs.

8.7 OTHER APPLICATIONS AND USES

In addition to the above, I have often used Perl to create various system monitors to continuously monitor the state of a system and/or its processes.

- When running on Unix, use *system* to invoke a "ps -ef|*processname*> checks" command. This command identifies all running process, filters them for the name *processname*, and write matches to a *checks* file. The checks file can then be opened and reviewed to verify that *processname* is running. If not, an error message can be displayed for corrective action.

- To verify that some host is *alive and well*, create and monitor a mechanism that creates a system *heartbeat*.

  - This may be as simple as monitoring a directory for new files that are created continuously.

- If SQL Server is running on that system, an agent can be created to periodically export the contents of a small table. Checking the date and time stamp of the exported file verifies that both the operating system and SQL Server are up and running.

- A Perl script can be written to create an output file each time run, then *sleep* for a specified period and repeat the process. Monitoring the date and time stamp of the output file confirms that the host and Perl script were active at that date and time.

- Next, a collection/monitoring script is needed to check the results of all monitoring scripts running by either directly checking to output directories in which these scripts run or by ftp/sftp-ing the results of these directories to a local directory. The monitoring script can then continuously check the health of a number of remote systems without requiring an analyst/administrator to continuously connect to each to perform a manual verification. When run on Unix, I always reset the display to *white on red* to make the information stand out.

If this monitoring script runs on Windows, it can be made even easier to use by not only displaying error messages when errors are found but also playing selected Windows sounds to get the attention of the analyst/administrator running the system checks. My personal favorites are the sound of glass breaking followed by a *tinkling* sound. They get your attention!

- Perl scripts can easily monitor a directory for new files that have been created and then take an appropriate action to forward or process the new files.

- The command-line option of Perl can be used for sophisticated editing of the file contents, for example, to enforce consistency of formatting of date/time strings.

8.8 LOADING DATA INTO TABLES

Hopefully by now, you have an understanding of how easy it is to use Perl to extract data from input file(s) and to create output files for analysis or review by analysts or administrators.

In some cases, simply reviewing new files may be sufficient. For example, DBAs can monitor an output directory for new files with warning and error messages regarding the *care and feeding* of their databases. Monitoring newly created files for current events/conditions will allow them to take whatever corrective action may be necessary. For example, a tablespace may be running out of space and needs to be extended.

If, however, such monitoring identifies problem symptoms that need to be investigated, these messages can be imported into a problem-tracking database and used by DBAs to identify and track the status of error messages that are being reviewed/investigated. A web-based interface for such a database is described in Chapter 11 to review and classify error records as *Reviewed* (no further action necessary), *Pending* (currently under investigation/analysis), and *Resolved* (problem/issue has been resolved). Using this approach requires importing the error messages captured into a database table.

In other cases, incremental changes on what is being monitored is insufficient, and a broader view of activity within the last day, week, or month is necessary to understand the scope and nature of what is being monitored. In this case, the files of change records must be imported into a database so that an analyst can query/review/summarize bulk activity to assess what is happening. Perhaps the best example of this is in the monitoring of proxy log files on government computer systems. Users of these systems know they are for official use only and that their activity will be monitored. Those warnings are often insufficient to prevent users from using government systems for other than official and/or authorized purposes.

For example, the script shown in Figures 8.1 and 8.2 can be used to build a monitoring system for *pornography*.

- First, files associated with *pornography* can be loaded as a set of search terms.

- Next, new proxy log records are reviewed to identify any internet activity associated with those terms.

- Finally, records that match one of these search terms can be imported into a *pornography* table for analysts to review in detail. This normally invokes review of all activity for a user over a period of time to identify real abuse versus a one-time *finger-check*/error.

  A web-based interface such as described in Chapter 11 can be created for analysts to allow them to classify records as *Reviewed* (no further analysis required), *Pending* (current records under review), and *Reported* (activity/records that have been reported).

Fortunately, files created with Perl can be easily imported into a database.

- Files can be directly imported into Microsoft Access, most commonly using a tab or comma delimited file as input.

- If using SQL Server, files can be imported into a table using SQL Server's *bcp* utility.

- If using Oracle, files are imported using Oracle's SQL*Loader utility.

Depending on the design and content of what is being monitored, the import function may be totally sufficient to update the database. In a more sophisticated application, such as monitoring and reporting on proxy log activity described in Chapter 11, newly imported rows need status flags set accordingly. Those can easily be handled within the database as part of import processing.

While the import processing is very straight forward, there are some subtleties that must be checked.

- The order of the data in the file to be imported will normally match the sequence of columns in the table's definition.

- Each row will normally have a key field/column embedded within the data record. In some cases, rows are identified only by an ever-ascending row value which is incremented automatically when new rows are imported.

- Imported files are driven/controlled by delimiters that separate the strings representing different columns. Check carefully to ensure that the delimiters chosen for use never appear within the character strings being imported.

- In some cases, post-processing of data in new rows is necessary. For example, in the proxy log monitoring discussed earlier, newly imported rows have *null* values for the Reviewed/Pending/Reported columns which should all be set by a database update to have *N* values, which flag new records that need to be reviewed by analysts.

8.9 SUMMARY

I have spent most of my work life with a database-centric point of view. In my later years as a developer of database systems, I have continually found user requirements that involved finding data within files of all types and extracting it, transforming it into *information* needed by the user community. Perl has been invaluable. Going forward, I would recommend including Perl (or Python) in every developer's *tool bag.*

QUESTIONS

1. What must be done to a PERL scripts being migrated from a UNIX to a Windows platform?

2. What are search patterns? What purpose do they serve?

3. Describe a pattern that will detect a date in the format of "mm-dd-yyyy."

4. Show the PERL command to change a date string "mm-dd-yyyy" to "yyyy-mm-dd."

5. What is the purpose of the *split* command? Give an example of how it can be used.

6. What is the purpose of the *index* operator? Give an example of how it can be used.

Refer to the PERL script shown in Figures 8.1 and 8.2.

7. What is the purpose of the $nterms variable?

8. What is the purpose of the "if" test in lines 31–42?

9. What is the purpose of the $match variable?

10. What records are written to the *Out* file?

11. If you wanted to expand the search to include additional terms, what would you do?

Refer to the PERL script shown in Figures 8.3 and 8.4.

12. In line 42, what is the purpose of the "\" character?

13. How are warning messages identified in the input file?

14. What are the output files produced when this script runs? Where are they stored?

15. What happens after the script runs and finishes searching for warning and error records?

REFERENCE

1. Medinets, D., *PERL 5 by Example*, Indianapolis, IN, Que Corporation, 1996, p. 203.

Building User Interfaces

9.1 MICROSOFT ACCESS IN A TYPICAL OFFICE ENVIRONMENT

As you might guess, the typical desktop environment for users in the Department of Defense (DOD) as well as in the Intelligence Community includes the Microsoft Office "Professional" or "Enterprise" software suite, which includes Microsoft Access. Yes, Microsoft Access is a *light-weight* database engine with limited capability to handle complex queries, but it is amazing how far you can *push* Access when that is all you have to work with.

9.1.1 General Capabilities

- As shown in Chapter 6, you can use Access to design, load, and query tables. In addition, Forms can be used to view or update subsets of data, and Reports can generate output of complex queries.

- Table links can be created to view and update tables residing in another database running on the user network. Links can be created for tables managed by Microsoft Access, Structured Query Language (SQL) Server, Oracle, and others.

- Complex queries for an SQL Server or Oracle database can be created in Access and classified as "Pass-Through" to forward the query directly the host database management system (DBMS) for execution.

- Very large Access databases can be supported by partitioning tables across multiple databases based on, for example, date ranges contained within the table. The user interface merely needs a *filter* to identify the data range of interest to the user, then opening the specific table-hosting data for that time period.

- Access contains embedded database administrator tools to shrink and *repair* the database, reclaiming free space and restoring tables and indexes.

9.1.2 Advantages

- Microsoft Office is standard software in essentially all government offices, including those in Intelligence Community and DOD.

- It is easy to import data into tables from flat files, Excel, or other databases.

- User functionality can be divided between a *Data* database having the core tables needed by users and a second database serving as the graphical user interface (GUI) to the data. The GUI would contain the query and update mechanisms and the Forms and Reports needed by users; its tables simply be links to the physical tables residing in the *Data* database. Each user would then be given a copy of the GUI database to run on their workstation.

- If/When necessary, a table can be *manually* viewed, sorted, and/or filtered to view data of interest. Those rows can subsequently be updated or deleted as needed.

9.1.3 Disadvantages

- Complex queries often require numerous work tables, queries, or macros to achieve a specific result. From the database administrator perspective, documentation for the design and functionality of the numerous components can prove difficult to write and maintain.

- Complex user displays can be difficult to create.

9.2 USE MICROSOFT ACCESS AS GUI

Microsoft Access can also be used simply as a GUI to view or update a database running on the user's network.

9.2.1 General Capabilities

- An Access database can be created in which the tables section only contains links to tables in another database.

- Access can be used to generate Windows-based screens to view or modify those tables.

- Pass-Through queries can be created to forward complex SQL queries to the database host.

- The GUI would be stored on each user's desktop computer.

9.2.2 Advantages

- Queries and Forms are normally quick and easy to design and test. Developers can get immediate feedback from users from the effectiveness and usefulness of the prototype being developed.

- Access is preinstalled on all DOD and Intelligence Community computers.

- ODBC links can be easily created to access SQL Server or Oracle databases running on the server.

- More complex queries can be passed to the server using the "Pass-Through" option. This passes the SQL for the query directly to the database on the server for interpretation and execution.

- As stated earlier, tables can be manually viewed, sorted, and/or filtered to display data of interest. These rows can then be updated or deleted as needed.

9.2.3 Disadvantages

- Complex queries are difficult to support. Multiple simple queries can be tied together to achieve a more complex result, but documenting the details of the design can be difficult.

- The GUI database must be installed on each user's computer.

- More complex user displays can be difficult to implement.

9.3 .NET FRAMEWORK

9.3.1 General Capabilities

- Microsoft's .NET Framework can generate complex Windows display of options and actions that can be performed.

- These implementations are *user aware* and can respond to the cursor position and mouse clicks.

- The software components are object oriented and typically use object-oriented design patterns.

- The .NET Framework is based on C++.

9.3.2 Advantages

- The Windows displays built in a .NET Framework are very powerful. Very complex windows can be displayed with *action* icons/buttons.

- These tools can interoperate with other Windows-based tools. For example, a display can be generated to interact with vendor software to monitor and control that vendor's surveillance cameras.

- Object-oriented "Design Patterns" are quite beneficial.

For example, the "Template" approach is quite effective in creating mechanisms to control different types of surveillance cameras. Essentially, all cameras require the same type of *agents* to control camera functions (tilt, zoom, etc.), but individual agents would contain the vendor-specific code to operate that type of camera.

9.3.3 Disadvantages

- The .NET Framework runs only on Microsoft Windows platforms.

- .NET implementations are totally dependent on the specific version of Microsoft operating system and internals used to build them.

- The .NET Framework and tools that run under it must be installed on each computer to be used.

- Development and support of .NET Framework tools are very complex and are deeply interwoven with Microsoft internals. In addition, they are difficult and complex to maintain.

- I found it difficult to update existing .NET-based tool because the behavior of the application can be mouse- or cursor-sensitive in which the developer does not *see* the code causing some result.

9.4 PHP

PHP is a widely used scripting language that can be used to develop web pages displaying information and options to users. Chapter 11 describes the creation and use of a web page to monitor database updates using PHP.

9.4.1 General Capabilities

- Options in each web page/window represent active links the user can select to open and process different web pages.

- Each web page has HTML component(s) to manage the display of data and/or options to the user and *hidden* code (invisible to web-based users) that check and act on parameters passed to the web page when opened.

- The *hidden* code can have embedded SQL statements to connect to, retrieve, and/or update data from a database.

9.4.2 Advantages

- Web pages built with PHP are independent of the operating system on client computers.

- Although hidden from users, the logic and SQL commands are seen in *clear text* by developers and are easy to read and maintain.

- PHP software can be downloaded at no cost.

9.4.3 Disadvantages

- The setup for a PHP-based implementation is somewhat complex.

- It requires (of course) a web browser running on the host.

- Typically, data encryption of web traffic is required.

- PHP requires database drivers for the DBMS to be used.

- PHP must be set up and activated on the host before development can begin.

9.5 JAVA

I have personally never developed web pages with JAVA. I have, however, worked in a support role in which a team of developers were using JAVA to build entire database applications for users.

9.5.1 General Capabilities

- JAVA applications can support complex displays and serve as a platform for database applications.

9.5.2 Advantages

- Development tools are commonly available.

9.5.3 Disadvantages

- Developers require additional training and use of development tools.

- JAVA is, in my opinion, not suitable for rapid prototyping.

QUESTIONS

1. When using Microsoft Access as a GUI, name two RDBMS's that can serve as the source for a database query.

2. When using Microsoft Access as a GUI, what is a linked table?

3. When using Microsoft Access as a GUI, how can a complex query using DBMS-specific SQL be executed?

4. By default, where is a Microsoft Access database installed? What users can run queries against the database?

5. Compare the use of Microsoft Access and PHP when performing a rapid prototype for a new database application.

A design team supporting a small group of analysts must do a rapid prototype to develop a GUI to be used to analyze data collected for the team.

6. What relational database management systems could be used to store the database and its tables?

7. Would a .NET framework be appropriate for use to develop the GUI? Why or why not?

8. Would Microsoft Access be appropriate for use as a GUI? Why or why not?

9. Would PHP be appropriate for use to develop the GUI? Why or why not?

Assume a university environment where hundreds of teachers and administrators have Windows-based computers varying in size and capacity and with a mixture of Windows 7 and Windows 10 operating systems. GUIs must now be developed to administer course and student information.

10. Would a .NET framework be appropriate for use? Why or why not?

11. Would Microsoft Access be appropriate for use? Why or why not?

12. Would PHP be appropriate for use? Why or why not?

Creating the University Database Application

In Chapter 6, we saw how Microsoft Access can be used to create and load tables, run simple queries, and create simple Forms. In the current chapter, we will see how to use Access to create a more complex application based on the University data model developed in Chapter 4. We will use Forms to create a Windows-based application to

- Enroll students into courses

- Enter grades for assignments

- Enter midterm and final grades

Let us begin by creating tables for the University database using the physical data model in Figure 4.7.

10.1 CREATE TABLES FOR UNIVERSITY ENVIRONMENT

Before we can create tables in a database, we must first create the relational database management system (RDBMS) system that will serve as a host to the tables and query mechanisms.

- From the Start menu, click on the Access label for your system (e.g., "Access 2016") to start the RDBMS software on your computer.

- Next, click "Blank Database" to start a new database management system instance.

- When the "Blank Database" screen opens, click on the folder icon and navigate to the directory in which the RDBMS is to be located. Next, change the file name to "University.accdb," and click "Create."

- The Table1 window opens in data entry mode with a default name for the first column as ID. Click the small "x" at the top right of the Table1 pane.

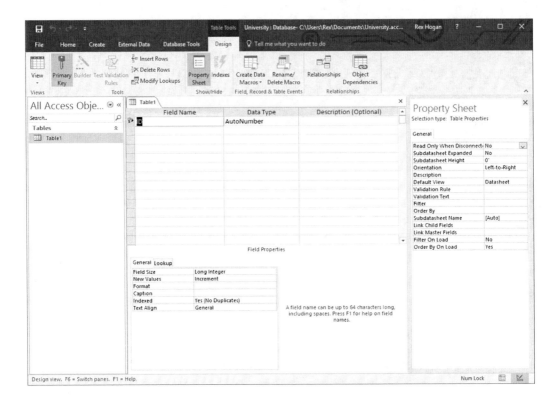

- A window will open for you to specify the table name, enter "School," then click "OK."

- We now have a window where we can enter the column names (under Field Name) and the data type for each.

  For the School table, enter the column name SchoolID and choose "Short Text" for a data type; in the lower part of the window, change the Field Size to 50 bytes.

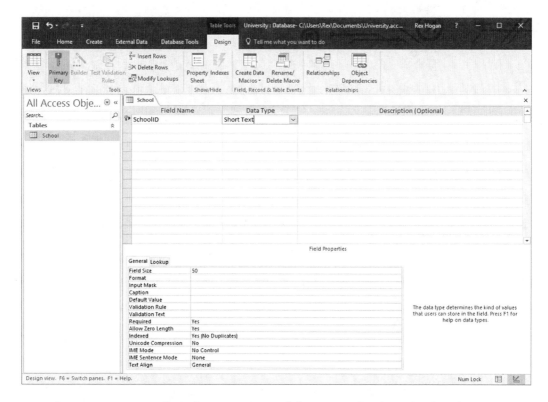

- Continue entering the column names and data types for the School table.

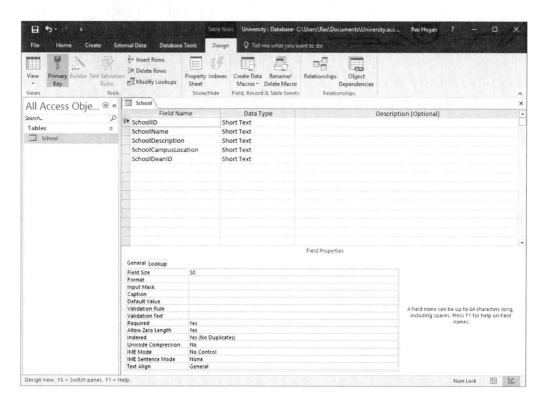

When entering data type for a column, note that Access does not support varchar, instead choose "Short Text" as a data type, and in the lower pane, change the field size to 50.

- Verify that the *key* symbol appears in the row(s) for the key column(s) for this table and click the small "x" on the School line to close the table. In response to "Do you want to save changes to the design of table 'School'," click "Yes."

- Referring to Figure 4.7, repeat this sequence to create all tables in the physical data model.

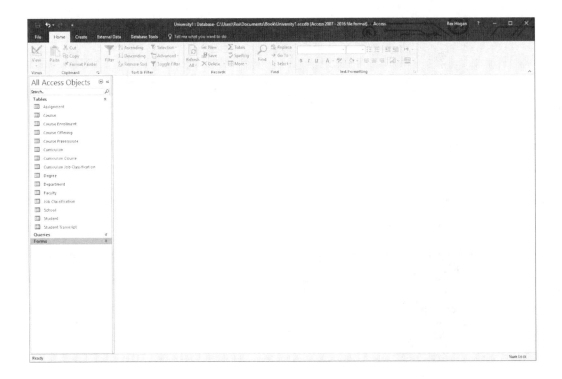

10.2 CREATE RELATIONSHIPS TO ENFORCE REFERENTIAL INTEGRITY

To set the Referential Integrity constraints between these tables, first select the "Database Tools" tab, then click on Relationships.

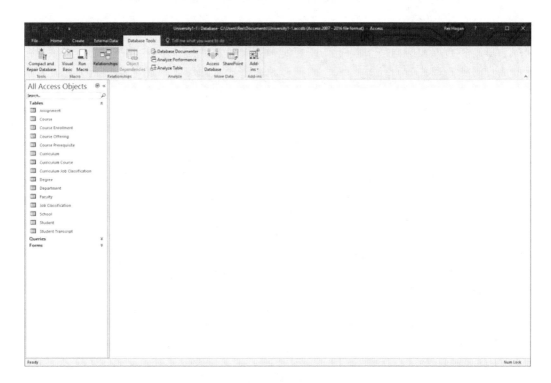

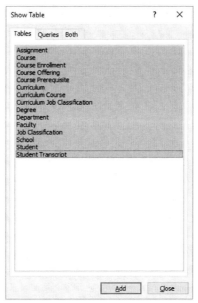

- Select all table names and then click Add; all tables will be displayed.

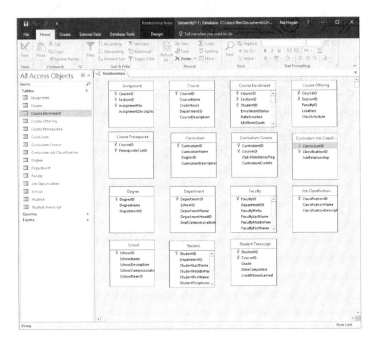

Next, rearrange the tables to reflect the layout used in Figure 4.6. (Minor revisions in the diagram are fine; it is just easier to group associated tables together.)

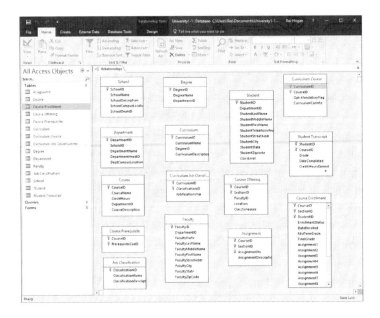

Now let us set the Referential Integrity constraints between tables.

- Note that the key of School (SchoolID) appears in Department. To set that relationship, click on SchoolID in School, then hold the mouse down and drag the arrow to SchoolID in Department. When you release the mouse, you see

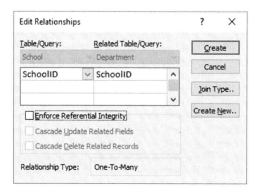

Click the "Enforce Referential Integrity" box, then "Create."

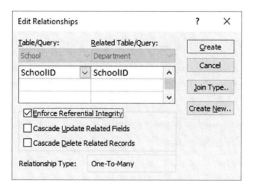

The one-to-many relationship is then created.

- Study each table and create additional one-to-many relationships as indicated. Compare your results to that shown in the following.

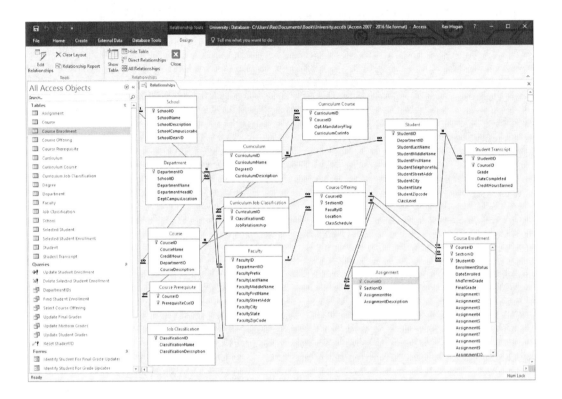

At this point, we are ready to start developing Forms-based mechanisms to enter students and associated grades. However, before starting developing any forms, I first edited the School, Department, Course, and Course Offering tables to add a couple of rows in each with test data. You will see the test data in the following screen shots as queries and forms are developed.

10.3 DESIGN A SCREEN TO ADD NEW STUDENTS

To add new students, we need a window/screen to support capturing/recording each column of information in the Student table.

In reviewing these columns, however, note that one column contains the DepartmentID for that student. Rather than having the person making the update type that value in (and taking a chance of a typing error), we'll use a pull-down menu in the form to select the DepartmentID from a list of valid values.

To develop the desired form, follow these steps:

- Select/Click on the Student table name.

- Next, click on Create, then Form.

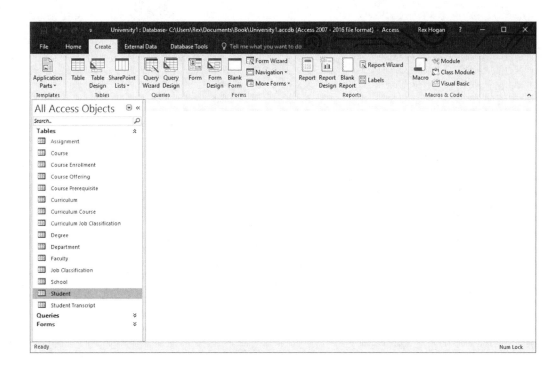

A screen will open with a "Student" form in design mode. Note that all columns from the Student table have been added to this window.

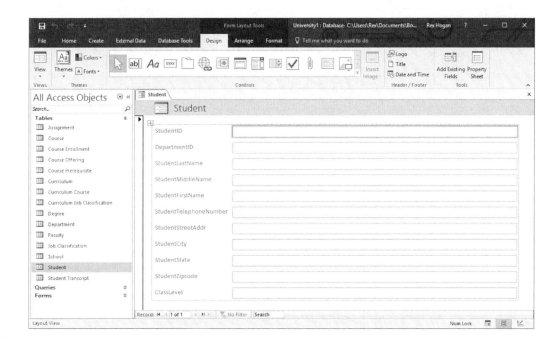

This form *could* be used *as is* with no changes; however, remember that we want to use a pull-down box for DepartmentID to choose an acceptable value rather than having to type the value.

To make this change

- Click on the DepartmentID row in the Student form design window.

- Right-click and select "Delete" to delete that item in the form window.

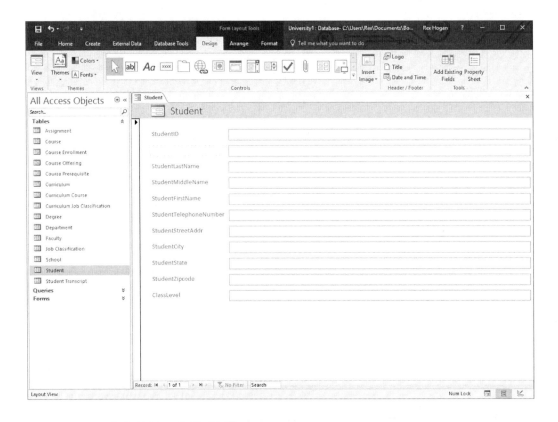

- Select the empty box to the right of where the DepartmentID label appeared, then right-click and select "Delete."

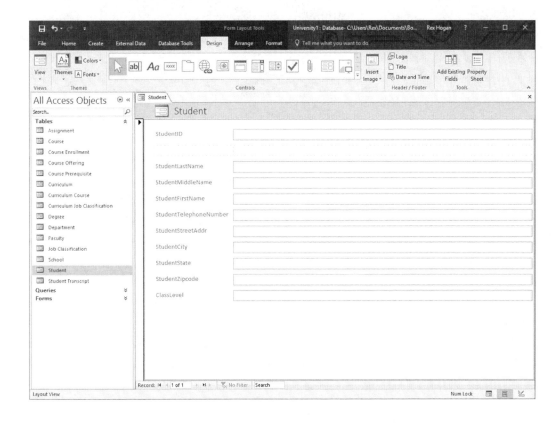

The form design has now been modified to allow a space for the DepartmentID drop-down box.

- Click the Design tab and scroll/find the drop-down box icon; click on that symbol as shown in the following.

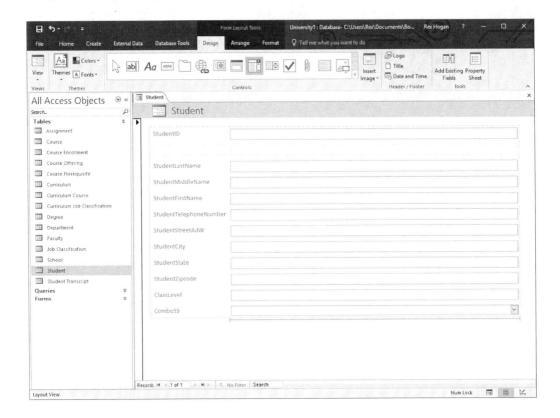

- Click on the box where the Combo box is to be created:

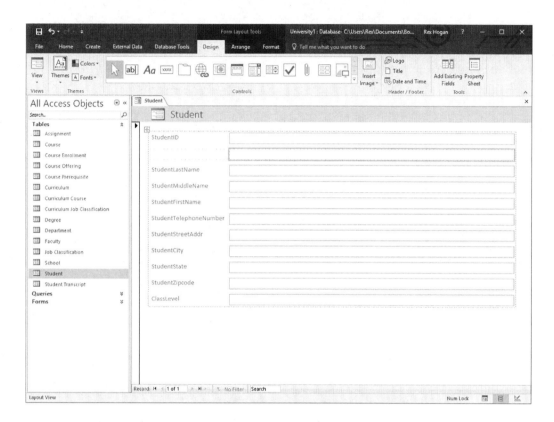

- After clicking the Combo box icon in the above-mentioned location, the following dialog opens:

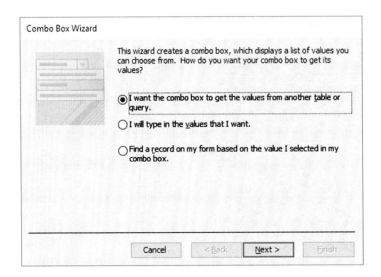

- Next, use the pull-down menu to select the Department table:

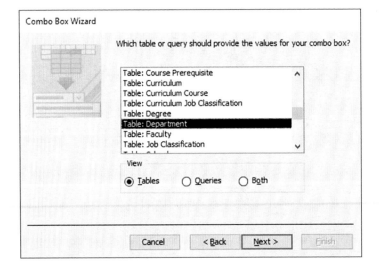

- Clicking Next opens the following window:

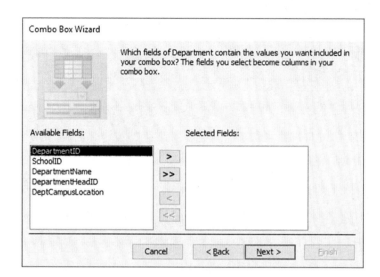

- First select DepartmentID as shown earlier, then click the ">" symbol to get the following:

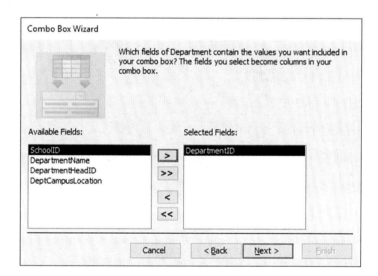

- We have now specified that we want a Combo box (a pull-down list of values) to see DepartmentID; the next window gives us the option of choosing a sort option.

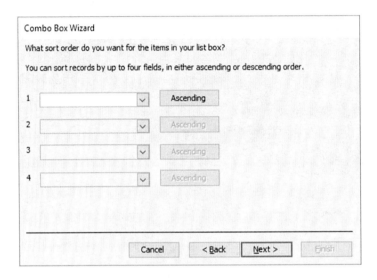

- Clicking Next gives us the following screen:

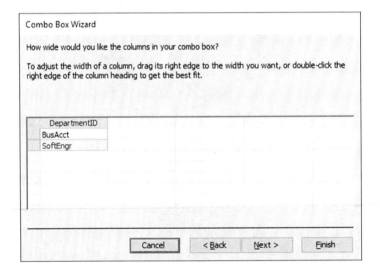

This screen gives us the option to adjust the width of the display; the values shown earlier show the test values previously entered for Departments.

- In the next window, choose the "Store" option and select DepartmentID to store the value retrieved into the form as DepartmentID.

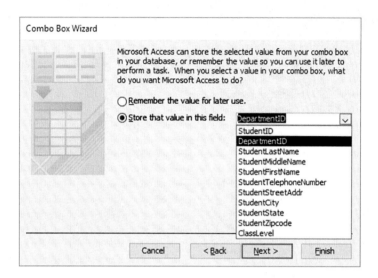

- Clicking Next brings up a window asking for a name for the list; enter DepartmentID.

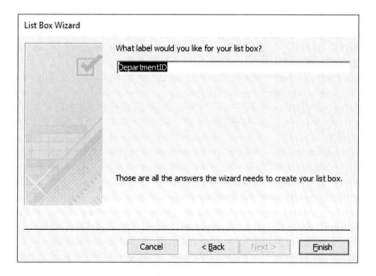

- The Form has now been modified to include the Combo box just created.

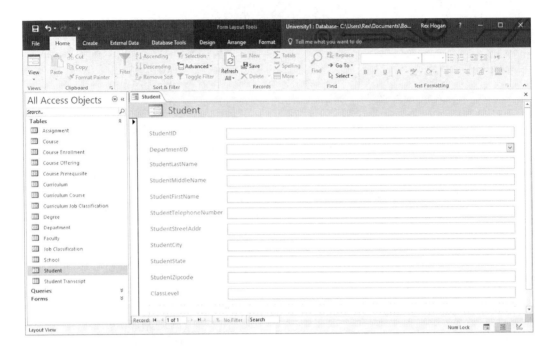

The Form has now been updated to include a drop-down list with all DepartmentIDs.

To finish the design of the form, we need to make one further modification. At the bottom of the form layout, add a "Save" button to add this information to the database.

- With the form in design mode, select the Design and Button options as shown in the following.

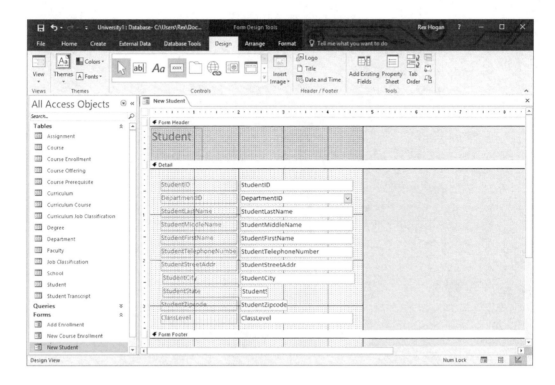

- Next, move the mouse to the bottom of the form and drag it open to form a box. Releasing the mouse gives the following:

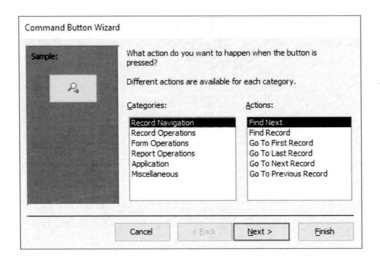

- Click on Form Operations, then Close Form.

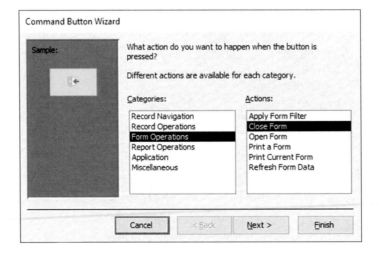

- Click Next, then select Text and enter "Save."

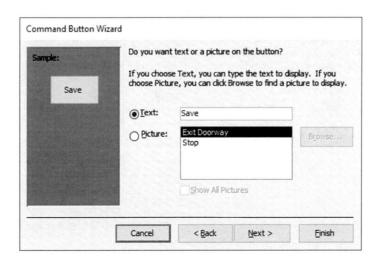

- Click Finish, then enter a meaning name at the top of the form.

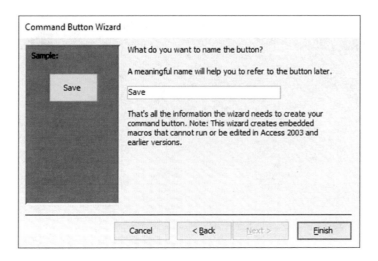

- Clicking Finish adds the Save button to the form.

- Close and save the form, assigning an appropriate name to the form (in this case, New Student Enrollment).

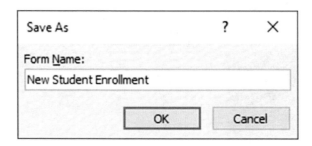

Opening the form opens a blank record where student information can be entered. Note the drop-down icon on the DepartmentID line.

- Clicking on that arrow displays a list of all DepartmentIDs. Choose the one appropriate for the student being enrolled.

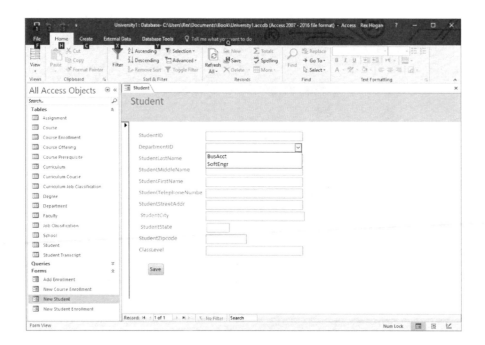

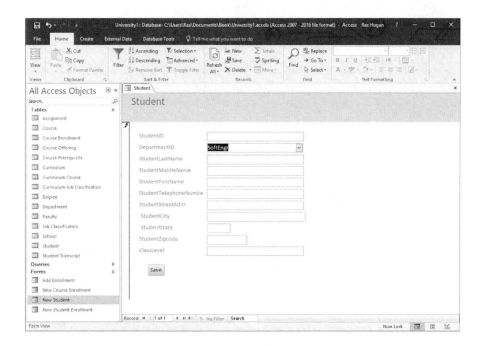

- Fill in the other information for that student, then click the Save button to add the information to the Student table and close the form.

- To use the form, click on Forms/New Student and the following screen opens. Note that the pull-down is populated with a list of DepartmentIDs in the Department table.

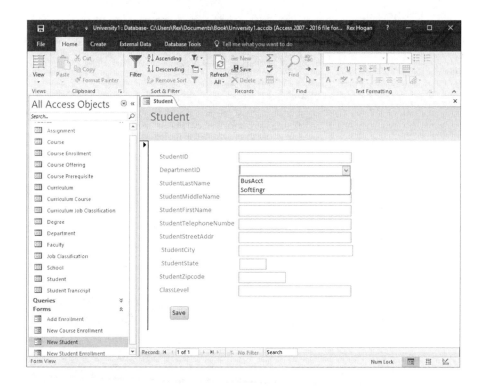

Select the DepartmentID for the new student, fill out the other items, and click Save to add that information to the Student table.

One of the last things we will do in this section is to create a "Main" page with controls to activate/perform all of the functions needed. We will add a button to that page to open this form when needed.

If you also need a form to modify Student information, follow the above-mentioned steps, but instead of creating a Combo box for DepartmentID, create a Combo box based on StudentID in Student. That form would then read and display all information for the selected student, and Save would close the form with those updates.

10.4 CREATE A SCREEN TO ENROLL STUDENTS IN A CLASS

The previous example illustrates how to create forms for simple tasks. Most applications require tools that are more sophisticated. When developing Forms-based tools with Microsoft Access, I typically start by creating *work tables* to hold key data that will be used in designing a query or form. To more easily identify this type table from a *core* table associated with the database, I've used the word "Selected" as the first word in the table name.

In thinking about the steps needed to enroll students, the following steps need to be taken:

- Using a form linked to a work table, capture the information about the student, course, and section involved.

- Save the form to update the work table with this information.

- Insert these data into the Course Enrollment table.

- Delete the information in the work table (to clear it for the next enrollment).

- Reopen the enrollment form to start a new enrollment record.

To create a form for enrolling students in a class:

Create a "Selected Student Enrollment" table patterned after the Course Enrollment table with those columns used when enrolled a student (CourseID, SectionID, StudentID, EnrollmentStatus, and DateEnrolled).

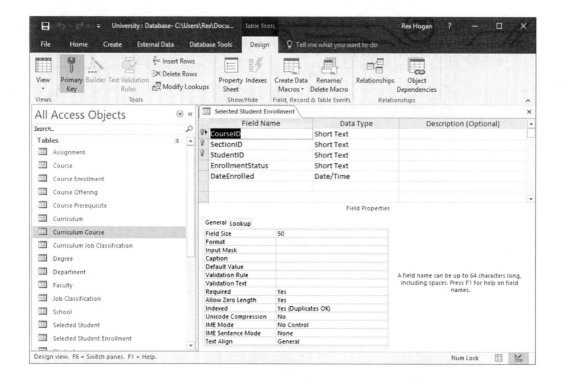

- Using this table as a source, create a form based on its contents.

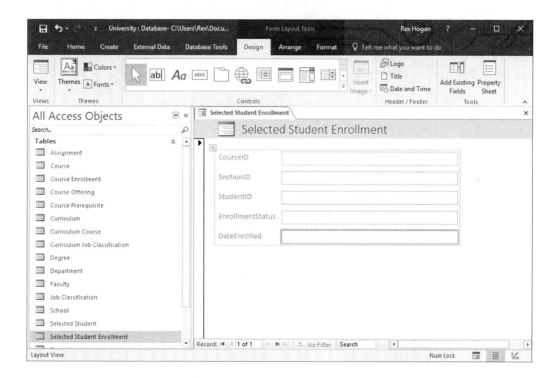

- Delete the CourseID row and replace it with a Combo box to look up DepartmentID values from the Course Offering table, that is, show a list of DepartmentIDs for all courses being offered.

- Delete the SectionID row and replace it with a Combo box to look up SectionID values from the Course Offering table.

When this Combo box is built, a query is created with the syntax "Select SectionID from [Course Offering];", and the list returned will contain all SectionID values for all course offerings. The query needs to be changed to include the CourseID value from the previous line; that is, show only SectionID values for the selected course.

To make this change, select the SectionID line just created and select the SectionID box.

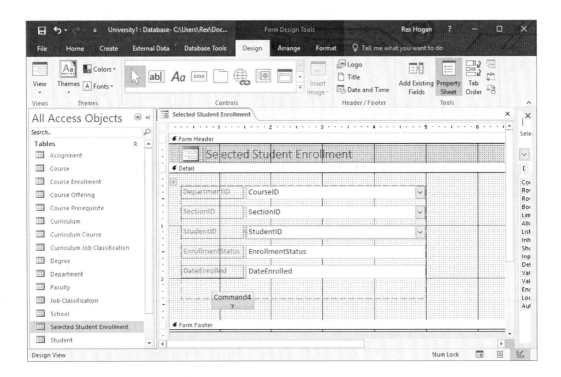

Right-click that box and click Properties to see the details behind the Combo box.

On the Data tab of the Property sheet, note the beginning of the "Select" clause for the Structured Query Language (SQL) query.

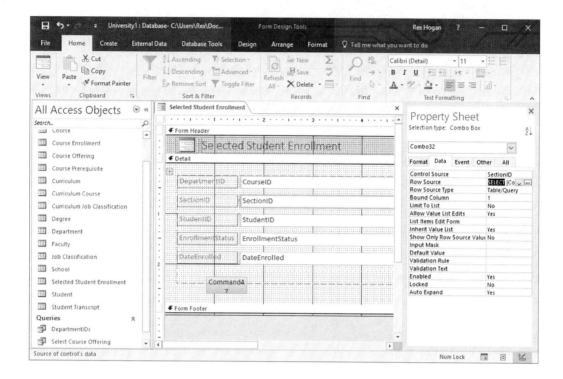

This query must be modified to include the CourseID value from the form. To get this value, go to the CourseID line and click on the CourseID box.

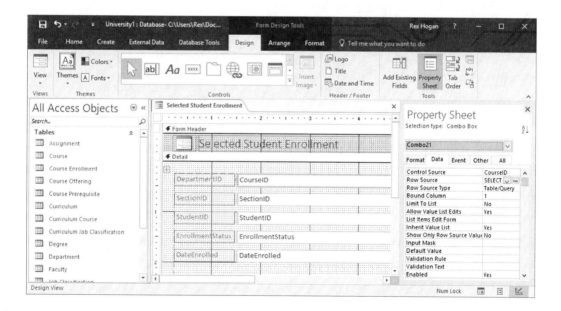

The Property sheet for this box shows at the top the internal name for this box/value; in this case, "Combo21" is displayed. This is the value that needs to be included in the SectionID query.

Going back to the SectionID query, click on the box with the three dots to open the query.

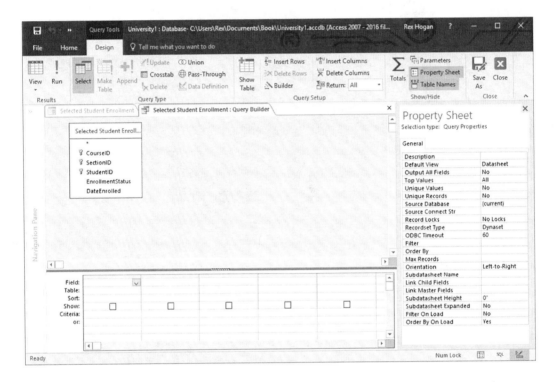

The design mode can be used to add the qualifier of CourseID = Combo10. I prefer to use the SQL mode, so right-click the design view and choose "SQL View" to get this display.

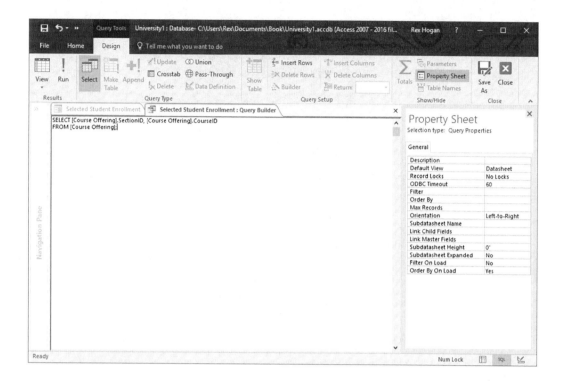

Modify this query to add the qualifier "Where [Course Offering].CourseID = Combo21;"

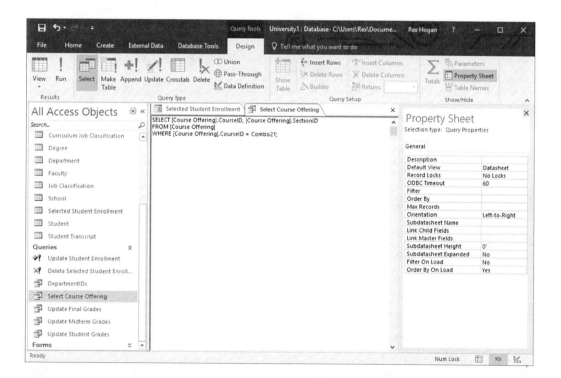

Click the x at the top right of the design window to close and save this change.

When using this form and clicking on the SectionID drop down, the list will now show SectionIDs for the CourseID selected on the form.

- Delete the StudentID line and replace it with a Combo box displaying the StudentID values from the Student table.

The basic changes in the form are now complete.

Next, with the form in Design mode, start to add a Button at the bottom of the form; when the first question comes up, click "Cancel." Next, click on the button just created, right-click, then pick "Build Event" at the top of the list of options shown.

Next, pick "Code Builder" from the options shown.

Clicking OK opens the following window.

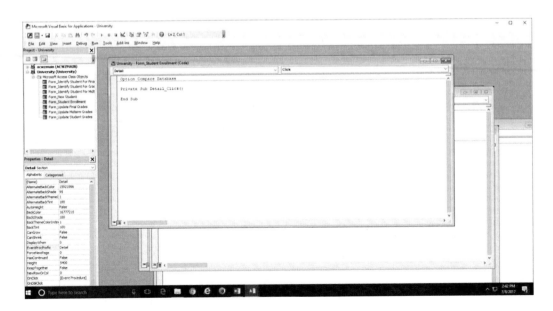

This is the window that we will use to enter commands to perform the following actions:

- Close the form (thereby saving data that was entered in the "Selected Student Enrollment" table).

- Run an INSERT command to add that data to the Class Enrollment table.

- Delete the data in the "Selected Student Enrollment" table.

- Reopen the form to clear it to enter another student.

Opening and closing forms are simple commands. Let us concentrate first on how to run the INSERT and DELETE commands; I recommend creating queries to perform both functions.

- For the INSERT command, use the Query wizard to start a new query and switch to "SQL View". Using the "INSERT INTO ..." syntax, enter the following command:

```
"INSERT INTO [Course Enrollment] ( CourseID, SectionID, StudentID,
EnrollmentStatus, DateEnrolled )
SELECT [Selected Student Enrollment].CourseID, [Selected Student
Enrollment].SectionID, [Selected Student Enrollment].StudentID,
[Selected Student Enrollment].EnrollmentStatus, [Selected Student
Enrollment].DateEnrolled
FROM [Selected Student Enrollment];"
```

- After saving the query, open it again in Design mode, right-click the upper pane, move the cursor down to "Query Type," and select "Append Query."

- The query can now be run manually to test it, if desired.

- For the DELETE command, use the Query wizard to start a new query and switch to "SQL View." Enter the following command:

```
"DELETE * FROM [Selected Student Enrollment];"
```

- Close and save this query. Run it manually to test it, if desired.

You are now ready to add commands to the button just created to add the functionality described earlier.

- With the form in Design mode, click on the button added earlier, right-click it, and choose "Build Event" at the top of the pop-up menu.

- Between the "Private Sub ..." line and the "End Sub" lines, insert the following commands:

```
DoCmd.Close acForm, "Selected Student Enrollment", acSaveYes
DoCmd.SetWarnings False
```

```
CurrentDb.Execute "Update Student Enrollment", dbFailOnError
DoCmd.OpenQuery "Delete Selected Student Enrollment",
acViewNormal, acEdit
DoCmd.SetWarnings True
DoCmd.OpenForm "Student Enrollment"
```

Note the "SetWarnings" commands. The INSERT and DELETE commands will notify/warn the user of pending updates; turning the warnings off for these commands makes for a smoother operation.

- Rename the label in the new button to "Save," and close the form, saving all updates.

The form is now ready for use.

10.5 CREATE A SCREEN TO ASSIGN GRADES

Now let us look at the steps necessary to create a screen to change grades for a student enrolled in a course.

Following the above-mentioned approach, perform the following steps:

- Create a work table "Selected Student" with columns DepartmentID, SectionID, and StudentID.

- Open the Query wizard to Design mode and add tables "Selected Student" and "Course Enrollment."

- Holding the mouse down, move the cursor between DepartmentID in the two tables; repeat that operation for SectionID and Student ID.

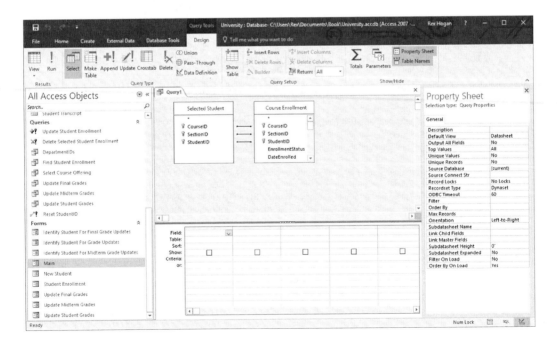

This directs SQL to join those two tables.

Next, specify which columns are to be displayed; moving left to right, click on a Field column and use the pull down to select first CourseID, SectionID, and StudentID from the Selected Student table.

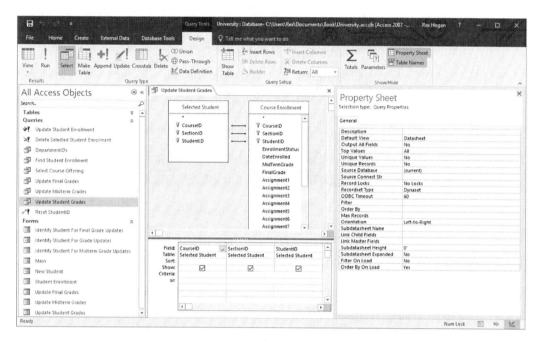

Continue adding Assignment columns from the Course Enrollment table until all Assignments are added.

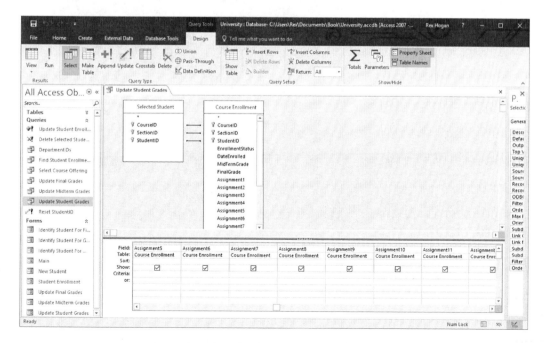

Now close and save the form.

Next, create a form based off this query; I chose "Update Student Grades" for the query name.

- Select the query "Update Student Grades" and use the Forms Query wizard to create a form based on that query.

  The form will open with simple boxes for each item.

- Delete and replace the CourseID, SectionID, and StudentID with Combo boxes reading data from the Course Enrollment table. As was done earlier, modify the SectionID query to add a CourseID qualifier based on the value chosen for CourseID, and StudentID based on the CourseID and SectionID values chosen.

  The StudentID SELECT statement will look something like:

```
SELECT [Course Enrollment].StudentID
FROM [Course Enrollment] WHERE [Course Enrollment] .CourseID =
Combo10 AND [Course Enrollment] .SectionID = Combo20;
```

- Rearrange the boxes displayed in the Design panel to be more readable; for example:

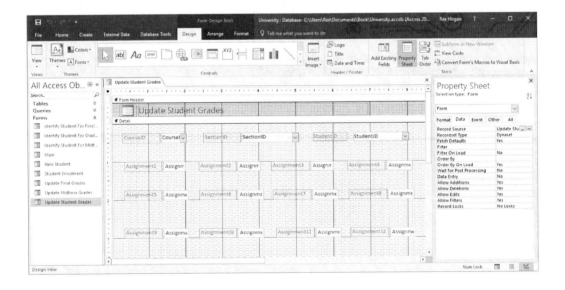

- As one final step, add a button at the bottom of the form. When the query wizard starts, cancel the operation, select the box and right-click it to open the "Build Event" option. Enter "DoCmd" commands modeled after that shown above to close the form, then reopen it.

The form can be closed and saved and is ready for use.

10.6 CREATE SCREENS TO ENTER MIDTERM AND FINAL GRADES

Finally, here are the steps to follow to create screens to enter midterm and final grades. For midterm grades:

- Following the aforementioned steps, use the Selected Student and Class Enrollment tables to create a query displaying only CourseID, SectionID, StudentID, and MidTerm Grade.

- Select this query and use the Forms query to create a new form.

- As was done earlier, change CourseID, SectionID, and StudentID to create Combo boxes for these elements based on Course Enrollment.

- Add a button at the bottom that will close and reopen the form just created.

For Final Grades:

- Once again, following the above-mentioned steps, use the Selected Student and Class Enrollment tables to create a query displaying only CourseID, SectionID, StudentID, and Final Grade.

- Select this query and use the Forms query to create a new form.

- As was done earlier, change CourseID, SectionID, and StudentID to create Combo boxes for these elements based on Course Enrollment.

- Add a button at the bottom that will close and reopen the form just created.

10.7 CREATE A "MAIN" MENU

As a final step, create a master screen allowing the user to select and run all of the functions created previously.

- Use the Forms wizard to create a black form.

- Add buttons to the form to open each of the forms created earlier.

- As the wizard for each button opens, choose Form Operations and Open Form.

- Next, pick the form name to be opened.

- Text labels can be added if desired to label different sections of the display.

- If desired, the background color can be changed.

- Save this form with an appropriate name, for example, "Main."

Your "Main" form will then look something like this:

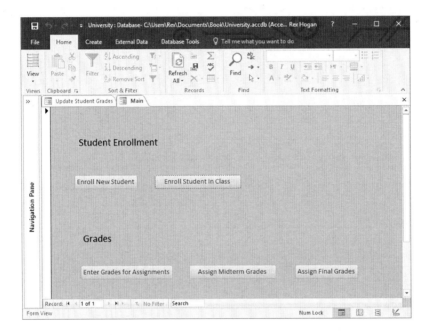

This "Dashboard" can then be used to invoke any of the functions created within the database.

Testing and using each component will show additional minor changes needed. For example, most forms opened may need to be modified to add a button to take the user to the "Main" page.

10.8 DEVELOPING APPLICATIONS FOR UNIVERSITY ADMINISTRATORS

If Microsoft Access is used to create a user interface for use by multiple staff members, the *core*/original database can be divided into two components.

- Begin by copying the original database into a "Data" database and again to a "User Interface" database.

- The "Data" database will contain only the core tables running on a *master* computer that is network accessible to the other staff members. All other components are deleted from the "Data" database.

- The User Interface database is modified by deleting all *data* tables (not the "work"/"Selected…" items) and recreating each table by linking each to the Access "Data" database. This User Interface database is given/copied to each user's workstation.

Hosting applications in this way supports the rapid development and testing of applications. As new versions of the application are created, users just need to be given a copy of the new User Interface for the application.

QUESTIONS

1. Describe the difference between a database Table, a View, and a Query.

2. By default, what columns have indexes created when a Table is defined?

3. What is a Form? How does it differ from a Query?

4. When using the Query wizard to create a query, what does the "View" mode/button do?

5. What are the different types of queries supported by Microsoft Access? What does each do?

6. What is a Pass-Through query? When/Why is it used?

7. What is an Update query? Why/When is this specified?

   The remaining questions are based on the Microsoft Access University Database.

8. What is the purpose of the "Reset StudentID" query?

   A query must be created to display all students associated with a specific department.

9. When using the query wizard, what tables are needed?

10. To run the query, what can be done to identify/select the DepartmentID of interest?

    A query is needed to show all students enrolled in any course for a specific department.

11. What tables must be included in the query?

12. When designing the query, how are specific columns included or excluded from the output display?

13. What is the purpose of the "Main" form, and what does it contain?

14. When using the Form wizard, what object is typically chosen as the basis for the Form design?

15. If the database design described in Section 10.3 were to be altered to store core data tables in SQL Server, what changes must be made to the table definitions?

PHP Implementation and Use

11.1 WHY PHP?

After loading data into a database, its overall usefulness to the user community will be driven by the type of user interface that can be developed to allow users to query and use the data.

- If all users are on the same network, Microsoft Access can be used to create and deploy user interfaces that are each linked to a *master* database containing the tables needed/used by users.

  This approach is fast and simple but limited by the functionality available in using Access. In addition, there may be significant overhead in deploying/maintaining the Access graphical user interface on each user's computer. There may also be design/implementation issues if users need to simultaneously read and update the same data.

- Microsoft's Visual Studio software suite allows you to create complex and powerful user interfaces/applications. However, because these applications must be deployed on each user's computer, these implementations create software dependencies for computers on which they are to be deployed and are dependent on the version of the Windows operating system used to develop the application. In addition, from the developer's point of view, applications that are sensitive/aware on mouse movements and actions are more difficult to develop and maintain.

- Java can be used but again has software dependencies and introduces a higher level of software complexity to design and deploy the application.

- PHP, on the other hand, provides a powerful but *developer-friendly* environment.[1]

  - PHP scripts reside on the web-based host where the database runs.

  - Clients can connect to this host using either Windows or UNIX operating systems.

  - PHP scripts are composed of HTML statements that are delivered to the user's browser, and PHP language statements that are *not* delivered to the user's browser. As such, PHP can be used to manage secure web pages.

  - The HTML component manages the output displayed to the user and reacts to user input to take some specific action or to branch to another web page.

  - PHP statements are written in *plain English* where the logic and commands are totally visible to the developer. This includes Structured Query Language (SQL) calls to connect to and query/update the database. This *what you see is what you get* framework is *so* much easier to develop and support database applications!

Section 7.3 covered the design and implementation of an SQLSvrLogs database. Next, Section 8.5 includes a description of how to use PERL to extract Warning and Error messages from an SQL Server log. This section ties this material together and shows how to develop a PHP web-based application that allows users to identify and review new Warning and Error log records as they occur.

Note that this process is based on the process of capturing log records of interest, importing them into SQL Server tables that include the message content plus columns/flags to denote Reviewed, Pending, and Resolved statuses, and providing a user interface to monitor and update this information as new updates are applied. All of these steps can run 24 × 7 and allow the user to focus on new log messages as they occur. In addition, the overall design and components are very generic in nature. This approach can easily be adapted to monitor and review log records in another database. For example, system administrators tasked with monitor proxy logs for internet traffic could use this approach using status flags to denote Reviewed, Pending, or Reported statuses.

Let us now review how to implement all of these components on a single host that serves as the web interface for tracking SQL Server log messages.

11.2 SYSTEM COMPONENTS

A web-based computer that serves as a host to a PHP-based database application requires a number of components to provide and manage that environment.

- The host itself must of course provide a web browser such as IIS or Apache. When using IIS, setup issues include

  - Establishing the *host's* web directory that will hold the scripts and HTML files that are to be accessed/used by external users.

- Creating a "Handler Mapping" that associated PHP scripts (i.e., files ending in ".php") with IIS's FastCGI module. This provides IIS with a high-performance mechanism for processing PHP scripts.

- Any supporting files for web page management would be placed in subdirectories in the directory defined earlier.

- PHP itself must be downloaded and installed. The installation itself is very straight-forward.

  - First, download the PHP software for your host.

  - Next, a few lines in the php.ini file must be edited per PHP's installation instructions to reflect the software environment on that computer. For example, there is an "open_basedir" variable that must be set to the web directory to be used for web scripts.

  - In addition, database drivers must be downloaded to match the database that will be used. These drivers are placed in PHP's "ext" directory, and the php.ini file updated to include the name of those drivers.

  The PHP configuration can be tested by (1) creating a file with the content "**<?php phpinfo(); ?>**"; (2) saving this file with the name "phpinfo.php" in the host's Web directory; then (3) opening a web browser and entering the following link http://localhost/phpinfo.php.

  If PHP is installed correctly, a report will be display showing the details of the PHP configuration and installation.

- The database management system to be used must of course be installed, along with the database itself and any required tables.

  - In the example application reviewed in Chapter 7, SQL Server 2008 R2 was installed on the host computer.

  - Next, an SQL Server database named "SQLSvrLogs" was created with tables to store the data needed by online users (see Section 7.3.1 for details).

  The tables referred to in this chapter are an extension of the material discussed in Section 8.5 for the review and analysis of Warning and Error messages from SQL Server logs. Tables "WarningRecords" and "ErrorRecords" have the following columns:

Column Name	Data Type	Allow Nulls
RecordKeys	Int	No
Message	Varchar(Max)	No
Reviewed	bit	Yes
Pending	bit	Yes
Resolved	bit	Yes

Note that the RecordKeys column is created within SQL Server using the *Identify* property. This causes SQL Server to automatically increment the value for row keys by "1" each time a new row is added. With this construct, individual rows can uniquely be identified/used for updates without having to define uniqueness within the content of the message strings themselves.

- To run in a 24 × 7 environment, a script must be created to periodically check for new files in a directory used to store updates. When found, each file must be imported using "bcp" into the appropriate table, then moved from the import *staging* directory to an *archive* directory.

As the tables being updated have more columns than the data being imported (the status flags/columns), a *format* file must be used to describe the contents of the file(s) being imported. To create the "LogRecords.fmt" format file, use the following command:

```
bcp SqlSvrLogs.dbo.WarningRecords format nul -c -f LogRecords.fmt -T
```

This format file contains descriptions for each column in the table.

As the file being imported will only contain the message information, the format file must be edited to reflect that only the Message column is being imported. The edited format file will now contain

```
10.0
1
1 SQLCHAR 0 0 "\r\n" 2 Message SQL_Latin1_General_CP1_CI_AS
```

The Warning and Error log messages created by the PERL script can now be imported using the following command syntax:

```
bcp SQLSvrLogs.dbo.WarningRecords IN <warninginputfile> -f LogRecords.
fmt -T
bcp SQLSvrLogs.dbo.ErrorRecords IN <errorinputfile> -f LogRecords.
fmt -T
```

- After new messages are imported into the WarningRecords and ErrorRecords tables, the Reviewed, Pending, and Resolved flags for each new row will have *null* values. After all new rows have been imported, an SQL Server process must run an SQL update that checks the WarningRecords and ErrorRecords that change all null status flags to "0" (i.e., *off*).

```
Update SQLSvrLogs.dbo.WarningRecords set Reviewed = 0 where Reviewed
is null;
Update SQLSvrLogs.dbo.WarningRecords set Pending = 0 where Pending
is null;
Update SQLSvrLogs.dbo.WarningRecords set Reported = 0 where Reported
is null;
Update SQLSvrLogs.dbo.ErrorRecords set Reviewed = 0 where Reviewed
is null;
Update SQLSvrLogs.dbo.ErrorRecords set Pending = 0 where Pending is
null;
Update SQLSvrLogs.dbo.ErrorRecords set Reported = 0 where Reported
is null;
```

Although the above-mentioned details may appear daunting or tedious, remember that all of these actions involve setting up a 24 × 7 system for processing database updates. Once created and activated, the imports and table flag updates run in a *hands off* mode with minimal *care and feeding* of database administrators (DBAs)/host administrators monitoring the host system processes.

- Data collection

  In creating a 24 × 7 operation for monitoring database log records, we need a background process that periodically checks for new log records and extracts warning and error records when found. These newly created files are then moved to the input directory being monitored for table updates.

  Section 8.5 contains a PERL script that monitors SQL Server logs for warning and error messages. This script can be set up to run continuously, for example, every 15 min, creating new files to be imported into the database. At the end of each cycle, new files found would be moved to the directory for table updates, and the script *sleeps* for the designated wait time. The script itself continues to run, requiring minimal attention from DBAs/system administrators to ensure all required processes are still active.

11.3 DESIGN OF WEB-BASED INTERFACE

A web-based interface for the application described earlier must support at a minimum the following functions[2]:

- A PHP script supporting user logon and authentication to enter/access supported functions.

- After users have logged on, a PHP script displaying links for the primary options provided for users.

- Each link in turn is mapped to the respective PHP script supporting that function. In this application, a PHP script is needed to view and manage warning records, and another to view and manage error records.

11.3.1 User Logon Options

- This web page will prompt the user for a user name and a password.

- In addition, all of the scripts provided for this sample application have *debug* options which, if selected here, will display to the user details of key script variables and SQL calls that can be used to verify the PHP script is functioning as intended.

  Note that this *debug* variable is passed continuously from one web page to the next as the user activates each link.

- At the bottom of the page is a *Logon* button, which passes the user name, password, and debug operation to the PHP script that authenticates the user.

When loaded from the host's web directory, the script produces the following display on the following page.

To log in, the user/analyst enters their logon name and password, then selects the Logon button.

If the user or developer is testing code changes and wants to see internal trace information from the subsequent page accesses and database calls, they would select the down arrow by the Debug question and choose *Yes* before selecting Logon.

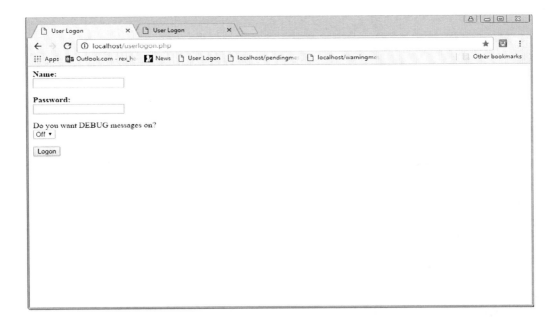

In this application, the name of the PHP script is UserLogon.php and appears below.

Note that when the form is submitted, the UserCredentials.php script is called. That script is reviewed under the section "User Authentication."

```
C:\Users\Rex\Documents\Book\Web\UserLogon.php - Notepad++                    —    □    ×
File  Edit  Search  View  Encoding  Language  Settings  Tools  Macro  Run  Plugins  Window  ?          X

UserLogon.php

 1   <html>
 2   <head>
 3    <title>User Logon</title>
 4    </head>
 5   <body>
 6   <?php
 7        $_POST['debug'] = "Off";
 8   ?>
 9   <form action="UserCredentials.php" method="POST">
10   <p><strong>Name:</strong><br/>
11       <input type="text" name="username" /></p>
12   <p><strong>Password:</strong><br/>
13       <input type="text" name="password" /></p>
14
15   <p>Do you want DEBUG messages on?<br>
16   <select name="debug">
17       <option value="Off">Off</option>
18       <option value="On">On</option>
19   </select>
20   </p>
21   <p><input type="submit" value="Logon" /></p>
22   </form>
23   </body>
24
25   <?php
26   if (isset($_POST['Logon'])) {
27       $debug = $_POST['debug'];
28       echo "<input type=\"hidden\" name=\"debug\" value=\"$debug\" />";
29       echo "debug reset to $debug <br>";
30   }
31   ?>
32   </html>

PHF length : 706   lines : 32          Ln : 1   Col : 7   Sel : 0 | 0          Windows (CR LF)    UTF-8          INS
```

UserLogon.php

11.3.2 User Authentication

As mentioned earlier, the UserCredentials.php script is called when the UserLogon.php Logon button is selected.

- This script takes the name and password provided by the user/analyst and attempts to log on to the SQL Server "SQLSvrLogs" database.

- If that logon is successful, the WebHeader.php script is called/loaded. If the logon fails, an error is displayed and a link is provided to redirect the user back to the User Logon page.

```php
<?php
$user = $_POST['username'];
$pwd = $_POST['password'];
$debug = $_POST['debug'];
$datab = "SQLSvrLogs";
echo "UserName=:$user:PWD=:$pwd:DB=:$datab:Debug=:$debug:<br />";
$serverName = "(local)";
$connectinfo = array("Database"=>$datab, "UID"=>$user, "PWD"=>$pwd);
// Authentication Verification
$conn = sqlsrv_connect($serverName, $connectinfo);
echo "<input type=\"hidden\" name=\"debug\" value=\"$debug\" />";
if( $conn ) {
    echo "Connection established!!!<br />";
    header("Location: WebHeader.php?debug=$debug");
}
else {
?>
<html>
<body>
    echo "Invalid username/password combination...try again...<br />
    <a href="http://localhost/UserLogon.php">ReEnter User Name and Password <br ></a>
</body>
</html>
<?php
}
?>
```

UserCredentials.php

11.3.3 Home Page User Options

The WebHeader.php script contains the primary links/options available to the user, producing the following display.

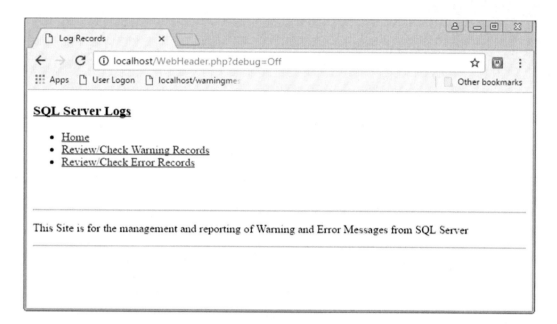

The links displayed are for the following functions:

- *Home*: A return to the *Home* WebHeader.php page. (This page is always loaded in subsequent pages and allows the user to get back to the primary option page.)

- *Review/check warning records*: The link to WarningMessages.php allows the user/ analyst to review new warning messages and provides a mechanism to change the various flags for those records.

- *Review/check error records*: The link to ErrorMessages.php allows the user/analyst to review new error messages and provides a mechanism to change the various flags for those records.

11.3.4 Review/Check Warning Records

When this link is selected, the following display is produced. Note that to demonstrate the functionality of this application, the SQL Server database used was loaded with records from the database's log file. The following shows four warning messages to be reviewed/ analyzed by the user/DBA.

Following on with this example, records two and four are not significant and can be ignored by setting their *Reviewed* flags. This is done by clicking the Selection boxes for these rows, clicking the arrow for Actions, and selecting the option *Set Reviewed Flags for these rows* as shown in the following.

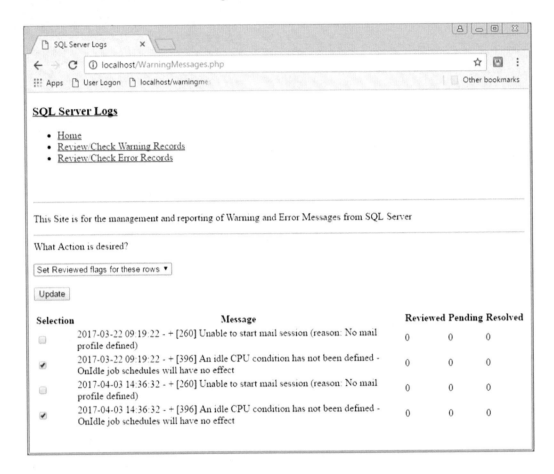

After making the above-mentioned selections and setting the Action desired, clicking the Update button reloads this script/web page, passes parameters to the database to update the Reviewed flags, then reruns the query to identify warning messages yet to be reviewed. By using this example, the output displayed is on the next page.

This cycle would then be repeated, allowing the user/analyst to

- Set Reviewed flags for records identifying insignificant events/states which can be ignored

- Set Pending flags for records that should be analyzed further

- Set Resolved flags for records that reflect issues or conditions that have been resolved

In this example, assume that the two remaining records should be researched further. To set these flags, click the Selection columns for these records, click the Actions pulldown and select the option *Set Pending flag for these rows* as shown in the display on the following page.

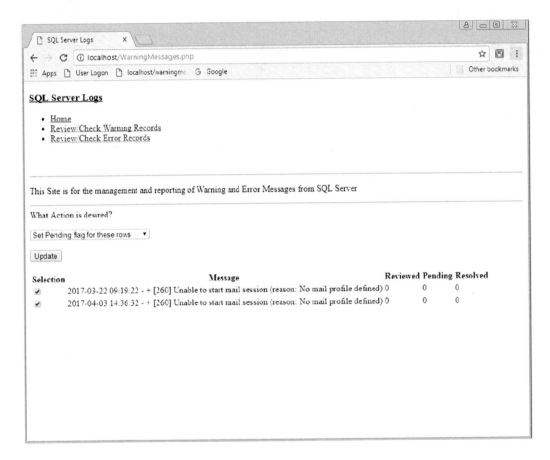

Clicking on *Update* will repeat the process of passing these options to this web page as it is reloaded, running the SQL updates associated with these records, and running the query to check for any additional records.

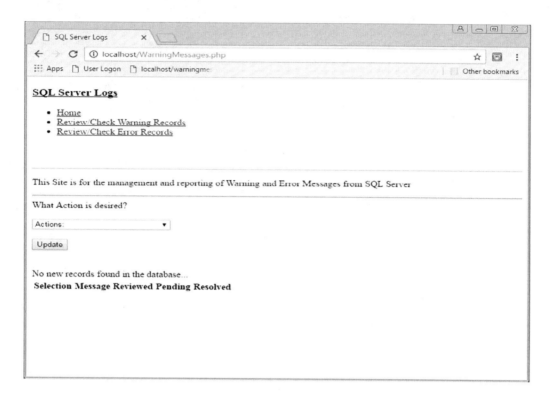

Note that no new additional warning records need to be reviewed.

Continuing on with this example, let us now check for warning records with a Pending status. To see those records, first click the Actions pull-down and select the option *Show all Pending Activity.*

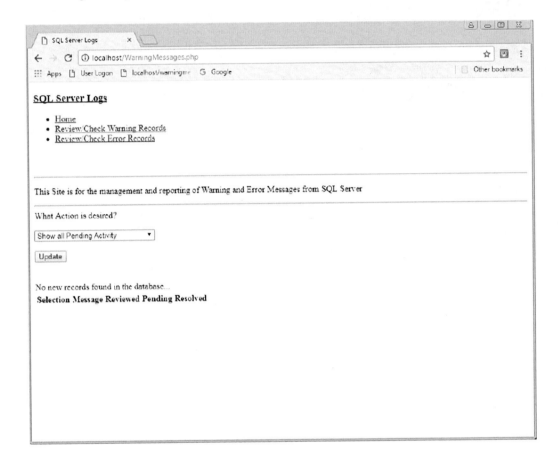

Clicking on the Update button produces the following display, showing the two records that were set to Pending in the last update earlier.

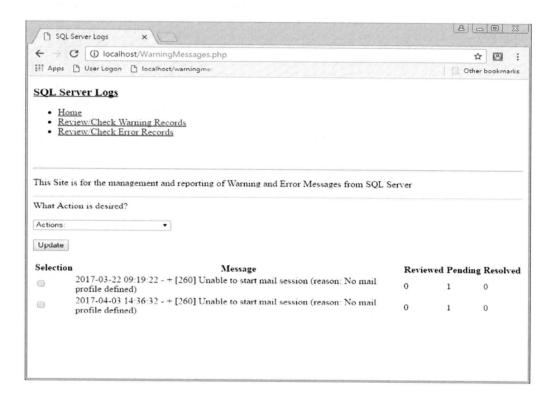

Assume that these conditions have been investigated and any required action taken to resolve the issue. To set these flags to Resolved, click the Selection boxes, then click the Action pull-down and select the option for *Set Resolved flag for these rows* as shown in the following.

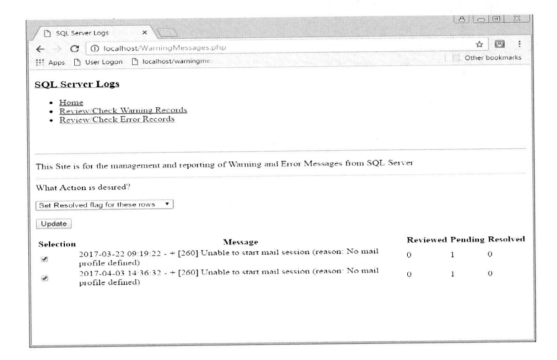

Clicking the Update button will reset these flags and update the display of records being reviewed.

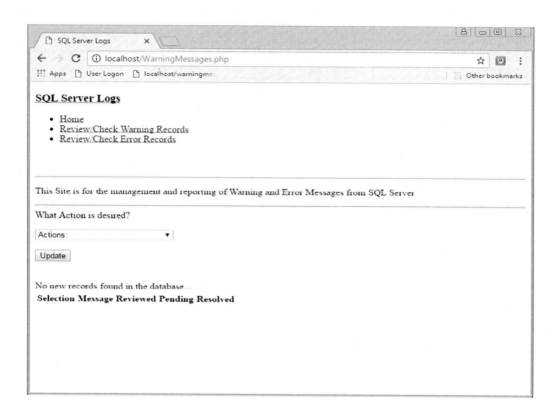

11.3.5 Review/Check Error Records

As with warning messages, the link to ErrorMessages.php allows the user/analyst to review error messages and provides a mechanism to change the various flags involved. Clicking on this link opens a similar display, only using the messages in the ErrorRecords table.

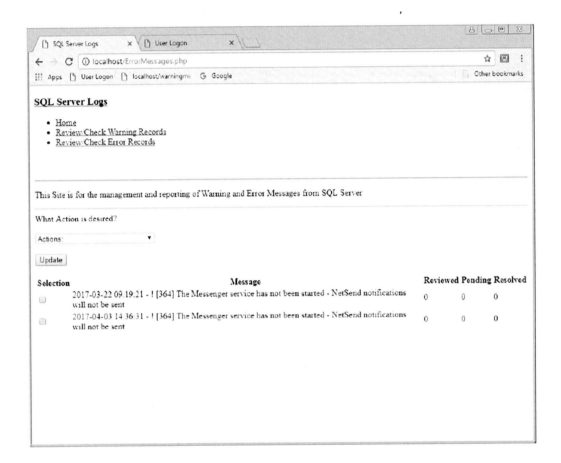

This page works identically to that shown in Section 11.3.4 except it is associated with the ErrorRecords table in the database.

11.4 SCRIPT LOGIC

Now let us review in detail how the WarningMessages.php script works.

11.4.1 Warning Records Logic

The WarningMessages.php script has more than 400 lines of code and is found in "Appendix A—WarningMessages.docx."

When the script is initially run, it performs several functions.

- The WebHeader.php is called to display/make available those links/options to the user.

- It uses a hidden script to log on and authenticate the user to the SQL Server database in preparation for subsequent user actions/updates.

- It displays a menu of pull-down options for subsequent actions selected by the user.

- It displays new warning messages (i.e., records whose Reviewed, Pending, and Resolved flags have not been set).

As described earlier, if the user chooses an action to update some record flags or requests a display of pending or resolved records, when the Update button is selected, the script/web page reloads with those options selected.

- If flag updates were requested, SQL updates are made to update the selected rows.

- Another query is then run to display records having no flags set.

- If an action is taken to display Pending or Resolved records, the default *query* SQL string is overwritten appropriately so that when the query is run for records to be displayed, the selected record types are retrieved/displayed.

- The user could of course simply select one of the links at the top of the display.

The user must then review the display and determine what subsequent action is needed or select a link at the top of the display to review a different set of messages.

With these different operations in mind, here is how they are implemented within WarningMessages.php:

Lines 11–14: A locally developed *trace*/Debug option. The script contains *trace* messages throughout that display message string at execution time if the *Debug* operation is turned on when the user logs in.

Lines 16–80: A startup/initialization function called when the script is loaded. If the Debug option is set, messages are set to display the value of key variables. It also handles Selection options when set.

Line 82: Saving the name of the web page loaded as the default for the next web page to be called.

Line 85: Displaying/Calling WebHeader.php.

Line 88: Calling the hidden script to logon and authenticate the user to the SQL Server database.

Line 90: Invoking the startup function.

Lines 91, 92: Checking for SQL data returned from a prior SQL *Select* call.

Lines 97–282: Logic to handle the *Action* operation selected on a prior execution.

Lines 101–123: Handling data returned from a prior SQL *Select* call to the database.

Lines 125–131: Option 1—Defining the query to be used.

Lines 134–169: Option 2—The logic to update the Reviewed flag/column for the selected records/rows in the database.

Lines 172–210: Option 3—The logic to update the Pending flag/column for the selected records/rows in the database.

Lines 213–251: Option 4—The logic to update the Resolved flag/column for the selected records/rows in the database.

Lines 254–264: Option 5—Reset the query statement to be issued for displaying warning records to show all records with the Pending flag set.

Lines 267–281: Option 6—Reset the query statement to be issued for displaying warning records to show all records with the Resolved flag set.

Lines 289–308: Logic to test for and preserve variables passed when a new web page is called.

Lines 311–326: Logic to handle the options in the *Actions* drop-down list.

Lines 341–387: Logic to deal with the query to be issued, to issue the SQL call to the database, and build a header display of the column names returned.

Lines 388–408: Logic to issue the SQL query and display results returned.

11.4.2 Error Records Logic

As mentioned earlier, the ErrorMessages.php script is identical to the WarningMessages. php script with two changes. In WarningMessages.php, all references to WarningMessages.php were changed to ErrorMessages.php, changing the name of the web pages/scripts to be used. In addition, all SQL references to WarningRecords were changed to ErrorRecords to change the name of the SQLSvrLogs table that is being queried or updated.

One final note, all scripts and displays in Chapters 8 and 9 were taken from a working Windows 7 computer configured and running as a web host with IIS and an SQL Server SQLSvrLogs database loaded with actual SQL Server log messages. All scripts and command-line instructions were taken from alive, running system. Together they hopefully illustrate how easy it is to design and create a system to perform real-time monitoring of events or log files, load items of interest into a database, and provide analysts with a web-based interface to review and categorize the collected information.

QUESTIONS

1. Name the system software necessary to provide a web-based interface to a database.

2. When setting up a PHP server, where are the PHP scripts stored/located?

3. What code can an external user see when using a PHP script?

4. What restrictions are there for client systems that must use this interface?

5. How does PHP know what type of relational database management system is being accessed?

6. In the scripts shown in the current chapter, what tables were accessed, and how were they updated?

7. Give the name of the software component that performs verification of the user's name and password.

8. In this application, where are user names and passwords stored and managed?

9. Give the name of the php scripts and how they are used.

10. The first display of WarningMessages.php has titles for each of the five columns of information from the database. Map each of the title names to columns in the database.

    This application is based on continuous updates from a PERL script that loads new rows into the associated tables. The display of data from these tables is based on bit settings at the time each query is run.

11. What are the bit settings for new rows after they are loaded into the database?

12. When and how are these bit settings changed?

    Figure 11.1 shows the initial display of WarningRecords in the database when the browser is first opened.

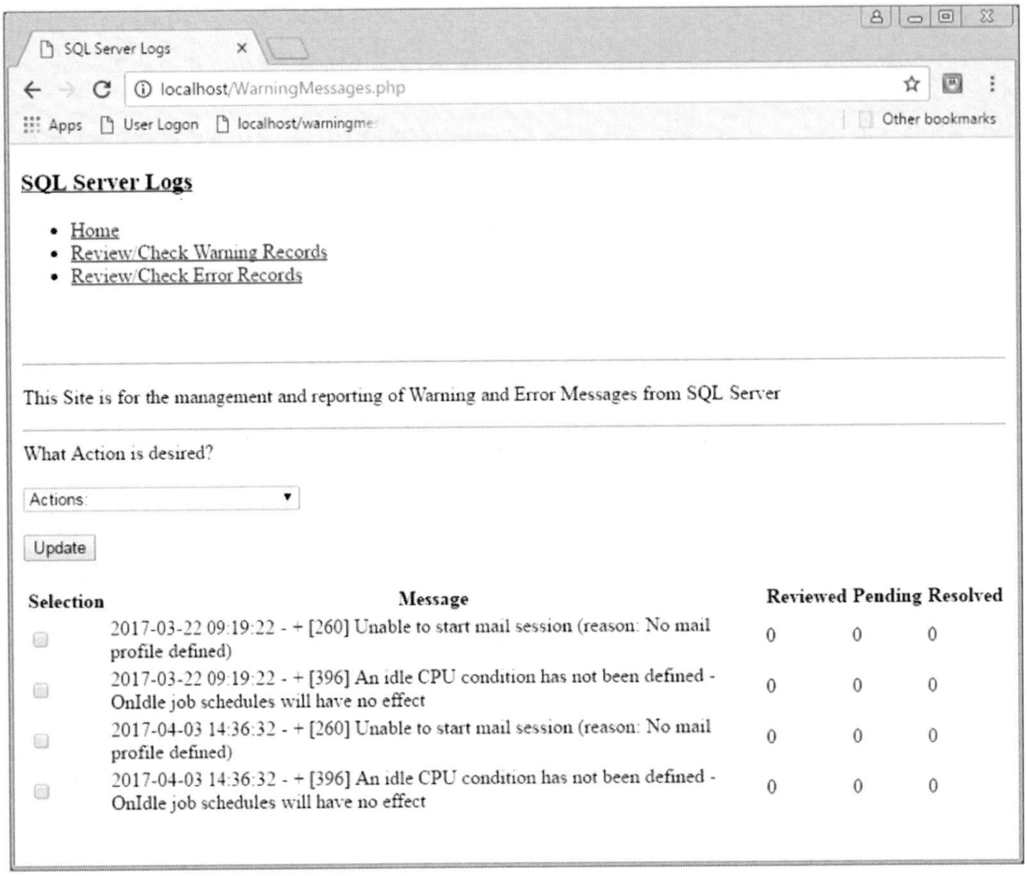

FIGURE 11.1   Warning messages.

13. If the first messages were considered important and the user wants to set the Pending flag until more research is done, what steps/selections are made by the user?

14. When making this update, how is the row being updated mapped to the information on the web page?

15. In the WebHeader.php web page, what does the *Review/Check Warning Records* label represent? What happens when it is selected?

REFERENCES

1. Valade, J., *PHP 5 for Dummies*, Indianapolis, IN, Wiley Publishing, 2004.

2. The World Wide Web Consortium (W3C) is an international community that develops open standards to ensure the long-term growth of the Web. Accessed from http://www.w3.org/.

Appendix A: Warning Messages

```
1    <!DOCTYPE html PUBLIC "-//W3C//DTD XHTML 1.0 Transitional//
     EN" "http://www.w3.org/TR/xhtml1/DTD/xhtml1-transitional.
     dtd">
2    <html xmlns="http://www.w3.org/1999/xhtml" xml:lang="en"
     lang="en" dir="ltr"> 3    <head>
4    <title>SQL Server Logs</title>
5    <meta http-equiv="Content-Type" content="text/html;
     charset=ISO-8859-1" />
6    <script type="text/javascript">
7    </script>
8    </head>
9    <body>
10   <?php
11   function trace($string) {
12     if ($_POST['debug'] == "On") {
13     echo "$string<br>";
14     }
15     }
16     function startup () {
17   //**********************************************************
18   // $_POST['debug'] = "On";
19   // $_POST['debug'] = "Off";
20
21       if (($_POST['debug']) == "On") {
22       $debug = $_POST['debug'];
23       trace ("***Message update logic***");
24       echo "...DEBUG set to $debug <br>";
25       if (isset($_POST['selection'])) {
26       $var = $_POST['selection'];
27       echo "...Selection is on and set to :$var:<br>";
28       }
29   else {
30      echo "...Selection is Off..<br>";
31       }
```

```
32          if (isset($_POST['TypeQuery'])) {
33          $var = $_POST['TypeQuery'];
34          echo "...TypeQuery is on and set to :$var:<br>";
35          }
36   else {
37       echo "...TypeQuery is Off..<br>";
38          }
39
40          if (isset($_POST['Query'])) {
41          $var = $_POST['Query'];
42          echo "...Query is on and set to :$var:<br>";
43          }
44   else {
45          echo "...Query is Off..<br>";
46          }
47
48          if (isset($_POST['formAction'])) {
49          $var = $_POST['formAction'];
50          echo "...formAction is on and set to :$var:<br>";
51          }
52   else {
53          echo "...formAction is  Off..<br>";
54          }
55          if (isset($_POST['selection'])) {
56          $var = $_POST['selection'];
57          $val = $var[0];
58          echo "...selection is on and set to :$var:$val:<br>";
59          }
60   else {
61          echo "...selection is Off..<br>";
62          }
63
64          if (isset($_POST['RecordKey'])) {
65          $val = $_POST['RecordKey'];
66          echo "...RecordKey is on and set to :$val:<br>";
67          }
68   else {
69          echo "...RecordKey is Off..<br>";
70          }
71          echo "<br>*************************<br>";
72
73      }
74   trace ("Initialization...");
75   if (isset($_POST['selection'])) {
76   $data = $_POST['selection'];
77   echo "<input type=\"hidden\" name=\"selection\" value=$data
     />";
```

```
78     trace ("Found selection, first values:$data:$reckey");
79     }
80    }
81
82  $self = $_SERVER['PHP_SELF'];
83  date_default_timezone_set('America/New_York');
84
85    include "WebHeader.php";
86  //***************** start php logic
87  // DB Variables
88  include "credentials.php"; // Connect to DB
89
90    startup();
91    $parms = array();
92  $options = array( "Scrollable" => SQLSRV_CURSOR_KEYSET );
93
94  //****************option processing
95  //**********************************************************
96  //**********************************************************
97     if (isset($_POST['formAction']) and $_POST['formAction']
       !== "") {
98     trace("Action Processing Selected...");
99     $action = $_POST['formAction'];
100    $data = $_POST['selection'];
101    if (!isset($_POST['RecordKey'])) {
102    $reckey = $data[0];
103     $_POST['RecordKey'] = $reckey;
104     }
105     trace ("Initializing with Record key = $reckey");
106     // echo "<input type=\"hidden\" name=\"RecordKey\"
        value=\"$reckey\" />";
107     if ($reckey === "A") {
108     echo "*****Record not selected*****...try
        again...<br><br>";
109     unset($_POST['formAction']);
110     $action = 0;
111     $_POST['Error'] = "On";
112     $debug = $_POST['debug'];
113     trace ("***Refresh values...first value = $reckey<br>");
114     echo "<form action=\"WarningMessages.php\" method =
        \"POST\">";
115     echo "<input type=\"hidden\" name=\"debug\"
        value= \"$debug\" />";
116     echo "<input type=\"submit\" name=\"link\" value=\"OK\"
        />";
117     }
118      else {
```

```
119      unset($_POST['Error']);
120      }
121      if ($_POST['debug'] == "On") {
122      echo "**Action option = $action<br>";
123      }
124 //*********************** option 1 Show all Warning
     records
125      if ($action == 1) {
126      trace ("Creating sql string for option 1");
127      $query = "SELECT Recordkey as Selection, Message,
         Reviewed, Pending, Resolved from WarningRecords ";
128      $_POST['Query'] = $query;
129      echo "<form action=\"WarningMessages.php\" method =
         \"POST\">";
130      echo "<input type=\"hidden\" name=\"debug\"
         value=\"$debug\" /Message,
         Reviewed, Pending, Resolved from WarningRecords>";
131      }
132
133 //*********************** option 2 Set Reviewed flags
     for these rows
134          else if ($action == 2) {
135          trace ("Processing options for action 2");
136          $parms = array();
137          if ((isset($_POST['selection'])) and
             ($_POST['selection'] !== "") ) {
138          trace ("Reviewed Flag Updates being processed...");
139          $data = $_POST['selection'];
140          $reckey = $data[0];
141          trace ("Using record key:" . $reckey . ":");
142          $debug = $_POST['debug'];
143          if ($_POST['debug'] == "On") {
144          echo "**Reviewed selected set value = $reckey<br>";
145          }
146          foreach ($data as $reckey) {
147          $string1 = 'Update WarningRecords set Reviewed = 1 ';
148          $string2 = 'Where RecordKey = ' . $reckey;
149          $sqlcmd = "$string1 $string2";
150          if ($_POST['debug'] == "On") {
151            echo "Command issued: $sqlcmd <br>";
152            }
153            if ($return = sqlsrv_query($conn, $sqlcmd)) {
154            if ($_POST['debug'] == "On") {
155            echo "REVIEWED flag set...<br>";
156            }
157            }
158      else {
```

```
159              echo "ah crap...<br>";
160              echo "Command issued: $sqlcmd <br>";
161              }
162              }
163              }
164              unset ($_POST['formAction']);
165              unset ($_POST['selection']);
166     // $query = "SELECT Message, Reviewed, Pending, Resolved
        from WarningRecords where Reviewed = 1";
167       echo "<form action=\"WarningMessages.php\" method =
          \"POST\">";
168       echo "<input type=\"hidden\" name=\"debug\" value=\"$debug\"
          />";
169     }
170
171     //*************************** option 3 Set Pending flags for
        these rows
172          else if ($action == 3) {
173          trace ("Processing updates for option 3");
174          $parms = array();
175          if ((isset($_POST['selection'])) and
             ($_POST['selection'] !== "") ) {
176          trace ("Pending Flag Updates being processed...");
177          $data = $_POST['selection'];
178          $reckey = $data[0];
179          trace ("Using record key:" . $reckey . ":");
180          $debug = $_POST['debug'];
181          if ($_POST['debug'] == "On") {
182          echo "**Reviewed selected set value = $reckey<br>";
183          }
184          foreach ($data as $reckey) {
185          $string1 = 'Update WarningRecords set Pending = 1 ';
186          $string2 = 'Where RecordKey = ' . $reckey;
187          $sqlcmd = "$string1 $string2"; 188    if ($_
             POST['debug'] == "On") {
189            echo "Command issued: $sqlcmd <br>";
190            }
191          if ($return = sqlsrv_query($conn, $sqlcmd)) {
192          if ($_POST['debug'] == "On") {
193          echo "Pending flag set...<br>";
194          }
195          }
196     else {
197              echo "ah crap...<br>";
198              echo "Command issued: $sqlcmd <br>";
199              }
200              }
```

```
201                    }
202               unset ($_POST['action']);
203               unset ($_POST['selection']);
204               unset ($_POST['RecordKey']);
205               $query = "SELECT Message, Reviewed, Pending,
                  Resolved from WarningRecords ";
206
207     echo "<form action=\"WarningMessages.php\" method =
        \"POST\">";
208     echo "<input type=\"hidden\" name=\"Query\"
        value=\"$query\" />";
209       echo "<input type=\"hidden\" name=\"debug\"
          value=\"$debug\" />";
210     }
211
212     //*************************** option 4 Set Resolved flags
        for these rows
213               else if ($action == 4) {
214               trace ("Processing updates for option 4");
215               $parms = array();
216               if ((isset($_POST['selection'])) and ($_
                  POST['selection'] !== "") ) {
217               trace ("Resolved Flag Updates being processed...");
218               $data = $_POST['selection'];
219               $reckey = $data[0];
220               trace ("Using record key:" . $reckey . ":");
221               $debug = $_POST['debug'];
222               if ($_POST['debug'] == "On") {
223               echo "**Reviewed selected set value = $reckey<br>";
224               }
225               foreach ($data as $reckey) {
226               $string1 = 'Update WarningRecords set Resolved = 1 ';
227               $string2 = 'Where RecordKey = ' . $reckey;
228               $sqlcmd = "$string1 $string2";
229               if ($_POST['debug'] == "On") {
230                 echo "Command issued: $sqlcmd <br>";
231                 }
232                 if ($return = sqlsrv_query($conn, $sqlcmd)) {
233                 if ($_POST['debug'] == "On") {
234                 echo "Resolved flag set...<br>";
235                 }
236                 }
237           else {
238               echo "ah crap...<br>";
239               echo "Command issued: $sqlcmd <br>";
240               }
241               }
```

```
242            }
243            unset ($_POST['action']);
244            unset ($_POST['selection']);
245            unset ($_POST['RecordKey']);
246            $query = "SELECT Message, Reviewed, Pending, Resolved
               from WarningRecords ";
247
248       echo "<form action=\"WarningMessages.php\" method =
          \"POST\">";
249       echo "<input type=\"hidden\" name=\"Query\" value=\"$query\"
          />";
250       echo "<input type=\"hidden\" name=\"debug\" value=\"$debug\"
          />";
251   }
252
253   //************************** option 5 Show all Pending
      activity
254     else if ($action == 5) {
255     trace ("Setting query for option 5");
256     $query1 = "SELECT Recordkey as Selection, Message,
        Reviewed, Pending, Resolved from WarningRecords ";
257     $query2 = " Where Pending = 1 and Resolved = 0";
258     $query = $query1 . $query2;
259     unset ($_POST['formAction']);
260     unset ($_POST['selection']);
261     $_POST['Query'] = $query;
262     echo "<form action=\"WarningMessages.php\" method =
        \"POST\">";
263   echo "<input type=\"hidden\" name=\"debug\" value=\"$debug\"
      />";
264     }
265
266   //************************** option 6 Show all Resolved
      activity
267     else if ($action == 6) {
268     trace ("setting query for option 6");
269
270     $query1 = "SELECT Recordkey as Selection, Message,
        Reviewed, Pending, Resolved from WarningRecords ";
271     $query2 = "Where Resolved = 1";
272     $query = $query1 . $query2;
273     unset ($_POST['formAction']);
274     echo "<form action=\"WarningMessages.php\" method =
        \"POST\">";
275     echo "<input type=\"hidden\" name=\"debug\" value=\"$debug\"
        />";
276     $_POST['Query'] = $query;
```

```
277        }
278      echo "<form action=\"WarningMessages.php\" method =
         \"POST\">";
279       echo "<input type=\"hidden\" name=\"debug\"
          value=\"$debug\" />";
280       echo "<input type=\"hidden\" name=\"formAction\"
          value=\"$action\" />";
281    }
282
283    //***************************************************************
284    //***************************************************************
285    //Display data based on default starting point or user
       selections from above
286
287    trace("Starting Query Logic");
288
289      if (isset($_POST['TypeQuery'])){
290      $query = $_POST['TypeQuery'];
291        trace ("query set to $query<br>");
292        }
293        if (isset($_POST['Query'])) {
294        $qval = $_POST['Query'];
295        trace ("Set query string to $qval<br>");
296        }
297
298        if (isset($_POST['formAction'])) {
299        $val = $_POST['formAction'];
300        trace ("Set formAction to $val<br>");
301        }
302
303      if (isset($_POST['debug'])) {
304      $debug = $_POST['debug'];
305      }
306    else {
307        $debug = "**";
308        }
309
310    ?>
311    <form action="<?php echo $self; ?>" method = "post">
312    <label for='formAction[]'>What Action is desired?</
       label><br><br>
313    <select name="formAction">
314    <option value="">Actions:</option>
315    <option value="1">  Show All Log Records </option>
316    <option value="2">  Set Reviewed flags for these rows</
       option>
```

```
317  <option value="3">  Set Pending flag for these rows</option>
318  <option value="4">  Set Resolved flag for these rows</
     option>
319  <option value="5">  Show all Pending Activity </option>
320  <option value="6">  Show all Resolved Activity </option>
321
322  </select>
323  <br>
324  <br>
325  <form action="<?php echo $self; ?>" method = "post">
326  <input type="submit" name="selection" name=formAction
     value="Update"><br>
327
328  <?php
329  //get value for debug for subsequent reposting of value
330  if (isset($_POST['debug'])) {
331    $debug = $_POST['debug'];
332    $select = $_POST['selection'];
333    trace ("Selection value = $select");
334    trace ("Display value = $display");
335    $query = $_POST['Query'];
336    trace("restored query to :$query:<br>");
337    }
338  else {
339    $debug = "**";
340    }
341    $parms = array();
342  $options = array( "Scrollable" => SQLSRV_CURSOR_KEYSET );
343    $colnames = array();
344    $header = "<th><a>Selection</a></th>";
345
346  //set default query
347    $string1 = "SELECT TOP 100 Recordkey as Selection, Message,
       Reviewed, Pending, Resolved ";
348    $string2 = " FROM WarningRecords  Where (Reviewed = 0 and
       Pending = 0 and Resolved = 0) ";
349  $query = $string1 . $string2;
350
351  if (isset($_POST['Query'])) {
352  $query = $_POST['Query'];
353    echo "<input type=\"hidden\" name=\"TypeQuery\"
       value=\"$query\" />";
354    trace ("reset value of query to :$query:<br>");
355    }
356    echo "<input type=\"hidden\" name=\"Query\" value=\"$query\"
       />";
```

```
357    echo "<input type=\"hidden\" name=\"TypeQuery\"
       value=\"$query\" />";
358    echo "<input type=\"hidden\" name=\"debug\" value=\"$debug\"
       />";
359
360    //Generate a header based on the sql query issued
361    trace ("SQL command:$query<br>");
362    $i = 0;
363    echo "<br />";
364    $return = sqlsrv_prepare($conn, $query);
365    foreach (sqlsrv_field_metadata ($return) as $fieldMetadata) {
366        foreach( $fieldMetadata as $name => $value) {
367        if ($name == 'Name') {
368        $i++;
369        if ($i > 1) {
370        $colnames[$i] = $value;
371        trace ("Name Offset $i: $value");
372        $header = $header . "<th>$colnames[$i]</th>";
373        }
374        }
375        }
376        }
377        $cols = $i;
378        ?>
379        <table class="FloatTitle" onMouseOver="javascript:trac
           kTableHighlight (event, '#99cc99');" onMouseOut="javasc
           ript:highlightTableRow(0);">
380        <thead>
381        <tr class="header" style='background-
           color:#666666;font-size:8pt;color:#fff;border:1px
           solid #c3c3c3;padding:3px;'>
382        </tr></thead>
383        <tbody>
384        <?php
385    //*********************************************** Display rows
       based on sql query
386    //***********************************************
387    echo "$header";
388    $return = sqlsrv_query ($conn, $query, $parms, $options);
389    if ($return == false) {
390        die ( print_r( sqlsrv_errors(), true));
391    }
392    $i = 0;
393    $numrows = sqlsrv_num_rows($return);
394    if ($numrows == 0) {
395    #print message when no rows found
396        echo "$string<br>";
```

```
397     echo "No new records found in the database...<br>";
398       }
399    trace ("Found " . $numrows . " rows in the database");
400    //********************************************** Normal
       (Default) Output Display
401    while ($row = sqlsrv_fetch_array ($return)) {
402        $i++;
403        echo "<tr class=\"d".($i & 1)."\">\n" .
404        "<td><input type=\"checkbox\" name=\"selection[]\"
           value =\"$row[0]\" /></td>";
405        for ($c = 1; $c < $cols; $c++) {
406        echo "<td>$row[$c]</td>\n";
407        }
408        }
409    #print message when no rows found
410    //echo ("Numrows:" . $numrows . ":<br>");
411      ?>
412      </body>
413
```

Appendix B: Error Messages

```
1    <!DOCTYPE html PUBLIC "-//W3C//DTD XHTML 1.0 Transitional//
     EN" "http://www.w3.org/TR/xhtml1/DTD/xhtml1-transitional.
     dtd">
2    <html xmlns="http://www.w3.org/1999/xhtml" xml:lang="en"
     lang="en" dir="ltr">
3    <head>
4    <title>SQL Server Logs</title>
5    <meta http-equiv="Content-Type" content="text/html;
     charset=ISO-8859-1" />
6    <script type="text/javascript">
7    </script>
8    </head>
9    <body>
10   <?php
11   function trace($string) {
12     if ($_POST['debug'] == "On") {
13     echo "$string<br>";
14     }
15     }
16   function startup () {
17   //************************************************************
18   // $_POST['debug'] = "On";
19   // $_POST['debug'] = "Off";
20
21      if (($_POST['debug']) == "On") {
22      $debug = $_POST['debug'];
23      trace ("***Message update logic***");
24      echo "...DEBUG set to $debug <br>";
25      if (isset($_POST['selection'])) {
26      $var = $_POST['selection'];
27      echo "...Selection is on and set to :$var:<br>";
28      }
29    else {
30      echo "...Selection is Off..<br>";
31      }
32      if (isset($_POST['TypeQuery'])) {
33      $var = $_POST['TypeQuery'];
```

```
34        echo "...TypeQuery is on and set to :$var:<br>";
35        }
36     else {
37        echo "...TypeQuery is Off..<br>";
38        }
39
40        if (isset($_POST['Query'])) {
41        $var = $_POST['Query'];
42        echo "...Query is on and set to :$var:<br>";
43        }
44     else {
45        echo "...Query is Off..<br>";
46        }
47
48        if (isset($_POST['formAction'])) {
49        $var = $_POST['formAction'];
50        echo "...formAction is on and set to :$var:<br>";
51        }
52     else {
53        echo "...formAction is  Off..<br>";
54        }
55        if (isset($_POST['selection'])) {
56        $var = $_POST['selection'];
57        $val = $var[0];
58        echo "...selection is on and set to :$var:$val:<br>";
59        }
60     else {
61        echo "...selection is Off..<br>";
62        }
63
64        if (isset($_POST['RecordKey'])) {
65        $val = $_POST['RecordKey'];
66        echo "...RecordKey is on and set to :$val:<br>";
67        }
68     else {
69        echo "...RecordKey is Off..<br>";
70        }
71        echo "<br>*************************<br>";
72
73     }
74     trace ("Initialization...");
75     if (isset($_POST['selection'])) {
76     $data = $_POST['selection'];
77     echo "<input type=\"hidden\" name=\"selection\" value=$data
       />";
78     trace ("Found selection, first values:$data:$reckey");
79     }
```

```
80  }
81
82  $self = $_SERVER['PHP_SELF'];
83  date_default_timezone_set('America/New_York');
84
85  include "WebHeader.php";
86  //***************** start php logic
87  // DB Variables
88  include "credentials.php"; // Connect to DB
89
90    startup();
91    $parms = array();
92  $options = array( "Scrollable" => SQLSRV_CURSOR_KEYSET );
93
94  //*****************option processing
95  //************************************************************
96  //************************************************************
97      if (isset($_POST['formAction']) and $_POST['formAction']
         !== "") {
98      trace("Action Processing Selected...");
99      $action = $_POST['formAction'];
100     $data = $_POST['selection'];
101     if (!isset($_POST['RecordKey'])) {
102     $reckey = $data[0];
103       $_POST['RecordKey'] = $reckey;
104       }
105       trace ("Initializing with Record key = $reckey");
106  // echo "<input type=\"hidden\" name=\"RecordKey\"
     value=\"$reckey\" />";
107       if ($reckey === "A") {
108       echo "*****Record not selected*****...try
          again...<br><br>";
109       unset($_POST['formAction']);
110       $action = 0;
111       $_POST['Error'] = "On";
112       $debug = $_POST['debug'];
113       trace ("***Refresh values...first value = $reckey<br>");
114       echo "<form action=\"ErrorMessages.php\" method =
          \"POST\">";
115       echo "<input type=\"hidden\" name=\"debug\"
          value=\"$debug\" />";
116       echo "<input type=\"submit\" name=\"link\" value=\"OK\"
          />";
117  }
118      else {
119        unset($_POST['Error']);
120        }
```

```
121        if ($_POST['debug'] == "On") {
122        echo "**Action option = $action<br>";
123        }
124   //************************* option 1 Show all Warning
      records
125        if ($action == 1) {
126        trace ("Creating sql string for option 1");
127        $query = "SELECT Recordkey as Selection, Message,
           Reviewed, Pending, Resolved from ErrorRecords ";
128        $_POST['Query'] = $query;
129        echo "<form action=\"ErrorMessages.php\" method =
           \"POST\">";
130        echo "<input type=\"hidden\" name=\"debug\"
           value=\"$debug\" /Message, Reviewed, Pending, Resolved
           from ErrorRecords>";
131        }
132
133   //************************* option 2 Set Reviewed flags
      for these rows
134          else if ($action == 2) {
135          trace ("Processing options for action 2");
136          $parms = array();
137          if ((isset($_POST['selection'])) and
             ($_POST['selection'] !== "") ) {
138          trace ("Reviewed Flag Updates being processed...");
139          $data = $_POST['selection'];
140          $reckey = $data[0];
141          trace ("Using record key:" . $reckey . ":");
142          $debug = $_POST['debug'];
143          if ($_POST['debug'] == "On") {
144          echo "**Reviewed selected set value = $reckey<br>";
145          }
146          foreach ($data as $reckey) {
147          $string1 = 'Update ErrorRecords set Reviewed = 1 ';
148          $string2 = 'Where RecordKey = ' . $reckey;
149          $sqlcmd = "$string1 $string2";
150          if ($_POST['debug'] == "On") {
151            echo "Command issued: $sqlcmd <br>";
152            }
153            if ($return = sqlsrv_query($conn, $sqlcmd)) {
154            if ($_POST['debug'] == "On") {
155            echo "REVIEWED flag set...<br>";
156            }
157            }
158          else {
159            echo "ah crap...<br>";
```

```
160        echo "Command issued: $sqlcmd <br>";
161            }
162            }
163            }
164        unset ($_POST['formAction']);
165        unset ($_POST['selection']);
166 // $query = "SELECT Message, Reviewed, Pending, Resolved
    from ErrorRecords where Reviewed = 1";
167   echo "<form action=\"ErrorMessages.php\" method =
    \"POST\">";
168   echo "<input type=\"hidden\" name=\"debug\" value=\"$debug\" />";
169   }
170
171 //*************************** option 3 Set Pending flags for
    these rows
172        else if ($action == 3) {
173        trace ("Processing updates for option 3");
174        $parms = array();
175        if ((isset($_POST['selection'])) and
           ($_POST['selection'] !== "") ) {
176        trace ("Pending Flag Updates being processed...");
177        $data = $_POST['selection'];
178        $reckey = $data[0];
179        trace ("Using record key:" . $reckey . ":");
180        $debug = $_POST['debug'];
181        if ($_POST['debug'] == "On") {
182        echo "**Reviewed selected set value = $reckey<br>";
183        }
184        foreach ($data as $reckey) {
185        $string1 = 'Update ErrorRecords set Pending = 1 ';
186        $string2 = 'Where RecordKey = ' . $reckey;
187        $sqlcmd = "$string1 $string2";
188        if ($_POST['debug'] == "On") {
189          echo "Command issued: $sqlcmd <br>";
190          }
191          if ($return = sqlsrv_query($conn, $sqlcmd)) {
192          if ($_POST['debug'] == "On") {
193          echo "Pending flag set...<br>";
194          }
195          }
196        else {
197          echo "ah crap...<br>";
198          echo "Command issued: $sqlcmd <br>";
199          }
200          }
201          }
```

```
202              unset ($_POST['action']);
203              unset ($_POST['selection']);
204              unset ($_POST['RecordKey']);
205              $query = "SELECT Message, Reviewed, Pending,
                 Resolved from ErrorRecords ";
206
207      echo "<form action=\"ErrorMessages.php\" method = \"POST
         \">";
208      echo "<input type=\"hidden\" name=\"Query\"
         value=\"$query\" />";
209      echo "<input type=\"hidden\" name=\"debug\"
         value=\"$debug\" />";
210  }
211
212 //*************************** option 4 Set Resolved flags for
    these rows
213          else if ($action == 4) {
214          trace ("Processing updates for option 4");
215          $parms = array();
216          if ((isset($_POST['selection'])) and
             ($_POST['selection'] !== "") ) {
217          trace ("Resolved Flag Updates being processed...");
218          $data = $_POST['selection'];
219          $reckey = $data[0];
220          trace ("Using record key:" . $reckey . ":");
221          $debug = $_POST['debug'];
222          if ($_POST['debug'] == "On") {
223          echo "**Reviewed selected set value = $reckey<br>";
224          }
225          foreach ($data as $reckey) {
226          $string1 = 'Update ErrorRecords set Resolved = 1 ';
227          $string2 = 'Where RecordKey = ' . $reckey;
228          $sqlcmd = "$string1 $string2";
229          if ($_POST['debug'] == "On") {
230              echo "Command issued: $sqlcmd <br>";
231              }
232              if ($return = sqlsrv_query($conn, $sqlcmd)) {
233              if ($_POST['debug'] == "On") {
234              echo "Resolved flag set...<br>";
235              }
236              }
237          else {
238            echo "ah crap...<br>";
239            echo "Command issued: $sqlcmd <br>";
240            }
241            }
```

```
242              }
243              unset ($_POST['action']);
244              unset ($_POST['selection']);
245              unset ($_POST['RecordKey']);
246              $query = "SELECT Message, Reviewed, Pending,
                 Resolved from ErrorRecords ";
247
248        echo "<form action=\"ErrorMessages.php\" method =
           \"POST\">";
249        echo "<input type=\"hidden\" name=\"Query\"
           value=\"$query\" />";
250        echo "<input type=\"hidden\" name=\"debug\"
           value=\"$debug\" />";
251        }
252
253  //*************************** option 5 Show all Pending
     activity
254    else if ($action == 5) {
255    trace ("Setting query for option 5");
256    $query1 = "SELECT Recordkey as Selection, Message,
       Reviewed, Pending, Resolved from ErrorRecords ";
257    $query2 = " Where Pending = 1 and Resolved = 0";
258    $query = $query1 . $query2;
259    unset ($_POST['formAction']);
260    unset ($_POST['selection']);
261    $_POST['Query'] = $query;
262    echo "<form action=\"ErrorMessages.php\" method =
       \"POST\">";
263    echo "<input type=\"hidden\" name=\"debug\"
       value=\"$debug\" />";
264      }
265
266  //*************************** option 6 Show all Resolved
     activity
267    else if ($action == 6) {
268    trace ("setting query for option 6");
269
270    $query1 = "SELECT Recordkey as Selection, Message,
       Reviewed, Pending, Resolved from ErrorRecords ";
271    $query2 = "Where Resolved = 1";
272    $query = $query1 . $query2;
273    unset ($_POST['formAction']);
274    echo "<form action=\"ErrorMessages.php\" method =
       \"POST\">";
275    echo "<input type=\"hidden\" name=\"debug\"
       value=\"$debug\" />";
```

```
276    $_POST['Query'] = $query;
277    }
278    echo "<form action=\"ErrorMessages.php\" method =
       \"POST\">";
279    echo "<input type=\"hidden\" name=\"debug\"
       value=\"$debug\" />";
280    echo "<input type=\"hidden\" name=\"formAction\"
       value=\"$action\" />";
281    }
282
283    //*********************************************************
284    //*********************************************************
285    //Display data based on default starting point or user
       selections from above
286
287    trace("Starting Query Logic");
288
289    if (isset($_POST['TypeQuery'])) {
290      $query = $_POST['TypeQuery'];
291      trace ("query set to $query<br>");
292      }
293      if (isset($_POST['Query'])) {
294      $qval = $_POST['Query'];
295      trace ("Set query string to $qval<br>");
296      }
297
298      if (isset($_POST['formAction'])) {
299      $val = $_POST['formAction'];
300      trace ("Set formAction to $val<br>");
301      }
302
303    if (isset($_POST['debug'])) {
304    $debug = $_POST['debug'];
305    }
306    else {
307      $debug = "**";
308      }
309
310    ?>
311    <form action="<?php echo $self; ?>" method = "post">
312    <label for='formAction[]'>What Action is desired?</
       label><br><br>
313    <select name="formAction">
314    <option value="">Actions:</option>
315    <option value="1">  Show All Log Records </option>
316    <option value="2">  Set Reviewed flags for these rows</option>
317    <option value="3">  Set Pending flag for these rows</option>
```

```
318   <option value="4">  Set Resolved flag for these rows</option>
319   <option value="5">  Show all Pending Activity </option>
320   <option value="6">  Show all Resolved Activity </option>
321
322   </select>
323   <br>
324   <br>
325   <form action="<?php echo $self; ?>" method = "post">
326   <input type="submit" name="selection" name=formAction
      value="Update"><br>
327
328   <?php
329   //get value for debug for subsequent reposting of value
330   if (isset($_POST['debug'])) {
331   $debug = $_POST ['debug'];
332     $select = $_POST['selection'];
333     trace ("Selection value = $select");
334     trace ("Display value = $display");
335     $query = $_POST['Query'];
336     trace("restored query to :$query:<br>");
337     }
338   else {
339     $debug = "**";
340     }
341     $parms = array();
342   $options = array( "Scrollable" => SQLSRV_CURSOR_KEYSET );
343     $colnames = array();
344     $header = "<th><a>Selection</a></th>";
345
346   //set default query
347   $string1 = "SELECT TOP 100 Recordkey as Selection, Message,
      Reviewed, Pending, Resolved ";
348   $string2 = " FROM ErrorRecords  Where (Reviewed = 0 and
      Pending = 0 and Resolved = 0) ";
349   $query = $string1 . $string2;
350
351   if (isset($_POST['Query'])) {
352   $query = $_POST['Query'];
353     echo "<input type=\"hidden\" name=\"TypeQuery\" value=
      \"$query\" />";
354     trace ("reset value of query to :$query:<br>");
355   }
356   echo "<input type=\"hidden\" name=\"Query\" value=\"$query\" />";
357   echo "<input type=\"hidden\" name=\"TypeQuery\"
      value=\"$query\" />";
358   echo "<input type=\"hidden\" name=\"debug\" value=\"$debug\"
      />";
```

```
359
360    //Generate a header based on the sql query issued
361      trace ("SQL command:$query<br>");
362      $i = 0;
363      echo "<br />";
364      $return = sqlsrv_prepare($conn, $query);
365    foreach (sqlsrv_field_metadata ($return) as $fieldMetadata) {
366          foreach( $fieldMetadata as $name => $value) {
367          if ($name == 'Name') {
368          $i++;
369          if ($i > 1) {
370          $colnames[$i] = $value;
371          trace ("Name Offset $i: $value");
372          $header = $header . "<th>$colnames[$i]</th>";
373          }
374          }
375          }
376          }
377          $cols = $i;
378          ?>
379          <table class="FloatTitle" onMouseOver="javascript:trac
             kTableHighlight(event, '#99cc99');" onMouseOut="javasc
             ript:highlightTableRow(0);">
380          <thead>
381          <tr class="header" style='background-
             color:#666666;font-size:8pt;color:#fff;border:1px
             solid #c3c3c3;padding:3px;'>
382          </tr></thead>
383          <tbody>
384          <?php
385    //***************************************** Display rows
       based on sql query 386    //*******************************
       ********
387      echo "$header";
388      $return = sqlsrv_query ($conn, $query, $parms, $options);
389      if ($return == false) {
390          die ( print_r( sqlsrv_errors(), true));
391      }
392      $i = 0;
393      $numrows = sqlsrv_num_rows($return);
394      if ($numrows == 0) {
395    #print message when no rows found
396        echo "$string<br>";
397        echo "No new records found in the database...<br>";
398        }
399      trace ("Found " . $numrows . " rows in the database");
```

```
400     //*********************************************** Normal
        (Default) Output Display
401   while ($row = sqlsrv_fetch_array ($return)) {
402         $i++;
403         echo "<tr class=\"d".($i & 1)."\">\n" .
404         "<td><input type=\"checkbox\" name=\"selection[]\"
            value =\"$row[0]\" /></td>";
405         for ($c = 1; $c < $cols; $c++) {
406         echo "<td>$row[$c]</td>\n";
407         }
408         }
409   #print message when no rows found
410   //echo ("Numrows:" . $numrows . ":<br>");
411     ?>
412     </body>
413
```

Appendix C: University DDL

```sql
CREATE TABLE [Assignment]
(
 [AssignmentNo]        char(18)    NOT NULL ,
 [CourseID]            varchar(50) NOT NULL ,
 [SectionID]           varchar(50) NOT NULL ,
 [AssignmentDescription] char(18)  NULL
)
go

ALTER TABLE [Assignment]
 ADD CONSTRAINT [XPKAssignment] PRIMARY KEY  CLUSTERED
([AssignmentNo] ASC,[CourseID] ASC,[SectionID] ASC)
go

CREATE TABLE [Course]
(
 [CourseID]            varchar(50) NOT NULL ,
 [DepartmentID]        varchar(50) NOT NULL ,
 [CourseName]          varchar(50) NULL ,
 [CreditHours]         varchar(50) NULL ,
 [CourseDescription]   varchar(50) NULL
)
go

ALTER TABLE [Course]
 ADD CONSTRAINT [XPKCourse] PRIMARY KEY  CLUSTERED ([CourseID] ASC)
go

CREATE TABLE [Course_Enrollment]
(
 [CourseID]            varchar(50) NOT NULL ,
 [SectionID]           varchar(50) NOT NULL ,
 [StudentID]           varchar(50) NOT NULL ,
 [DateEnrolled]        datetime    NULL ,
```

```
 [MidtermGrade]          char(18)   NULL ,
 [FinalGrade]            char(18)   NULL
)
go


ALTER TABLE [Course_Enrollment]
 ADD CONSTRAINT [XPKCourse_Enrollment] PRIMARY KEY  CLUSTERED
([CourseID] ASC,[SectionID] ASC,[StudentID] ASC)
go


CREATE TABLE [Course_Offering]
(
 [CourseID]              varchar(50)  NOT NULL ,
 [SectionID]             varchar(50)  NOT NULL ,
 [FacultyID]             varchar(50)  NOT NULL ,
 [Location]              varchar(50)  NULL ,
 [ClassSchedule]         varchar(50)  NULL
)
go


ALTER TABLE [Course_Offering]
 ADD CONSTRAINT [XPKCourse_Offering] PRIMARY KEY  CLUSTERED
([CourseID] ASC,[SectionID] ASC)
go


CREATE TABLE [Course_Prerequisite]
(
 [CourseID]              varchar(50)  NOT NULL ,
 [PrerequisiteCseID]     varchar(50)  NOT NULL
)
go


ALTER TABLE [Course_Prerequisite]
 ADD CONSTRAINT [XPKCourse_Prerequisite] PRIMARY KEY  CLUSTERED
([CourseID] ASC,[PrerequisiteCseID] ASC)
go


CREATE TABLE [Curriculum]
(
 [CurriculumID]          char(18,50)  NOT NULL ,
 [DegreeID]              varchar(50)  NOT NULL ,
 [CurriculumName]        varchar(50)  NULL ,
 [CurriculumDescription] varchar(50)  NULL
)
go
```

```
ALTER TABLE [Curriculum]
 ADD CONSTRAINT [XPKCurriculum] PRIMARY KEY  CLUSTERED
([CurriculumID] ASC)
go


CREATE TABLE [Curriculum_Course]
(
 [CurriculumID]        char(18,50)   NOT NULL ,
 [CourseID]            varchar(50)   NOT NULL ,
 [Opt_MandatoryFlag]   varchar(50)   NULL ,
 [CurriculumCseInfo]   varchar(50)   NULL
)
go


ALTER TABLE [Curriculum_Course]
 ADD CONSTRAINT [XPKCurriculum_Course] PRIMARY KEY  CLUSTERED
([CurriculumID] ASC,[CourseID] ASC)
go


CREATE TABLE [Curriculum_Job_Classification]
(
 [ClassificationID]    varchar(50)   NOT NULL ,
 [CurriculumID]        char(18,50)   NOT NULL ,
 [Job_Relationship]    varchar(50)   NULL
)
go


ALTER TABLE [Curriculum_Job_Classification]
 ADD CONSTRAINT [XPKCurriculum_Job_Classification] PRIMARY KEY
CLUSTERED ([ClassificationID] ASC,[CurriculumID] ASC)
go


CREATE TABLE [Degree]
(
 [DegreeID]            varchar(50)   NOT NULL ,
 [DepartmentID]        varchar(50)   NOT NULL ,
 [DegreeName]          char(18,50)   NULL
)
go


ALTER TABLE [Degree]
 ADD CONSTRAINT [XPKDegree] PRIMARY KEY  CLUSTERED ([DegreeID] ASC)
go


CREATE TABLE [Department]
(
 [DepartmentID]            varchar(50)   NOT NULL ,
```

```
 [SchoolID]            varchar(50)   NOT NULL ,
 [DepartmentName]      varchar(50)   NULL ,
 [DepartmentHeadID]    varchar(50)   NULL ,
 [DeptCampusLocation]  varchar(50)   NULL
)
go


ALTER TABLE [Department]
 ADD CONSTRAINT [XPKDepartment] PRIMARY KEY  CLUSTERED
([DepartmentID] ASC)
go


CREATE TABLE [Faculty]
(
 [FacultyID]           varchar(50)   NOT NULL ,
 [DepartmentID]        varchar(50)   NULL ,
 [FacultyPrefix]       varchar(50)   NULL ,
 [FacultyLastName]     varchar(50)   NULL ,
 [FacultyMiddleName]   varchar(50)   NULL ,
 [FacultyFirstName]    varchar(50)   NULL ,
 [FacultyStreetAddr]   varchar(50)   NULL ,
 [FacultyCity]         varchar(50)   NULL ,
 [FacultyState]        varchar(50)   NULL ,
 [FacultyZipCode]      varchar(50)   NULL
)
go


ALTER TABLE [Faculty]
 ADD CONSTRAINT [XPKFaculty] PRIMARY KEY  CLUSTERED ([FacultyID]
 ASC)
go


CREATE TABLE [Job_Classification]
(
 [ClassificationID]          varchar(50)   NOT NULL ,
 [ClassificationName]        varchar(50)   NULL ,
 [ClassificationDescription] varchar(50)   NULL
)
go


ALTER TABLE [Job_Classification]
 ADD CONSTRAINT [XPKJob_Classification] PRIMARY KEY  CLUSTERED
([ClassificationID] ASC)
go
```

```
CREATE TABLE [School]
(
 [SchoolID]              varchar(50)  NOT NULL ,
 [SchoolName]            varchar(50)  NULL ,
 [SchoolDescription]     varchar(50)  NULL ,
 [SchoolCampusLocation]  varchar(50)  NULL ,
 [SchoolDeanID]          varchar(50)  NULL
)
go

ALTER TABLE [School]
 ADD CONSTRAINT [XPKSchool] PRIMARY KEY  CLUSTERED ([SchoolID]
 ASC)
go

CREATE TABLE [Student]
(
 [StudentID]               varchar(50)  NOT NULL ,
 [DepartmentID]            varchar(50)  NULL ,
 [StudentLastName]         varchar(50)  NULL ,
 [StudentMiddleName]       varchar(50)  NULL ,
 [StudentFirstName]        varchar(50)  NULL ,
 [StudentTelephoneNumber]  varchar(50)  NULL ,
 [StudentStreetAddr]       varchar(50)  NULL ,
 [StudentCity]             varchar(50)  NULL ,
 [StudentState]            varchar(50)  NULL ,
 [StudentZipCode]          varchar(50)  NULL ,
 [ClassLevel]              varchar(50)  NULL
)
go

ALTER TABLE [Student]
 ADD CONSTRAINT [XPKStudent] PRIMARY KEY  CLUSTERED ([StudentID] ASC)
go

CREATE TABLE [Student_Grade]
(
 [CourseID]    varchar(50)  NOT NULL ,
 [SectionID]   varchar(50)  NOT NULL ,
 [StudentID]   varchar(50)  NOT NULL ,
 [Week1]       varchar(50)  NULL ,
 [Week2]       varchar(50)  NULL ,
 [Week3]       varchar(50)  NULL ,
 [xxx]         varchar(50)  NULL ,
 [Week16]      varchar(50)  NULL
)
go
```

```
ALTER TABLE [Student_Grade]
 ADD CONSTRAINT [XPKStudent_Grade] PRIMARY KEY  CLUSTERED
([CourseID] ASC,[SectionID] ASC,[StudentID] ASC)
go

CREATE TABLE [Student_Transcript]
(
 [CourseID]            varchar(50)  NOT NULL ,
 [StudentID]           varchar(50)  NOT NULL ,
 [Grade]               varchar(50)  NULL ,
 [DateCompleted]       datetime  NULL ,
 [CreditHoursEarned]   varchar(50)  NULL
)
go

ALTER TABLE [Student_Transcript]
 ADD CONSTRAINT [XPKStudent_Transcript] PRIMARY KEY  CLUSTERED
([CourseID] ASC,[StudentID] ASC)
go

ALTER TABLE [Assignment]
 ADD CONSTRAINT [R_14] FOREIGN KEY ([CourseID],[SectionID])
REFERENCES [Course_Offering]([CourseID],[SectionID])
go

ALTER TABLE [Assignment]
 ADD CONSTRAINT [R_31] FOREIGN KEY ([CourseID],[SectionID])
REFERENCES [Course_Offering]([CourseID],[SectionID])
go

ALTER TABLE [Course]
 ADD CONSTRAINT [R_21] FOREIGN KEY ([DepartmentID]) REFERENCES
[Department]([DepartmentID])
go

ALTER TABLE [Course_Enrollment]
 ADD CONSTRAINT [R_13] FOREIGN KEY ([CourseID],[SectionID])
REFERENCES [Course_Offering]([CourseID],[SectionID])
go

ALTER TABLE [Course_Enrollment]
 ADD CONSTRAINT [R_18] FOREIGN KEY ([StudentID]) REFERENCES
[Student]([StudentID])
go
```

```
ALTER TABLE [Course_Enrollment]
 ADD CONSTRAINT [R_32] FOREIGN KEY ([CourseID],[SectionID])
REFERENCES [Course_Offering]([CourseID],[SectionID])
go

ALTER TABLE [Course_Enrollment]
 ADD CONSTRAINT [R_33] FOREIGN KEY ([StudentID]) REFERENCES
[Student]([StudentID])
go

ALTER TABLE [Course_Offering]
 ADD CONSTRAINT [R_11] FOREIGN KEY ([CourseID]) REFERENCES
[Course]([CourseID])
go

ALTER TABLE [Course_Offering]
 ADD CONSTRAINT [R_12] FOREIGN KEY ([FacultyID]) REFERENCES
[Faculty]([FacultyID])
go

ALTER TABLE [Course_Offering]
 ADD CONSTRAINT [R_29] FOREIGN KEY ([CourseID]) REFERENCES
[Course]([CourseID])
go

ALTER TABLE [Course_Offering]
 ADD CONSTRAINT [R_30] FOREIGN KEY ([FacultyID]) REFERENCES
[Faculty]([FacultyID])
go

ALTER TABLE [Course_Prerequisite]
 ADD CONSTRAINT [R_5] FOREIGN KEY ([CourseID]) REFERENCES [Course]
([CourseID])
go

ALTER TABLE [Course_Prerequisite]
 ADD CONSTRAINT [R_22] FOREIGN KEY ([CourseID]) REFERENCES
[Course]([CourseID])
go

ALTER TABLE [Curriculum]
 ADD CONSTRAINT [R_24] FOREIGN KEY ([DegreeID]) REFERENCES
[Degree]([DegreeID])
go
```

```
ALTER TABLE [Curriculum_Course]
 ADD CONSTRAINT [R_25] FOREIGN KEY ([CurriculumID]) REFERENCES
[Curriculum]([CurriculumID])
go

ALTER TABLE [Curriculum_Course]
 ADD CONSTRAINT [R_26] FOREIGN KEY ([CourseID]) REFERENCES
[Course]([CourseID])
go

ALTER TABLE [Curriculum_Job_Classification]
 ADD CONSTRAINT [R_6] FOREIGN KEY ([ClassificationID]) REFERENCES
[Job_Classification]([ClassificationID])
go

ALTER TABLE [Curriculum_Job_Classification]
 ADD CONSTRAINT [R_23] FOREIGN KEY ([ClassificationID]) REFERENCES
[Job_Classification]([ClassificationID])
go

ALTER TABLE [Curriculum_Job_Classification]
 ADD CONSTRAINT [R_28] FOREIGN KEY ([CurriculumID]) REFERENCES
[Curriculum]([CurriculumID])
go

ALTER TABLE [Degree]
 ADD CONSTRAINT [R_19] FOREIGN KEY ([DepartmentID]) REFERENCES
[Department]([DepartmentID])
go

ALTER TABLE [Department]
ADD CONSTRAINT [R_1] FOREIGN KEY ([SchoolID]) REFERENCES [School]
([SchoolID])
go

ALTER TABLE [Department]
 ADD CONSTRAINT [R_2] FOREIGN KEY ([SchoolID]) REFERENCES [School]
([SchoolID])
go

ALTER TABLE [Department]
 ADD CONSTRAINT [R_20] FOREIGN KEY ([SchoolID]) REFERENCES
[School]([SchoolID])
go

ALTER TABLE [Student_Grade]
 ADD CONSTRAINT [R_27] FOREIGN KEY ([CourseID],[SectionID],[StudentID
]) REFERENCES [Course_Enrollment]([CourseID],[SectionID],[StudentID])
go
```

```
ALTER TABLE [Student_Transcript]
 ADD CONSTRAINT [R_36] FOREIGN KEY ([StudentID]) REFERENCES
[Student]([StudentID])
go


CREATE TRIGGER tI_Assignment ON Assignment FOR INSERT AS
/* erwin Builtin Trigger */
/* INSERT trigger on Assignment */
BEGIN
   DECLARE @numrows int,
           @nullcnt int,
           @validcnt int,
           @errno    int,
           @severity int,
           @state    int,
           @errmsg   varchar(255)
  SELECT @numrows = @@rowcount
  /* erwin Builtin Trigger */
  /* Course_Offering  Assignment on child insert restrict */
  /* ERWIN_RELATION:CHECKSUM="00031487", PARENT_OWNER="",
PARENT_TABLE="Course_Offering"
    CHILD_OWNER="", CHILD_TABLE="Assignment"
    P2C_VERB_PHRASE="", C2P_VERB_PHRASE="",
    FK_CONSTRAINT="R_31", FK_COLUMNS="CourseID""SectionID" */
  IF
    /* %ChildFK(" OR",UPDATE) */
    UPDATE(CourseID) OR
    UPDATE(SectionID)
  BEGIN
    SELECT @nullcnt = 0
    SELECT @validcnt = count(*)
      FROM inserted,Course_Offering
        WHERE
          /* %JoinFKPK(inserted,Course_Offering) */
          inserted.CourseID = Course_Offering.CourseID and
          inserted.SectionID = Course_Offering.SectionID
    /* %NotnullFK(inserted," IS NULL","select @nullcnt = count(*)
from inserted where"," and") */

    IF @validcnt + @nullcnt != @numrows
    BEGIN
      SELECT @errno  = 30002,
             @errmsg = 'Cannot insert Assignment because Course_
Offering does not exist.'
      GOTO error
    END
  END
```

```
  /* erwin Builtin Trigger */
  /* Course_Offering  Assignment on child insert restrict */
  /* ERWIN_RELATION:CHECKSUM="00000000", PARENT_OWNER="",
PARENT_TABLE="Course_Offering"
    CHILD_OWNER="", CHILD_TABLE="Assignment"
    P2C_VERB_PHRASE="", C2P_VERB_PHRASE="",
    FK_CONSTRAINT="R_14", FK_COLUMNS="CourseID""SectionID" */
  IF
    /* %ChildFK(" OR",UPDATE) */
    UPDATE(CourseID) OR
    UPDATE(SectionID)
  BEGIN
    SELECT @nullcnt = 0
    SELECT @validcnt = count(*)
      FROM inserted,Course_Offering
        WHERE
          /* %JoinFKPK(inserted,Course_Offering) */
          inserted.CourseID = Course_Offering.CourseID and
          inserted.SectionID = Course_Offering.SectionID
    /* %NotnullFK(inserted," IS NULL","select @nullcnt = count(*)
from inserted where"," and") */

    IF @validcnt + @nullcnt != @numrows
    BEGIN
      SELECT @errno  = 30002,
             @errmsg = 'Cannot insert Assignment because Course_
Offering does not exist.'
      GOTO error
    END
  END

  /* erwin Builtin Trigger */
  RETURN
error:
   RAISERROR (@errmsg, -- Message text.
              @severity, -- Severity (0~25).
              @state) -- State (0~255).
   rollback transaction
END

go

CREATE TRIGGER tU_Assignment ON Assignment FOR UPDATE AS
/* erwin Builtin Trigger */
/* UPDATE trigger on Assignment */
BEGIN
  DECLARE  @numrows int,
           @nullcnt int,
```

```
            @validcnt int,
            @insAssignmentNo char(18),
            @insCourseID varchar(50),
            @insSectionID varchar(50),
            @errno    int,
            @severity int,
            @state    int,
            @errmsg   varchar(255)


  SELECT @numrows = @@rowcount
  /* erwin Builtin Trigger */
  /* Course_Offering  Assignment on child update restrict */
  /* ERWIN_RELATION:CHECKSUM="00032302", PARENT_OWNER="",
PARENT_TABLE="Course_Offering"
    CHILD_OWNER="", CHILD_TABLE="Assignment"
    P2C_VERB_PHRASE="", C2P_VERB_PHRASE="",
    FK_CONSTRAINT="R_31", FK_COLUMNS="CourseID""SectionID" */
  IF
    /* %ChildFK(" OR",UPDATE) */
    UPDATE(CourseID) OR
    UPDATE(SectionID)
  BEGIN
    SELECT @nullcnt = 0
    SELECT @validcnt = count(*)
      FROM inserted,Course_Offering
        WHERE
          /* %JoinFKPK(inserted,Course_Offering) */
          inserted.CourseID = Course_Offering.CourseID and
          inserted.SectionID = Course_Offering.SectionID
    /* %NotnullFK(inserted," IS NULL","select @nullcnt = count(*)
from inserted where"," AND") */

    IF @validcnt + @nullcnt != @numrows
    BEGIN
      SELECT @errno  = 30007,
             @errmsg = 'Cannot update Assignment because Course_
Offering does not exist.'
      GOTO error
    END
  END

  /* erwin Builtin Trigger */
  /* Course_Offering  Assignment on child update restrict */
  /* ERWIN_RELATION:CHECKSUM="00000000", PARENT_OWNER="",
PARENT_TABLE="Course_Offering"
    CHILD_OWNER="", CHILD_TABLE="Assignment"
    P2C_VERB_PHRASE="", C2P_VERB_PHRASE="",
```

```
    FK_CONSTRAINT="R_14", FK_COLUMNS="CourseID""SectionID" */
  IF
    /* %ChildFK(" OR",UPDATE) */
    UPDATE(CourseID) OR
    UPDATE(SectionID)
  BEGIN
    SELECT @nullcnt = 0
    SELECT @validcnt = count(*)
      FROM inserted,Course_Offering
        WHERE
          /* %JoinFKPK(inserted,Course_Offering) */
          inserted.CourseID = Course_Offering.CourseID and
          inserted.SectionID = Course_Offering.SectionID
    /* %NotnullFK(inserted," IS NULL","select @nullcnt = count(*)
from inserted where"," AND") */

    IF @validcnt + @nullcnt != @numrows
    BEGIN
      SELECT @errno  = 30007,
             @errmsg = 'Cannot update Assignment because Course_
Offering does not exist.'
      GOTO error
    END
  END

  /* erwin Builtin Trigger */
  RETURN
error:
  RAISERROR (@errmsg, -- Message text.
             @severity, -- Severity (0~25).
             @state) -- State (0~255).
    rollback transaction
END

go

CREATE TRIGGER tD_Course ON Course FOR DELETE AS
/* erwin Builtin Trigger */
/* DELETE trigger on Course */
BEGIN
  DECLARE @errno    int,
          @severity int,
          @state    int,
          @errmsg   varchar(255)
    /* erwin Builtin Trigger */
    /* Course  Course_Offering on parent delete restrict */
    /* ERWIN_RELATION:CHECKSUM="000536a7", PARENT_OWNER="",
PARENT_TABLE="Course"
    CHILD_OWNER="", CHILD_TABLE="Course_Offering"
```

```
    P2C_VERB_PHRASE="", C2P_VERB_PHRASE="",
    FK_CONSTRAINT="R_29", FK_COLUMNS="CourseID" */
    IF EXISTS (
      SELECT * FROM deleted,Course_Offering
      WHERE
        /* %JoinFKPK(Course_Offering,deleted," = "," AND") */
        Course_Offering.CourseID = deleted.CourseID
    )
    BEGIN
      SELECT @errno  = 30001,
             @errmsg = 'Cannot delete Course because Course_
Offering exists.'
      GOTO error
    END
    /* erwin Builtin Trigger */
    /* Course  Curriculum_Course on parent delete restrict */
    /* ERWIN_RELATION:CHECKSUM="00000000", PARENT_OWNER="",
PARENT_TABLE="Course"
    CHILD_OWNER="", CHILD_TABLE="Curriculum_Course"
    P2C_VERB_PHRASE="", C2P_VERB_PHRASE="",
    FK_CONSTRAINT="R_26", FK_COLUMNS="CourseID" */
    IF EXISTS (
      SELECT * FROM deleted,Curriculum_Course
      WHERE
        /* %JoinFKPK(Curriculum_Course,deleted," = "," AND") */
        Curriculum_Course.CourseID = deleted.CourseID
    )
    BEGIN
      SELECT @errno  = 30001,
             @errmsg = 'Cannot delete Course because Curriculum_
Course exists.'
      GOTO error
    END

    /* erwin Builtin Trigger */
    /* Course  Course_Prerequisite on parent delete restrict */
    /* ERWIN_RELATION:CHECKSUM="00000000", PARENT_OWNER="",
PARENT_TABLE="Course"
    CHILD_OWNER="", CHILD_TABLE="Course_Prerequisite"
    P2C_VERB_PHRASE="", C2P_VERB_PHRASE="",
    FK_CONSTRAINT="R_22", FK_COLUMNS="CourseID" */
    IF EXISTS (
      SELECT * FROM deleted,Course_Prerequisite
      WHERE
        /* %JoinFKPK(Course_Prerequisite,deleted," = "," AND") */
        Course_Prerequisite.CourseID = deleted.CourseID
    )
```

```
      BEGIN
        SELECT @errno  = 30001,
                @errmsg = 'Cannot delete Course because Course_
Prerequisite exists.'
        GOTO error
      END


      /* erwin Builtin Trigger */
      /* Course  Course_Offering on parent delete restrict */
      /* ERWIN_RELATION:CHECKSUM="00000000", PARENT_OWNER="",
PARENT_TABLE="Course"
      CHILD_OWNER="", CHILD_TABLE="Course_Offering"
      P2C_VERB_PHRASE="", C2P_VERB_PHRASE="",
      FK_CONSTRAINT="R_11", FK_COLUMNS="CourseID" */
      IF EXISTS (
        SELECT * FROM deleted,Course_Offering
        WHERE
          /*  %JoinFKPK(Course_Offering,deleted," = "," AND") */
          Course_Offering.CourseID = deleted.CourseID
      )
      BEGIN
        SELECT @errno  = 30001,
                @errmsg = 'Cannot delete Course because Course_
Offering exists.'
        GOTO error
      END


      /* erwin Builtin Trigger */
      /* Course  Course_Prerequisite on parent delete restrict */
      /* ERWIN_RELATION:CHECKSUM="00000000", PARENT_OWNER="",
PARENT_TABLE="Course"
      CHILD_OWNER="", CHILD_TABLE="Course_Prerequisite"
      P2C_VERB_PHRASE="", C2P_VERB_PHRASE="",
      FK_CONSTRAINT="R_5", FK_COLUMNS="CourseID" */
      IF EXISTS (
        SELECT * FROM deleted,Course_Prerequisite
        WHERE
          /*  %JoinFKPK(Course_Prerequisite,deleted," = "," AND") */
          Course_Prerequisite.CourseID = deleted.CourseID
      )
      BEGIN
        SELECT @errno  = 30001,
                @errmsg = 'Cannot delete Course because Course_
Prerequisite exists.'
        GOTO error
      END
```

```
     /* erwin Builtin Trigger */
     RETURN
error:
   RAISERROR (@errmsg, -- Message text.
              @severity, -- Severity (0~25).
              @state) -- State (0~255).
     rollback transaction
END

go

CREATE TRIGGER tI_Course ON Course FOR INSERT AS
/* erwin Builtin Trigger */
/* INSERT trigger on Course */
BEGIN
   DECLARE @numrows int,
           @nullcnt int,
           @validcnt int,
           @errno   int,
           @severity int,
           @state     int,
           @errmsg  varchar(255)

  SELECT @numrows = @@rowcount
  /* erwin Builtin Trigger */
  /* Department  Course on child insert restrict */
  /* ERWIN_RELATION:CHECKSUM="00017ce4", PARENT_OWNER="",
PARENT_TABLE="Department"
    CHILD_OWNER="", CHILD_TABLE="Course"
    P2C_VERB_PHRASE="", C2P_VERB_PHRASE="",
    FK_CONSTRAINT="R_21", FK_COLUMNS="DepartmentID" */
  IF
    /* %ChildFK(" OR",UPDATE) */
    UPDATE(DepartmentID)
  BEGIN
    SELECT @nullcnt = 0
    SELECT @validcnt = count(*)
      FROM inserted,Department
        WHERE
          /* %JoinFKPK(inserted,Department) */
          inserted.DepartmentID = Department.DepartmentID
    /* %NotnullFK(inserted," IS NULL","select @nullcnt = count(*)
from inserted where"," and") */

    IF @validcnt + @nullcnt != @numrows
    BEGIN
      SELECT @errno  = 30002,
```

```
              @errmsg = 'Cannot insert Course because Department
does not exist.'
      GOTO error
    END
  END

  /* erwin Builtin Trigger */
  RETURN
error:
   RAISERROR (@errmsg, -- Message text.
              @severity, -- Severity (0~25).
              @state) -- State (0~255).
    rollback transaction
END

go

CREATE TRIGGER tU_Course ON Course FOR UPDATE AS
/* erwin Builtin Trigger */
/* UPDATE trigger on Course */
BEGIN
  DECLARE   @numrows int,
            @nullcnt int,
            @validcnt int,
            @insCourseID varchar(50),
            @errno   int,
            @severity int,
            @state    int,
            @errmsg  varchar(255)

  SELECT @numrows = @@rowcount
  /* erwin Builtin Trigger */
  /* Course  Course_Offering on parent update restrict */
  /* ERWIN_RELATION:CHECKSUM="0006ee2e", PARENT_OWNER="",
PARENT_TABLE="Course"
    CHILD_OWNER="", CHILD_TABLE="Course_Offering"
    P2C_VERB_PHRASE="", C2P_VERB_PHRASE="",
    FK_CONSTRAINT="R_29", FK_COLUMNS="CourseID" */
  IF
    /* %ParentPK(" OR",UPDATE) */
    UPDATE(CourseID)
  BEGIN
    IF EXISTS (
      SELECT * FROM deleted,Course_Offering
      WHERE
        /*  %JoinFKPK(Course_Offering,deleted," = "," AND") */
        Course_Offering.CourseID = deleted.CourseID
```

```
    )
  BEGIN
    SELECT @errno  = 30005,
           @errmsg = 'Cannot update Course because Course_
Offering exists.'
    GOTO error
  END
END


/* erwin Builtin Trigger */
/* Course  Curriculum_Course on parent update restrict */
/* ERWIN_RELATION:CHECKSUM="00000000", PARENT_OWNER="",
PARENT_TABLE="Course"
  CHILD_OWNER="", CHILD_TABLE="Curriculum_Course"
  P2C_VERB_PHRASE="", C2P_VERB_PHRASE="",
  FK_CONSTRAINT="R_26", FK_COLUMNS="CourseID" */
IF
  /* %ParentPK(" OR",UPDATE) */
  UPDATE(CourseID)
BEGIN
  IF EXISTS (
    SELECT * FROM deleted,Curriculum_Course
    WHERE
      /*  %JoinFKPK(Curriculum_Course,deleted," = "," AND") */
      Curriculum_Course.CourseID = deleted.CourseID
  )
  BEGIN
    SELECT @errno  = 30005,
           @errmsg = 'Cannot update Course because Curriculum_
Course exists.'
    GOTO error
  END
END


/* erwin Builtin Trigger */
/* Course  Course_Prerequisite on parent update restrict */
/* ERWIN_RELATION:CHECKSUM="00000000", PARENT_OWNER="",
PARENT_TABLE="Course"
  CHILD_OWNER="", CHILD_TABLE="Course_Prerequisite"
  P2C_VERB_PHRASE="", C2P_VERB_PHRASE="",
  FK_CONSTRAINT="R_22", FK_COLUMNS="CourseID" */
IF
  /* %ParentPK(" OR",UPDATE) */
  UPDATE(CourseID)
BEGIN
  IF EXISTS (
    SELECT * FROM deleted,Course_Prerequisite
```

```
      WHERE
        /*  %JoinFKPK(Course_Prerequisite,deleted," = "," AND") */
        Course_Prerequisite.CourseID = deleted.CourseID
    )
    BEGIN
      SELECT @errno  = 30005,
             @errmsg = 'Cannot update Course because Course_
Prerequisite exists.'
      GOTO error
    END
  END


  /* erwin Builtin Trigger */
  /* Course  Course_Offering on parent update restrict */
  /* ERWIN_RELATION:CHECKSUM="00000000", PARENT_OWNER="",
PARENT_TABLE="Course"
    CHILD_OWNER="", CHILD_TABLE="Course_Offering"
    P2C_VERB_PHRASE="", C2P_VERB_PHRASE="",
    FK_CONSTRAINT="R_11", FK_COLUMNS="CourseID" */
  IF
    /* %ParentPK(" OR",UPDATE) */
    UPDATE(CourseID)
  BEGIN
    IF EXISTS (
      SELECT * FROM deleted,Course_Offering
      WHERE
        /*  %JoinFKPK(Course_Offering,deleted," = "," AND") */
        Course_Offering.CourseID = deleted.CourseID
    )
    BEGIN
      SELECT @errno  = 30005,
             @errmsg = 'Cannot update Course because Course_
Offering exists.'
      GOTO error
    END
  END

  /* erwin Builtin Trigger */
  /* Course  Course_Prerequisite on parent update restrict */
  /* ERWIN_RELATION:CHECKSUM="00000000", PARENT_OWNER="",
PARENT_TABLE="Course"
    CHILD_OWNER="", CHILD_TABLE="Course_Prerequisite"
    P2C_VERB_PHRASE="", C2P_VERB_PHRASE="",
    FK_CONSTRAINT="R_5", FK_COLUMNS="CourseID" */
  IF
```

```
    /* %ParentPK(" OR",UPDATE) */
    UPDATE(CourseID)
  BEGIN
    IF EXISTS (
      SELECT * FROM deleted,Course_Prerequisite
      WHERE
        /*  %JoinFKPK(Course_Prerequisite,deleted," = "," AND") */
        Course_Prerequisite.CourseID = deleted.CourseID
    )
    BEGIN
      SELECT @errno  = 30005,
             @errmsg = 'Cannot update Course because Course_
Prerequisite exists.'
      GOTO error
    END
  END

  /* erwin Builtin Trigger */
  /* Department  Course on child update restrict */
  /* ERWIN_RELATION:CHECKSUM="00000000", PARENT_OWNER="",
PARENT_TABLE="Department"
    CHILD_OWNER="", CHILD_TABLE="Course"
    P2C_VERB_PHRASE="", C2P_VERB_PHRASE="",
    FK_CONSTRAINT="R_21", FK_COLUMNS="DepartmentID" */
  IF
    /* %ChildFK(" OR",UPDATE) */
    UPDATE(DepartmentID)
  BEGIN
    SELECT @nullcnt = 0
    SELECT @validcnt = count(*)
      FROM inserted,Department
        WHERE
          /* %JoinFKPK(inserted,Department) */
          inserted.DepartmentID = Department.DepartmentID
    /* %NotnullFK(inserted," IS NULL","select @nullcnt = count(*)
from inserted where"," AND") */

    IF @validcnt + @nullcnt != @numrows
    BEGIN
      SELECT @errno  = 30007,
             @errmsg = 'Cannot update Course because Department
does not exist.'
      GOTO error
    END
  END
```

```
  /* erwin Builtin Trigger */
  RETURN
error:
   RAISERROR (@errmsg, -- Message text.
              @severity, -- Severity (0~25).
              @state) -- State (0~255).
    rollback transaction
END

go

CREATE TRIGGER tD_Course_Enrollment ON Course_Enrollment FOR
DELETE AS
/* erwin Builtin Trigger */
/* DELETE trigger on Course_Enrollment */
BEGIN
  DECLARE @errno    int,
          @severity int,
          @state    int,
          @errmsg   varchar(255)
    /* erwin Builtin Trigger */
    /* Course_Enrollment  Student_Grade on parent delete restrict
*/
    /* ERWIN_RELATION:CHECKSUM="000156e7", PARENT_OWNER="",
PARENT_TABLE="Course_Enrollment"
    CHILD_OWNER="", CHILD_TABLE="Student_Grade"
    P2C_VERB_PHRASE="", C2P_VERB_PHRASE="",
    FK_CONSTRAINT="R_27", FK_COLUMNS="StudentID""CourseID"
"SectionID" */
    IF EXISTS (
      SELECT * FROM deleted,Student_Grade
      WHERE
        /* %JoinFKPK(Student_Grade,deleted," = "," AND") */
        Student_Grade.CourseID = deleted.CourseID AND
        Student_Grade.SectionID = deleted.SectionID AND
        Student_Grade.StudentID = deleted.StudentID
    )
    BEGIN
      SELECT @errno  = 30001,
             @errmsg = 'Cannot delete Course_Enrollment because
Student_Grade exists.'
      GOTO error
    END

    /* erwin Builtin Trigger */
    RETURN
 error:
```

```
        RAISERROR (@errmsg, -- Message text.
                   @severity, -- Severity (0~25).
                   @state) -- State (0~255).
        rollback transaction
END

go

CREATE TRIGGER tI_Course_Enrollment ON Course_Enrollment FOR
INSERT AS
/* erwin Builtin Trigger */
/* INSERT trigger on Course_Enrollment */
BEGIN
    DECLARE @numrows int,
            @nullcnt int,
            @validcnt int,
            @errno   int,
            @severity int,
            @state    int,
            @errmsg   varchar(255)

  SELECT @numrows = @@rowcount
  /* erwin Builtin Trigger */
  /* Student   Course_Enrollment on child insert restrict */
  /* ERWIN_RELATION:CHECKSUM="0005e02c", PARENT_OWNER="",
PARENT_TABLE="Student"
    CHILD_OWNER="", CHILD_TABLE="Course_Enrollment"
    P2C_VERB_PHRASE="", C2P_VERB_PHRASE="",
    FK_CONSTRAINT="R_33", FK_COLUMNS="StudentID" */
  IF
    /* %ChildFK(" OR",UPDATE) */
    UPDATE(StudentID)
  BEGIN
    SELECT @nullcnt = 0
    SELECT @validcnt = count(*)
      FROM inserted,Student
        WHERE
          /* %JoinFKPK(inserted,Student) */
          inserted.StudentID = Student.StudentID
    /* %NotnullFK(inserted," IS NULL","select @nullcnt = count(*)
from inserted where"," and") */

    IF @validcnt + @nullcnt != @numrows
    BEGIN
      SELECT @errno  = 30002,
             @errmsg = 'Cannot insert Course_Enrollment because
Student does not exist.'
```

```
      GOTO error
    END
  END


  /* erwin Builtin Trigger */
  /* Course_Offering  Course_Enrollment on child insert restrict
*/
  /* ERWIN_RELATION:CHECKSUM="00000000", PARENT_OWNER="",
PARENT_TABLE="Course_Offering"
    CHILD_OWNER="", CHILD_TABLE="Course_Enrollment"
    P2C_VERB_PHRASE="", C2P_VERB_PHRASE="",
    FK_CONSTRAINT="R_32", FK_COLUMNS="CourseID""SectionID" */
  IF
    /* %ChildFK(" OR",UPDATE) */
    UPDATE(CourseID) OR
    UPDATE(SectionID)
  BEGIN
    SELECT @nullcnt = 0
    SELECT @validcnt = count(*)
      FROM inserted,Course_Offering
        WHERE
          /* %JoinFKPK(inserted,Course_Offering) */
          inserted.CourseID = Course_Offering.CourseID and
          inserted.SectionID = Course_Offering.SectionID
    /* %NotnullFK(inserted," IS NULL","select @nullcnt = count(*)
from inserted where"," and") */

    IF @validcnt + @nullcnt != @numrows
    BEGIN
      SELECT @errno  = 30002,
             @errmsg = 'Cannot insert Course_Enrollment because
Course_Offering does not exist.'
        GOTO error
    END
  END


  /* erwin Builtin Trigger */
  /* Student  Course_Enrollment on child insert restrict */
  /* ERWIN_RELATION:CHECKSUM="00000000", PARENT_OWNER="",
PARENT_TABLE="Student"
    CHILD_OWNER="", CHILD_TABLE="Course_Enrollment"
    P2C_VERB_PHRASE="", C2P_VERB_PHRASE="",
    FK_CONSTRAINT="R_18", FK_COLUMNS="StudentID" */
  IF
    /* %ChildFK(" OR",UPDATE) */
    UPDATE(StudentID)
```

```
   BEGIN
     SELECT @nullcnt = 0
     SELECT @validcnt = count(*)
       FROM inserted,Student
         WHERE
           /* %JoinFKPK(inserted,Student) */
           inserted.StudentID = Student.StudentID
     /* %NotnullFK(inserted," IS NULL","select @nullcnt = count(*)
from inserted where"," and") */

     IF @validcnt + @nullcnt != @numrows
     BEGIN
       SELECT @errno  = 30002,
              @errmsg = 'Cannot insert Course_Enrollment because
Student does not exist.'
       GOTO error
     END
   END


   /* erwin Builtin Trigger */
   /* Course_Offering  Course_Enrollment on child insert restrict
*/
   /* ERWIN_RELATION:CHECKSUM="00000000", PARENT_OWNER="",
PARENT_TABLE="Course_Offering"
     CHILD_OWNER="", CHILD_TABLE="Course_Enrollment"
     P2C_VERB_PHRASE="", C2P_VERB_PHRASE="",
     FK_CONSTRAINT="R_13", FK_COLUMNS="CourseID""SectionID" */
   IF
     /* %ChildFK(" OR",UPDATE) */
     UPDATE(CourseID) OR
     UPDATE(SectionID)
   BEGIN
     SELECT @nullcnt = 0
     SELECT @validcnt = count(*)
       FROM inserted,Course_Offering
         WHERE
           /* %JoinFKPK(inserted,Course_Offering) */
           inserted.CourseID = Course_Offering.CourseID and
           inserted.SectionID = Course_Offering.SectionID
     /* %NotnullFK(inserted," IS NULL","select @nullcnt = count(*)
from inserted where"," and") */

     IF @validcnt + @nullcnt != @numrows
     BEGIN
       SELECT @errno  = 30002,
```

```
            @errmsg = 'Cannot insert Course_Enrollment because
Course_Offering does not exist.'
        GOTO error
      END
    END


    /* erwin Builtin Trigger */
    RETURN
error:
    RAISERROR (@errmsg, -- Message text.
               @severity, -- Severity (0~25).
               @state) -- State (0~255).
      rollback transaction
END


go

CREATE TRIGGER tU_Course_Enrollment ON Course_Enrollment FOR
UPDATE AS
/* erwin Builtin Trigger */
/* UPDATE trigger on Course_Enrollment */
BEGIN
  DECLARE  @numrows int,
           @nullcnt int,
           @validcnt int,
           @insCourseID varchar(50),
           @insSectionID varchar(50),
           @insStudentID varchar(50),
           @errno    int,
           @severity int,
           @state    int,
           @errmsg  varchar(255)


  SELECT @numrows = @@rowcount
  /* erwin Builtin Trigger */
  /* Course_Enrollment  Student_Grade on parent update restrict */
  /* ERWIN_RELATION:CHECKSUM="00075239", PARENT_OWNER="",
PARENT_TABLE="Course_Enrollment"
    CHILD_OWNER="", CHILD_TABLE="Student_Grade"
    P2C_VERB_PHRASE="", C2P_VERB_PHRASE="",
    FK_CONSTRAINT="R_27", FK_COLUMNS="CourseID""StudentID"
"SectionID" */
  IF
    /* %ParentPK(" OR",UPDATE) */
    UPDATE(CourseID) OR
    UPDATE(SectionID) OR
```

```
   UPDATE(StudentID)
 BEGIN
   IF EXISTS (
     SELECT * FROM deleted,Student_Grade
     WHERE
       /* %JoinFKPK(Student_Grade,deleted," = "," AND") */
       Student_Grade.CourseID = deleted.CourseID AND
       Student_Grade.SectionID = deleted.SectionID AND
       Student_Grade.StudentID = deleted.StudentID
   )
   BEGIN
     SELECT @errno  = 30005,
            @errmsg = 'Cannot update Course_Enrollment because
Student_Grade exists.'
     GOTO error
   END
 END


 /* erwin Builtin Trigger */
 /* Student  Course_Enrollment on child update restrict */
 /* ERWIN_RELATION:CHECKSUM="00000000", PARENT_OWNER="",
PARENT_TABLE="Student"
   CHILD_OWNER="", CHILD_TABLE="Course_Enrollment"
   P2C_VERB_PHRASE="", C2P_VERB_PHRASE="",
   FK_CONSTRAINT="R_33", FK_COLUMNS="StudentID" */
 IF
   /* %ChildFK(" OR",UPDATE) */
   UPDATE(StudentID)
 BEGIN
   SELECT @nullcnt = 0
   SELECT @validcnt = count(*)
     FROM inserted,Student
       WHERE
         /* %JoinFKPK(inserted,Student) */
         inserted.StudentID = Student.StudentID
   /* %NotnullFK(inserted," IS NULL","select @nullcnt = count(*)
from inserted where"," AND") */

   IF @validcnt + @nullcnt != @numrows
   BEGIN
     SELECT @errno  = 30007,
            @errmsg = 'Cannot update Course_Enrollment because
Student does not exist.'
     GOTO error
   END
 END
```

```
/* erwin Builtin Trigger */
/* Course_Offering  Course_Enrollment on child update restrict
*/
/* ERWIN_RELATION:CHECKSUM="00000000", PARENT_OWNER="",
PARENT_TABLE="Course_Offering"
   CHILD_OWNER="", CHILD_TABLE="Course_Enrollment"
   P2C_VERB_PHRASE="", C2P_VERB_PHRASE="",
   FK_CONSTRAINT="R_32", FK_COLUMNS="CourseID""SectionID" */
IF
  /* %ChildFK(" OR",UPDATE) */
  UPDATE(CourseID) OR
  UPDATE(SectionID)
BEGIN
  SELECT @nullcnt = 0
  SELECT @validcnt = count(*)
    FROM inserted,Course_Offering
      WHERE
        /* %JoinFKPK(inserted,Course_Offering) */
        inserted.CourseID = Course_Offering.CourseID and
        inserted.SectionID = Course_Offering.SectionID
  /* %NotnullFK(inserted," IS NULL","select @nullcnt = count(*)
from inserted where"," AND") */

  IF @validcnt + @nullcnt != @numrows
  BEGIN
    SELECT @errno  = 30007,
           @errmsg = 'Cannot update Course_Enrollment because
Course_Offering does not exist.'
    GOTO error
  END
END


/* erwin Builtin Trigger */
/* Student  Course_Enrollment on child update restrict */
/* ERWIN_RELATION:CHECKSUM="00000000", PARENT_OWNER="",
PARENT_TABLE="Student"
   CHILD_OWNER="", CHILD_TABLE="Course_Enrollment"
   P2C_VERB_PHRASE="", C2P_VERB_PHRASE="",
   FK_CONSTRAINT="R_18", FK_COLUMNS="StudentID" */
IF
  /* %ChildFK(" OR",UPDATE) */
  UPDATE(StudentID)
BEGIN
  SELECT @nullcnt = 0
  SELECT @validcnt = count(*)
    FROM inserted,Student
```

```
      WHERE
          /* %JoinFKPK(inserted,Student) */
          inserted.StudentID = Student.StudentID
      /* %NotnullFK(inserted," IS NULL","select @nullcnt = count(*)
from inserted where"," AND") */

      IF @validcnt + @nullcnt != @numrows
      BEGIN
        SELECT @errno  = 30007,
               @errmsg = 'Cannot update Course_Enrollment because
Student does not exist.'
          GOTO error
      END
    END


    /* erwin Builtin Trigger */
    /* Course_Offering  Course_Enrollment on child update restrict
*/
    /* ERWIN_RELATION:CHECKSUM="00000000", PARENT_OWNER="",
PARENT_TABLE="Course_Offering"
        CHILD_OWNER="", CHILD_TABLE="Course_Enrollment"
        P2C_VERB_PHRASE="", C2P_VERB_PHRASE="",
        FK_CONSTRAINT="R_13", FK_COLUMNS="CourseID""SectionID" */
    IF
      /* %ChildFK(" OR",UPDATE) */
      UPDATE(CourseID) OR
      UPDATE(SectionID)
    BEGIN
      SELECT @nullcnt = 0
      SELECT @validcnt = count(*)
        FROM inserted,Course_Offering
          WHERE
              /* %JoinFKPK(inserted,Course_Offering) */
              inserted.CourseID = Course_Offering.CourseID and
              inserted.SectionID = Course_Offering.SectionID
      /* %NotnullFK(inserted," IS NULL","select @nullcnt = count(*)
from inserted where"," AND") */

      IF @validcnt + @nullcnt != @numrows
      BEGIN
        SELECT @errno  = 30007,
               @errmsg = 'Cannot update Course_Enrollment because
Course_Offering does not exist.'
          GOTO error
      END
    END
```

```
   /* erwin Builtin Trigger */
   RETURN
error:
   RAISERROR (@errmsg, -- Message text.
              @severity, -- Severity (0~25).
              @state) -- State (0~255).
     rollback transaction
END

go

CREATE TRIGGER tD_Course_Offering ON Course_Offering FOR DELETE AS
/* erwin Builtin Trigger */
/* DELETE trigger on Course_Offering */
BEGIN
  DECLARE  @errno    int,
           @severity int,
           @state    int,
           @errmsg   varchar(255)
     /* erwin Builtin Trigger */
     /* Course_Offering  Course_Enrollment on parent delete
restrict */
     /* ERWIN_RELATION:CHECKSUM="00048585", PARENT_OWNER="",
PARENT_TABLE="Course_Offering"
     CHILD_OWNER="", CHILD_TABLE="Course_Enrollment"
     P2C_VERB_PHRASE="", C2P_VERB_PHRASE="",
     FK_CONSTRAINT="R_32", FK_COLUMNS="CourseID""SectionID" */
     IF EXISTS (
       SELECT * FROM deleted,Course_Enrollment
       WHERE
         /*  %JoinFKPK(Course_Enrollment,deleted," = "," AND") */
         Course_Enrollment.CourseID = deleted.CourseID AND
         Course_Enrollment.SectionID = deleted.SectionID
     )
     BEGIN
       SELECT @errno  = 30001,
              @errmsg = 'Cannot delete Course_Offering because
Course_Enrollment exists.'
       GOTO error
     END

     /* erwin Builtin Trigger */
     /* Course_Offering  Assignment on parent delete restrict */
     /* ERWIN_RELATION:CHECKSUM="00000000", PARENT_OWNER="",
PARENT_TABLE="Course_Offering"
     CHILD_OWNER="", CHILD_TABLE="Assignment"
     P2C_VERB_PHRASE="", C2P_VERB_PHRASE="",
```

```
      FK_CONSTRAINT="R_31", FK_COLUMNS="CourseID""SectionID" */
      IF EXISTS (
        SELECT * FROM deleted,Assignment
        WHERE
          /*  %JoinFKPK(Assignment,deleted," = "," AND") */
          Assignment.CourseID = deleted.CourseID AND
          Assignment.SectionID = deleted.SectionID
      )
      BEGIN
        SELECT @errno  = 30001,
               @errmsg = 'Cannot delete Course_Offering because
Assignment exists.'
        GOTO error
      END


      /* erwin Builtin Trigger */
      /* Course_Offering  Assignment on parent delete restrict */
      /* ERWIN_RELATION:CHECKSUM="00000000", PARENT_OWNER="",
PARENT_TABLE="Course_Offering"
      CHILD_OWNER="", CHILD_TABLE="Assignment"
      P2C_VERB_PHRASE="", C2P_VERB_PHRASE="",
      FK_CONSTRAINT="R_14", FK_COLUMNS="CourseID""SectionID" */
      IF EXISTS (
        SELECT * FROM deleted,Assignment
        WHERE
          /*  %JoinFKPK(Assignment,deleted," = "," AND") */
          Assignment.CourseID = deleted.CourseID AND
          Assignment.SectionID = deleted.SectionID
      )
      BEGIN
        SELECT @errno  = 30001,
               @errmsg = 'Cannot delete Course_Offering because
Assignment exists.'
        GOTO error
      END


      /* erwin Builtin Trigger */
      /* Course_Offering  Course_Enrollment on parent delete
restrict */
      /* ERWIN_RELATION:CHECKSUM="00000000", PARENT_OWNER="",
PARENT_TABLE="Course_Offering"
      CHILD_OWNER="", CHILD_TABLE="Course_Enrollment"
      P2C_VERB_PHRASE="", C2P_VERB_PHRASE="",
      FK_CONSTRAINT="R_13", FK_COLUMNS="CourseID""SectionID" */
      IF EXISTS (
        SELECT * FROM deleted,Course_Enrollment
```

```
    WHERE
      /*  %JoinFKPK(Course_Enrollment,deleted," = "," AND") */
      Course_Enrollment.CourseID = deleted.CourseID AND
      Course_Enrollment.SectionID = deleted.SectionID
    )
  BEGIN
    SELECT @errno  = 30001,
           @errmsg = 'Cannot delete Course_Offering because
Course_Enrollment exists.'
      GOTO error
    END


    /* erwin Builtin Trigger */
    RETURN
error:
   RAISERROR (@errmsg, -- Message text.
              @severity, -- Severity (0~25).
              @state) -- State (0~255).
   rollback transaction
END

go

CREATE TRIGGER tI_Course_Offering ON Course_Offering FOR INSERT AS
/* erwin Builtin Trigger */
/* INSERT trigger on Course_Offering */
BEGIN
   DECLARE @numrows int,
           @nullcnt int,
           @validcnt int,
           @errno   int,
           @severity int,
           @state    int,
           @errmsg  varchar(255)

  SELECT @numrows = @@rowcount
  /* erwin Builtin Trigger */
  /* Faculty  Course_Offering on child insert restrict */
  /* ERWIN_RELATION:CHECKSUM="00053126", PARENT_OWNER="",
PARENT_TABLE="Faculty"
    CHILD_OWNER="", CHILD_TABLE="Course_Offering"
    P2C_VERB_PHRASE="", C2P_VERB_PHRASE="",
    FK_CONSTRAINT="R_30", FK_COLUMNS="FacultyID" */
  IF
    /* %ChildFK(" OR",UPDATE) */
    UPDATE(FacultyID)
```

```
    BEGIN
      SELECT @nullcnt = 0
      SELECT @validcnt = count(*)
        FROM inserted,Faculty
          WHERE
            /* %JoinFKPK(inserted,Faculty) */
            inserted.FacultyID = Faculty.FacultyID
      /* %NotnullFK(inserted," IS NULL","select @nullcnt = count(*)
  from inserted where"," and") */

      IF @validcnt + @nullcnt != @numrows
      BEGIN
        SELECT @errno  = 30002,
               @errmsg = 'Cannot insert Course_Offering because
  Faculty does not exist.'
        GOTO error
      END
    END
    /* erwin Builtin Trigger */
    /* Course  Course_Offering on child insert restrict */
    /* ERWIN_RELATION:CHECKSUM="00000000", PARENT_OWNER="",
  PARENT_TABLE="Course"
      CHILD_OWNER="", CHILD_TABLE="Course_Offering"
      P2C_VERB_PHRASE="", C2P_VERB_PHRASE="",
      FK_CONSTRAINT="R_29", FK_COLUMNS="CourseID" */
    IF
      /* %ChildFK(" OR",UPDATE) */
      UPDATE(CourseID)
    BEGIN
      SELECT @nullcnt = 0
      SELECT @validcnt = count(*)
        FROM inserted,Course
          WHERE
            /* %JoinFKPK(inserted,Course) */
            inserted.CourseID = Course.CourseID
      /* %NotnullFK(inserted," IS NULL","select @nullcnt = count(*)
  from inserted where"," and") */

      IF @validcnt + @nullcnt != @numrows
      BEGIN
        SELECT @errno  = 30002,
               @errmsg = 'Cannot insert Course_Offering because
  Course does not exist.'
        GOTO error
      END
    END
```

```
/* erwin Builtin Trigger */
/* Faculty  Course_Offering on child insert restrict */
/* ERWIN_RELATION:CHECKSUM="00000000", PARENT_OWNER="",
PARENT_TABLE="Faculty"
   CHILD_OWNER="", CHILD_TABLE="Course_Offering"
   P2C_VERB_PHRASE="", C2P_VERB_PHRASE="",
   FK_CONSTRAINT="R_12", FK_COLUMNS="FacultyID" */
IF
   /* %ChildFK(" OR",UPDATE) */
   UPDATE(FacultyID)
BEGIN
   SELECT @nullcnt = 0
   SELECT @validcnt = count(*)
     FROM inserted,Faculty
       WHERE
         /* %JoinFKPK(inserted,Faculty) */
         inserted.FacultyID = Faculty.FacultyID
   /* %NotnullFK(inserted," IS NULL","select @nullcnt = count(*)
from inserted where"," and") */

   IF @validcnt + @nullcnt != @numrows
   BEGIN
     SELECT @errno  = 30002,
            @errmsg = 'Cannot insert Course_Offering because
Faculty does not exist.'
     GOTO error
   END
END

/* erwin Builtin Trigger */
/* Course  Course_Offering on child insert restrict */
/* ERWIN_RELATION:CHECKSUM="00000000", PARENT_OWNER="",
PARENT_TABLE="Course"
   CHILD_OWNER="", CHILD_TABLE="Course_Offering"
   P2C_VERB_PHRASE="", C2P_VERB_PHRASE="",
   FK_CONSTRAINT="R_11", FK_COLUMNS="CourseID" */
IF
   /* %ChildFK(" OR",UPDATE) */
   UPDATE(CourseID)
BEGIN
   SELECT @nullcnt = 0
   SELECT @validcnt = count(*)
     FROM inserted,Course
       WHERE
         /* %JoinFKPK(inserted,Course) */
         inserted.CourseID = Course.CourseID
```

```
    /* %NotnullFK(inserted," IS NULL","select @nullcnt = count(*)
from inserted where"," and") */


    IF @validcnt + @nullcnt != @numrows
    BEGIN
      SELECT @errno  = 30002,
             @errmsg = 'Cannot insert Course_Offering because
Course does not exist.'
      GOTO error
    END
  END


  /* erwin Builtin Trigger */
  RETURN
error:
   RAISERROR (@errmsg, -- Message text.
              @severity, -- Severity (0~25).
              @state) -- State (0~255).
   rollback transaction
END


go


CREATE TRIGGER tU_Course_Offering ON Course_Offering FOR UPDATE AS
/* erwin Builtin Trigger */
/* UPDATE trigger on Course_Offering */
BEGIN
  DECLARE  @numrows int,
           @nullcnt int,
           @validcnt int,
           @insCourseID varchar(50),
           @insSectionID varchar(50),
           @errno   int,
           @severity int,
           @state    int,
           @errmsg  varchar(255)


  SELECT @numrows = @@rowcount
  /* erwin Builtin Trigger */
  /* Course_Offering  Course_Enrollment on parent update restrict
*/
  /* ERWIN_RELATION:CHECKSUM="000a4fc9", PARENT_OWNER="",
PARENT_TABLE="Course_Offering"
    CHILD_OWNER="", CHILD_TABLE="Course_Enrollment"
    P2C_VERB_PHRASE="", C2P_VERB_PHRASE="",
    FK_CONSTRAINT="R_32", FK_COLUMNS="CourseID""SectionID" */
```

```
IF
  /* %ParentPK(" OR",UPDATE) */
  UPDATE(CourseID) OR
  UPDATE(SectionID)
BEGIN
  IF EXISTS (
    SELECT * FROM deleted,Course_Enrollment
    WHERE
      /* %JoinFKPK(Course_Enrollment,deleted," = "," AND") */
      Course_Enrollment.CourseID = deleted.CourseID AND
      Course_Enrollment.SectionID = deleted.SectionID
  )
  BEGIN
    SELECT @errno  = 30005,
           @errmsg = 'Cannot update Course_Offering because
Course_Enrollment exists.'
    GOTO error
  END
END

/* erwin Builtin Trigger */
/* Course_Offering  Assignment on parent update restrict */
/* ERWIN_RELATION:CHECKSUM="00000000", PARENT_OWNER="",
PARENT_TABLE="Course_Offering"
  CHILD_OWNER="", CHILD_TABLE="Assignment"
  P2C_VERB_PHRASE="", C2P_VERB_PHRASE="",
  FK_CONSTRAINT="R_31", FK_COLUMNS="CourseID""SectionID" */
IF
  /* %ParentPK(" OR",UPDATE) */
  UPDATE(CourseID) OR
  UPDATE(SectionID)
BEGIN
  IF EXISTS (
    SELECT * FROM deleted,Assignment
    WHERE
      /* %JoinFKPK(Assignment,deleted," = "," AND") */
      Assignment.CourseID = deleted.CourseID AND
      Assignment.SectionID = deleted.SectionID
  )
  BEGIN
    SELECT @errno  = 30005,
           @errmsg = 'Cannot update Course_Offering because
Assignment exists.'
    GOTO error
  END
END
```

```
  /* erwin Builtin Trigger */
  /* Course_Offering  Assignment on parent update restrict */
  /* ERWIN_RELATION:CHECKSUM="00000000", PARENT_OWNER="",
PARENT_TABLE="Course_Offering"
    CHILD_OWNER="", CHILD_TABLE="Assignment"
    P2C_VERB_PHRASE="", C2P_VERB_PHRASE="",
    FK_CONSTRAINT="R_14", FK_COLUMNS="CourseID""SectionID" */
  IF
    /* %ParentPK(" OR",UPDATE) */
    UPDATE(CourseID) OR
    UPDATE(SectionID)
  BEGIN
    IF EXISTS (
      SELECT * FROM deleted,Assignment
      WHERE
        /* %JoinFKPK(Assignment,deleted," = "," AND") */
        Assignment.CourseID = deleted.CourseID AND
        Assignment.SectionID = deleted.SectionID
    )
    BEGIN
      SELECT @errno  = 30005,
             @errmsg = 'Cannot update Course_Offering because
Assignment exists.'
        GOTO error
    END
  END
  /* erwin Builtin Trigger */
  /* Course_Offering  Course_Enrollment on parent update restrict
*/
  /* ERWIN_RELATION:CHECKSUM="00000000", PARENT_OWNER="",
PARENT_TABLE="Course_Offering"
    CHILD_OWNER="", CHILD_TABLE="Course_Enrollment"
    P2C_VERB_PHRASE="", C2P_VERB_PHRASE="",
    FK_CONSTRAINT="R_13", FK_COLUMNS="CourseID""SectionID" */
  IF
    /* %ParentPK(" OR",UPDATE) */
    UPDATE(CourseID) OR
    UPDATE(SectionID)
  BEGIN
    IF EXISTS (
      SELECT * FROM deleted,Course_Enrollment
      WHERE
        /* %JoinFKPK(Course_Enrollment,deleted," = "," AND") */
        Course_Enrollment.CourseID = deleted.CourseID AND
        Course_Enrollment.SectionID = deleted.SectionID
    )
```

```
    BEGIN
      SELECT @errno  = 30005,
              @errmsg = 'Cannot update Course_Offering because
Course_Enrollment exists.'
        GOTO error
    END
  END


  /* erwin Builtin Trigger */
  /* Faculty  Course_Offering on child update restrict */
  /* ERWIN_RELATION:CHECKSUM="00000000", PARENT_OWNER="",
PARENT_TABLE="Faculty"
    CHILD_OWNER="", CHILD_TABLE="Course_Offering"
    P2C_VERB_PHRASE="", C2P_VERB_PHRASE="",
    FK_CONSTRAINT="R_30", FK_COLUMNS="FacultyID" */
  IF
    /* %ChildFK(" OR",UPDATE) */
    UPDATE(FacultyID)
  BEGIN
    SELECT @nullcnt = 0
    SELECT @validcnt = count(*)
      FROM inserted,Faculty
        WHERE
          /* %JoinFKPK(inserted,Faculty) */
          inserted.FacultyID = Faculty.FacultyID
    /* %NotnullFK(inserted," IS NULL","select @nullcnt = count(*)
from inserted where"," AND") */

    IF @validcnt + @nullcnt != @numrows
    BEGIN
      SELECT @errno  = 30007,
              @errmsg = 'Cannot update Course_Offering because
Faculty does not exist.'
        GOTO error
    END
  END
  /* erwin Builtin Trigger */
  /* Course  Course_Offering on child update restrict */
  /* ERWIN_RELATION:CHECKSUM="00000000", PARENT_OWNER="",
PARENT_TABLE="Course"
    CHILD_OWNER="", CHILD_TABLE="Course_Offering"
    P2C_VERB_PHRASE="", C2P_VERB_PHRASE="",
    FK_CONSTRAINT="R_29", FK_COLUMNS="CourseID" */
  IF
    /* %ChildFK(" OR",UPDATE) */
    UPDATE(CourseID)
```

```
  BEGIN
    SELECT @nullcnt = 0
    SELECT @validcnt = count(*)
      FROM inserted,Course
        WHERE
          /* %JoinFKPK(inserted,Course) */
          inserted.CourseID = Course.CourseID
    /* %NotnullFK(inserted," IS NULL","select @nullcnt = count(*)
from inserted where"," AND") */

    IF @validcnt + @nullcnt != @numrows
    BEGIN
      SELECT @errno  = 30007,
             @errmsg = 'Cannot update Course_Offering because
Course does not exist.'
      GOTO error
    END
  END


  /* erwin Builtin Trigger */
  /* Faculty  Course_Offering on child update restrict */
  /* ERWIN_RELATION:CHECKSUM="00000000", PARENT_OWNER="",
PARENT_TABLE="Faculty"
    CHILD_OWNER="", CHILD_TABLE="Course_Offering"
    P2C_VERB_PHRASE="", C2P_VERB_PHRASE="",
    FK_CONSTRAINT="R_12", FK_COLUMNS="FacultyID" */
  IF
    /* %ChildFK(" OR",UPDATE) */
    UPDATE(FacultyID)
  BEGIN
    SELECT @nullcnt = 0
    SELECT @validcnt = count(*)
      FROM inserted,Faculty
        WHERE
          /* %JoinFKPK(inserted,Faculty) */
          inserted.FacultyID = Faculty.FacultyID
    /* %NotnullFK(inserted," IS NULL","select @nullcnt = count(*)
from inserted where"," AND") */

    IF @validcnt + @nullcnt != @numrows
    BEGIN
      SELECT @errno  = 30007,
             @errmsg = 'Cannot update Course_Offering because
Faculty does not exist.'
      GOTO error
    END
  END
```

```
  /* erwin Builtin Trigger */
  /* Course  Course_Offering on child update restrict */
  /* ERWIN_RELATION:CHECKSUM="00000000", PARENT_OWNER="",
PARENT_TABLE="Course"
    CHILD_OWNER="", CHILD_TABLE="Course_Offering"
    P2C_VERB_PHRASE="", C2P_VERB_PHRASE="",
    FK_CONSTRAINT="R_11", FK_COLUMNS="CourseID" */
  IF
    /* %ChildFK(" OR",UPDATE) */
    UPDATE(CourseID)
  BEGIN
    SELECT @nullcnt = 0
    SELECT @validcnt = count(*)
      FROM inserted,Course
        WHERE
          /* %JoinFKPK(inserted,Course) */
          inserted.CourseID = Course.CourseID
    /* %NotnullFK(inserted," IS NULL","select @nullcnt = count(*)
from inserted where"," AND") */

    IF @validcnt + @nullcnt != @numrows
    BEGIN
      SELECT @errno  = 30007,
             @errmsg = 'Cannot update Course_Offering because
Course does not exist.'
      GOTO error
    END
  END


  /* erwin Builtin Trigger */
  RETURN
error:
    RAISERROR (@errmsg, -- Message text.
               @severity, -- Severity (0~25).
               @state) -- State (0~255).
    rollback transaction
END

go

CREATE TRIGGER tI_Course_Prerequisite ON Course_Prerequisite FOR
INSERT AS
/* erwin Builtin Trigger */
/* INSERT trigger on Course_Prerequisite */
BEGIN
    DECLARE @numrows int,
            @nullcnt int,
```

```
            @validcnt int,
            @errno    int,
            @severity int,
            @state    int,
            @errmsg   varchar(255)

SELECT @numrows = @@rowcount
/* erwin Builtin Trigger */
/* Course  Course_Prerequisite on child insert restrict */
/* ERWIN_RELATION:CHECKSUM="0002b871", PARENT_OWNER="",
PARENT_TABLE="Course"
  CHILD_OWNER="", CHILD_TABLE="Course_Prerequisite"
  P2C_VERB_PHRASE="", C2P_VERB_PHRASE="",
  FK_CONSTRAINT="R_22", FK_COLUMNS="CourseID" */
IF
  /* %ChildFK(" OR",UPDATE) */
  UPDATE(CourseID)
BEGIN
  SELECT @nullcnt = 0
  SELECT @validcnt = count(*)
    FROM inserted,Course
      WHERE
        /* %JoinFKPK(inserted,Course) */
        inserted.CourseID = Course.CourseID
  /* %NotnullFK(inserted," IS NULL","select @nullcnt = count(*)
from inserted where"," and") */

  IF @validcnt + @nullcnt != @numrows
  BEGIN
    SELECT @errno  = 30002,
           @errmsg = 'Cannot insert Course_Prerequisite because
Course does not exist.'
    GOTO error
  END
END
/* erwin Builtin Trigger */
/* Course  Course_Prerequisite on child insert restrict */
/* ERWIN_RELATION:CHECKSUM="00000000", PARENT_OWNER="",
PARENT_TABLE="Course"
  CHILD_OWNER="", CHILD_TABLE="Course_Prerequisite"
  P2C_VERB_PHRASE="", C2P_VERB_PHRASE="",
  FK_CONSTRAINT="R_5", FK_COLUMNS="CourseID" */
IF
  /* %ChildFK(" OR",UPDATE) */
  UPDATE(CourseID)
BEGIN
  SELECT @nullcnt = 0
```

```
    SELECT @validcnt = count(*)
      FROM inserted,Course
        WHERE
          /* %JoinFKPK(inserted,Course) */
          inserted.CourseID = Course.CourseID
    /* %NotnullFK(inserted," IS NULL","select @nullcnt = count(*)
from inserted where"," and") */

    IF @validcnt + @nullcnt != @numrows
    BEGIN
      SELECT @errno  = 30002,
             @errmsg = 'Cannot insert Course_Prerequisite because
Course does not exist.'
      GOTO error
    END
  END


  /* erwin Builtin Trigger */
  RETURN
error:
   RAISERROR (@errmsg, -- Message text.
              @severity, -- Severity (0~25).
              @state) -- State (0~255).
    rollback transaction
END

go

CREATE TRIGGER tU_Course_Prerequisite ON Course_Prerequisite FOR
UPDATE AS
/* erwin Builtin Trigger */
/* UPDATE trigger on Course_Prerequisite */
BEGIN
  DECLARE   @numrows int,
            @nullcnt int,
            @validcnt int,
            @insCourseID varchar(50),
            @insPrerequisiteCseID varchar(50),
            @errno   int,
            @severity int,
            @state    int,
            @errmsg   varchar(255)

  SELECT @numrows = @@rowcount
  /* erwin Builtin Trigger */
  /* Course  Course_Prerequisite on child update restrict */
  /* ERWIN_RELATION:CHECKSUM="0002c28b", PARENT_OWNER="",
PARENT_TABLE="Course"
```

```
   CHILD_OWNER="", CHILD_TABLE="Course_Prerequisite"
   P2C_VERB_PHRASE="", C2P_VERB_PHRASE="",
   FK_CONSTRAINT="R_22", FK_COLUMNS="CourseID" */
 IF
   /* %ChildFK(" OR",UPDATE) */
   UPDATE(CourseID)
 BEGIN
   SELECT @nullcnt = 0
   SELECT @validcnt = count(*)
     FROM inserted,Course
       WHERE
         /* %JoinFKPK(inserted,Course) */
         inserted.CourseID = Course.CourseID
   /* %NotnullFK(inserted," IS NULL","select @nullcnt = count(*)
from inserted where"," AND") */

   IF @validcnt + @nullcnt != @numrows
   BEGIN
     SELECT @errno  = 30007,
            @errmsg = 'Cannot update Course_Prerequisite because
Course does not exist.'
     GOTO error
   END
 END

 /* erwin Builtin Trigger */
 /* Course  Course_Prerequisite on child update restrict */
 /* ERWIN_RELATION:CHECKSUM="00000000", PARENT_OWNER="",
PARENT_TABLE="Course"
   CHILD_OWNER="", CHILD_TABLE="Course_Prerequisite"
   P2C_VERB_PHRASE="", C2P_VERB_PHRASE="",
   FK_CONSTRAINT="R_5", FK_COLUMNS="CourseID" */
 IF
   /* %ChildFK(" OR",UPDATE) */
   UPDATE(CourseID)
 BEGIN
   SELECT @nullcnt = 0
   SELECT @validcnt = count(*)
     FROM inserted,Course
       WHERE
         /* %JoinFKPK(inserted,Course) */
         inserted.CourseID = Course.CourseID
   /* %NotnullFK(inserted," IS NULL","select @nullcnt = count(*)
from inserted where"," AND") */

   IF @validcnt + @nullcnt != @numrows
   BEGIN
     SELECT @errno  = 30007,
```

```
                @errmsg = 'Cannot update Course_Prerequisite because
Course does not exist.'
      GOTO error
    END
  END


  /* erwin Builtin Trigger */
  RETURN
error:
   RAISERROR (@errmsg, -- Message text.
              @severity, -- Severity (0~25).
              @state) -- State (0~255).
    rollback transaction
END


go

CREATE TRIGGER tD_Curriculum ON Curriculum FOR DELETE AS
/* erwin Builtin Trigger */
/* DELETE trigger on Curriculum */
BEGIN
  DECLARE  @errno   int,
           @severity int,
           @state   int,
           @errmsg  varchar(255)
    /* erwin Builtin Trigger */
    /* Curriculum  Curriculum_Job_Classification on parent delete
restrict */
    /* ERWIN_RELATION:CHECKSUM="00024e0d", PARENT_OWNER="",
PARENT_TABLE="Curriculum"
    CHILD_OWNER="", CHILD_TABLE="Curriculum_Job_Classification"
    P2C_VERB_PHRASE="", C2P_VERB_PHRASE="",
    FK_CONSTRAINT="R_28", FK_COLUMNS="CurriculumID" */
    IF EXISTS (
      SELECT * FROM deleted,Curriculum_Job_Classification
      WHERE
        /*  %JoinFKPK(Curriculum_Job_Classification,deleted," =
"," AND") */
        Curriculum_Job_Classification.CurriculumID = deleted.
CurriculumID
    )
    BEGIN
      SELECT @errno  = 30001,
             @errmsg = 'Cannot delete Curriculum because
Curriculum_Job_Classification exists.'
      GOTO error
    END
```

```
    /* erwin Builtin Trigger */
    /* Curriculum  Curriculum_Course on parent delete restrict */
    /* ERWIN_RELATION:CHECKSUM="00000000", PARENT_OWNER="",
PARENT_TABLE="Curriculum"
    CHILD_OWNER="", CHILD_TABLE="Curriculum_Course"
    P2C_VERB_PHRASE="", C2P_VERB_PHRASE="",
    FK_CONSTRAINT="R_25", FK_COLUMNS="CurriculumID" */
    IF EXISTS (
      SELECT * FROM deleted,Curriculum_Course
      WHERE
        /*  %JoinFKPK(Curriculum_Course,deleted," = "," AND") */
        Curriculum_Course.CurriculumID = deleted.CurriculumID
    )
    BEGIN
      SELECT @errno  = 30001,
             @errmsg = 'Cannot delete Curriculum because
Curriculum_Course exists.'
      GOTO error
    END

    /* erwin Builtin Trigger */
    RETURN
error:
  RAISERROR (@errmsg, -- Message text.
             @severity, -- Severity (0~25).
             @state) -- State (0~255).
    rollback transaction
END

go

CREATE TRIGGER tI_Curriculum ON Curriculum FOR INSERT AS
/* erwin Builtin Trigger */
/* INSERT trigger on Curriculum */
BEGIN
   DECLARE @numrows int,
           @nullcnt int,
           @validcnt int,
           @errno   int,
           @severity int,
           @state    int,
           @errmsg  varchar(255)

  SELECT @numrows = @@rowcount
  /* erwin Builtin Trigger */
  /* Degree  Curriculum on child insert restrict */
  /* ERWIN_RELATION:CHECKSUM="000160a1", PARENT_OWNER="",
PARENT_TABLE="Degree"
```

```
    CHILD_OWNER="", CHILD_TABLE="Curriculum"
    P2C_VERB_PHRASE="", C2P_VERB_PHRASE="",
    FK_CONSTRAINT="R_24", FK_COLUMNS="DegreeID" */
  IF
    /* %ChildFK(" OR",UPDATE) */
    UPDATE(DegreeID)
  BEGIN
    SELECT @nullcnt = 0
    SELECT @validcnt = count(*)
      FROM inserted,Degree
        WHERE
          /* %JoinFKPK(inserted,Degree) */
          inserted.DegreeID = Degree.DegreeID
    /* %NotnullFK(inserted," IS NULL","select @nullcnt = count(*)
from inserted where"," and") */

    IF @validcnt + @nullcnt != @numrows
    BEGIN
      SELECT @errno  = 30002,
             @errmsg = 'Cannot insert Curriculum because Degree
does not exist.'
      GOTO error
    END
  END

  /* erwin Builtin Trigger */
  RETURN
error:
   RAISERROR (@errmsg, -- Message text.
              @severity, -- Severity (0~25).
              @state) -- State (0~255).
   rollback transaction
END

go

CREATE TRIGGER tU_Curriculum ON Curriculum FOR UPDATE AS
/* erwin Builtin Trigger */
/* UPDATE trigger on Curriculum */
BEGIN
  DECLARE  @numrows int,
           @nullcnt int,
           @validcnt int,
           @insCurriculumID char(18,50),
           @errno   int,
           @severity int,
           @state   int,
           @errmsg  varchar(255)
```

```
  SELECT @numrows = @@rowcount
  /* erwin Builtin Trigger */
  /* Curriculum  Curriculum_Job_Classification on parent update
restrict */
  /* ERWIN_RELATION:CHECKSUM="0003cdcd", PARENT_OWNER="",
PARENT_TABLE="Curriculum"
    CHILD_OWNER="", CHILD_TABLE="Curriculum_Job_Classification"
    P2C_VERB_PHRASE="", C2P_VERB_PHRASE="",
    FK_CONSTRAINT="R_28", FK_COLUMNS="CurriculumID" */
  IF
    /* %ParentPK(" OR",UPDATE) */
    UPDATE(CurriculumID)
  BEGIN
    IF EXISTS (
      SELECT * FROM deleted,Curriculum_Job_Classification
      WHERE
        /*  %JoinFKPK(Curriculum_Job_Classification,deleted," =
"," AND") */
        Curriculum_Job_Classification.CurriculumID = deleted.
CurriculumID
    )
    BEGIN
      SELECT @errno  = 30005,
             @errmsg = 'Cannot update Curriculum because
Curriculum_Job_Classification exists.'
      GOTO error
    END
  END


  /* erwin Builtin Trigger */
  /* Curriculum  Curriculum_Course on parent update restrict */
  /* ERWIN_RELATION:CHECKSUM="00000000", PARENT_OWNER="",
PARENT_TABLE="Curriculum"
    CHILD_OWNER="", CHILD_TABLE="Curriculum_Course"
    P2C_VERB_PHRASE="", C2P_VERB_PHRASE="",
    FK_CONSTRAINT="R_25", FK_COLUMNS="CurriculumID" */
  IF
    /* %ParentPK(" OR",UPDATE) */
    UPDATE(CurriculumID)
  BEGIN
    IF EXISTS (
      SELECT * FROM deleted,Curriculum_Course
      WHERE
        /*  %JoinFKPK(Curriculum_Course,deleted," = "," AND") */
        Curriculum_Course.CurriculumID = deleted.CurriculumID
    )
```

```
    BEGIN
      SELECT @errno  = 30005,
             @errmsg = 'Cannot update Curriculum because
Curriculum_Course exists.'
       GOTO error
    END
  END


  /* erwin Builtin Trigger */
  /* Degree  Curriculum on child update restrict */
  /* ERWIN_RELATION:CHECKSUM="00000000", PARENT_OWNER="",
PARENT_TABLE="Degree"
    CHILD_OWNER="", CHILD_TABLE="Curriculum"
    P2C_VERB_PHRASE="", C2P_VERB_PHRASE="",
    FK_CONSTRAINT="R_24", FK_COLUMNS="DegreeID" */
  IF
    /* %ChildFK(" OR",UPDATE) */
    UPDATE(DegreeID)
  BEGIN
    SELECT @nullcnt = 0
    SELECT @validcnt = count(*)
      FROM inserted,Degree
        WHERE
          /* %JoinFKPK(inserted,Degree) */
          inserted.DegreeID = Degree.DegreeID
    /* %NotnullFK(inserted," IS NULL","select @nullcnt = count(*)
from inserted where"," AND") */

    IF @validcnt + @nullcnt != @numrows
    BEGIN
      SELECT @errno  = 30007,
             @errmsg = 'Cannot update Curriculum because Degree
does not exist.'
       GOTO error
    END
  END


  /* erwin Builtin Trigger */
  RETURN
error:
   RAISERROR (@errmsg, -- Message text.
              @severity, -- Severity (0~25).
              @state) -- State (0~255).
    rollback transaction
END

go
```

```
CREATE TRIGGER tI_Curriculum_Course ON Curriculum_Course FOR
INSERT AS
/* erwin Builtin Trigger */
/* INSERT trigger on Curriculum_Course */
BEGIN
   DECLARE @numrows int,
           @nullcnt int,
           @validcnt int,
           @errno   int,
           @severity int,
           @state    int,
           @errmsg  varchar(255)
  SELECT @numrows = @@rowcount
  /* erwin Builtin Trigger */
  /* Course  Curriculum_Course on child insert restrict */
  /* ERWIN_RELATION:CHECKSUM="0002aed3", PARENT_OWNER="",
PARENT_TABLE="Course"
    CHILD_OWNER="", CHILD_TABLE="Curriculum_Course"
    P2C_VERB_PHRASE="", C2P_VERB_PHRASE="",
    FK_CONSTRAINT="R_26", FK_COLUMNS="CourseID" */
  IF
    /* %ChildFK(" OR",UPDATE) */
    UPDATE(CourseID)
  BEGIN
    SELECT @nullcnt = 0
    SELECT @validcnt = count(*)
      FROM inserted,Course
        WHERE
          /* %JoinFKPK(inserted,Course) */
          inserted.CourseID = Course.CourseID
    /* %NotnullFK(inserted," IS NULL","select @nullcnt = count(*)
from inserted where"," and") */

    IF @validcnt + @nullcnt != @numrows
    BEGIN
      SELECT @errno  = 30002,
             @errmsg = 'Cannot insert Curriculum_Course because
Course does not exist.'
      GOTO error
    END
  END
  /* erwin Builtin Trigger */
  /* Curriculum  Curriculum_Course on child insert restrict */
  /* ERWIN_RELATION:CHECKSUM="00000000", PARENT_OWNER="",
PARENT_TABLE="Curriculum"
    CHILD_OWNER="", CHILD_TABLE="Curriculum_Course"
    P2C_VERB_PHRASE="", C2P_VERB_PHRASE="",
```

```
    FK_CONSTRAINT="R_25", FK_COLUMNS="CurriculumID" */
  IF
    /* %ChildFK(" OR",UPDATE) */
    UPDATE(CurriculumID)
  BEGIN
    SELECT @nullcnt = 0
    SELECT @validcnt = count(*)
      FROM inserted,Curriculum
        WHERE
          /* %JoinFKPK(inserted,Curriculum) */
          inserted.CurriculumID = Curriculum.CurriculumID
    /* %NotnullFK(inserted," IS NULL","select @nullcnt = count(*)
from inserted where"," and") */

    IF @validcnt + @nullcnt != @numrows
    BEGIN
      SELECT @errno  = 30002,
             @errmsg = 'Cannot insert Curriculum_Course because
Curriculum does not exist.'
      GOTO error
    END
  END

  /* erwin Builtin Trigger */
  RETURN
error:
   RAISERROR (@errmsg, -- Message text.
              @severity, -- Severity (0~25).
              @state) -- State (0~255).
    rollback transaction
END

go

CREATE TRIGGER tU_Curriculum_Course ON Curriculum_Course FOR
UPDATE AS
/* erwin Builtin Trigger */
/* UPDATE trigger on Curriculum_Course */
BEGIN
  DECLARE   @numrows int,
            @nullcnt int,
            @validcnt int,
            @insCurriculumID char(18,50),
            @insCourseID varchar(50),
            @errno   int,
            @severity int,
            @state    int,
            @errmsg  varchar(255)
```

```
SELECT @numrows = @@rowcount
/* erwin Builtin Trigger */
/* Course  Curriculum_Course on child update restrict */
/* ERWIN_RELATION:CHECKSUM="0002c09b", PARENT_OWNER="",
PARENT_TABLE="Course"
   CHILD_OWNER="", CHILD_TABLE="Curriculum_Course"
   P2C_VERB_PHRASE="", C2P_VERB_PHRASE="",
   FK_CONSTRAINT="R_26", FK_COLUMNS="CourseID" */
IF
   /* %ChildFK(" OR",UPDATE) */
   UPDATE(CourseID)
BEGIN
   SELECT @nullcnt = 0
   SELECT @validcnt = count(*)
     FROM inserted,Course
       WHERE
         /* %JoinFKPK(inserted,Course) */
         inserted.CourseID = Course.CourseID
   /* %NotnullFK(inserted," IS NULL","select @nullcnt = count(*)
from inserted where"," AND") */

   IF @validcnt + @nullcnt != @numrows
   BEGIN
     SELECT @errno  = 30007,
            @errmsg = 'Cannot update Curriculum_Course because
Course does not exist.'
     GOTO error
   END
 END


/* erwin Builtin Trigger */
/* Curriculum  Curriculum_Course on child update restrict */
/* ERWIN_RELATION:CHECKSUM="00000000", PARENT_OWNER="",
PARENT_TABLE="Curriculum"
   CHILD_OWNER="", CHILD_TABLE="Curriculum_Course"
   P2C_VERB_PHRASE="", C2P_VERB_PHRASE="",
   FK_CONSTRAINT="R_25", FK_COLUMNS="CurriculumID" */
IF
   /* %ChildFK(" OR",UPDATE) */
   UPDATE(CurriculumID)
BEGIN
   SELECT @nullcnt = 0
   SELECT @validcnt = count(*)
     FROM inserted,Curriculum
       WHERE
         /* %JoinFKPK(inserted,Curriculum) */
         inserted.CurriculumID = Curriculum.CurriculumID
```

```
    /* %NotnullFK(inserted," IS NULL","select @nullcnt = count(*)
from inserted where"," AND") */


    IF @validcnt + @nullcnt != @numrows
    BEGIN
      SELECT @errno  = 30007,
             @errmsg = 'Cannot update Curriculum_Course because
Curriculum does not exist.'
      GOTO error
    END
  END


  /* erwin Builtin Trigger */
  RETURN
error:
   RAISERROR (@errmsg, -- Message text.
              @severity, -- Severity (0~25).
              @state) -- State (0~255).
   rollback transaction
END

go

CREATE TRIGGER tI_Curriculum_Job_Classification ON Curriculum_Job_
Classification FOR INSERT AS
/* erwin Builtin Trigger */
/* INSERT trigger on Curriculum_Job_Classification */
BEGIN
   DECLARE @numrows int,
           @nullcnt int,
           @validcnt int,
           @errno   int,
           @severity int,
           @state    int,
           @errmsg  varchar(255)

  SELECT @numrows = @@rowcount
  /* erwin Builtin Trigger */
  /* Curriculum  Curriculum_Job_Classification on child insert
restrict */
  /* ERWIN_RELATION:CHECKSUM="0004c8eb", PARENT_OWNER="",
PARENT_TABLE="Curriculum"
    CHILD_OWNER="", CHILD_TABLE="Curriculum_Job_Classification"
    P2C_VERB_PHRASE="", C2P_VERB_PHRASE="",
    FK_CONSTRAINT="R_28", FK_COLUMNS="CurriculumID" */
  IF
    /* %ChildFK(" OR",UPDATE) */
    UPDATE(CurriculumID)
```

```
  BEGIN
    SELECT @nullcnt = 0
    SELECT @validcnt = count(*)
      FROM inserted,Curriculum
        WHERE
          /* %JoinFKPK(inserted,Curriculum) */
          inserted.CurriculumID = Curriculum.CurriculumID
    /* %NotnullFK(inserted," IS NULL","select @nullcnt = count(*)
from inserted where"," and") */

    IF @validcnt + @nullcnt != @numrows
    BEGIN
      SELECT @errno  = 30002,
             @errmsg = 'Cannot insert Curriculum_Job_
Classification because Curriculum does not exist.'
      GOTO error
    END
  END

  /* erwin Builtin Trigger */
  /* Job_Classification  Curriculum_Job_Classification on child
insert restrict */
  /* ERWIN_RELATION:CHECKSUM="00000000", PARENT_OWNER="",
PARENT_TABLE="Job_Classification"
    CHILD_OWNER="", CHILD_TABLE="Curriculum_Job_Classification"
    P2C_VERB_PHRASE="", C2P_VERB_PHRASE="",
    FK_CONSTRAINT="R_23", FK_COLUMNS="ClassificationID" */
  IF
    /* %ChildFK(" OR",UPDATE) */
    UPDATE(ClassificationID)
  BEGIN
    SELECT @nullcnt = 0
    SELECT @validcnt = count(*)
      FROM inserted,Job_Classification
        WHERE
          /* %JoinFKPK(inserted,Job_Classification) */
          inserted.ClassificationID = Job_Classification.
ClassificationID
    /* %NotnullFK(inserted," IS NULL","select @nullcnt = count(*)
from inserted where"," and") */

    IF @validcnt + @nullcnt != @numrows
    BEGIN
      SELECT @errno  = 30002,
             @errmsg = 'Cannot insert Curriculum_Job_
Classification because Job_Classification does not exist.'
      GOTO error
    END
  END
```

```
  /* erwin Builtin Trigger */
  /* Job_Classification  Curriculum_Job_Classification on child
insert restrict */
  /* ERWIN_RELATION:CHECKSUM="00000000", PARENT_OWNER="",
PARENT_TABLE="Job_Classification"
    CHILD_OWNER="", CHILD_TABLE="Curriculum_Job_Classification"
    P2C_VERB_PHRASE="", C2P_VERB_PHRASE="",
    FK_CONSTRAINT="R_6", FK_COLUMNS="ClassificationID" */
  IF
    /* %ChildFK(" OR",UPDATE) */
    UPDATE(ClassificationID)
  BEGIN
    SELECT @nullcnt = 0
    SELECT @validcnt = count(*)
      FROM inserted,Job_Classification
        WHERE
          /* %JoinFKPK(inserted,Job_Classification) */
          inserted.ClassificationID = Job_Classification.
ClassificationID
    /* %NotnullFK(inserted," IS NULL","select @nullcnt = count(*)
from inserted where"," and") */

    IF @validcnt + @nullcnt != @numrows
    BEGIN
      SELECT @errno  = 30002,
             @errmsg = 'Cannot insert Curriculum_Job_
Classification because Job_Classification does not exist.'
      GOTO error
    END
  END

  /* erwin Builtin Trigger */
  RETURN
error:
   RAISERROR (@errmsg, -- Message text.
              @severity, -- Severity (0~25).
              @state) -- State (0~255).
    rollback transaction
END

go

CREATE TRIGGER tU_Curriculum_Job_Classification ON Curriculum_Job_
Classification FOR UPDATE AS
/* erwin Builtin Trigger */
/* UPDATE trigger on Curriculum_Job_Classification */
BEGIN
  DECLARE  @numrows int,
           @nullcnt int,
```

```
          @validcnt int,
          @insClassificationID varchar(50),
          @insCurriculumID char(18,50),
          @errno   int,
          @severity int,
          @state    int,
          @errmsg  varchar(255)

   SELECT @numrows = @@rowcount
   /* erwin Builtin Trigger */
   /* Curriculum  Curriculum_Job_Classification on child update
restrict */
   /* ERWIN_RELATION:CHECKSUM="0004b030", PARENT_OWNER="",
PARENT_TABLE="Curriculum"
      CHILD_OWNER="", CHILD_TABLE="Curriculum_Job_Classification"
      P2C_VERB_PHRASE="", C2P_VERB_PHRASE="",
      FK_CONSTRAINT="R_28", FK_COLUMNS="CurriculumID" */
   IF
     /* %ChildFK(" OR",UPDATE) */
     UPDATE(CurriculumID)
   BEGIN
     SELECT @nullcnt = 0
     SELECT @validcnt = count(*)
       FROM inserted,Curriculum
         WHERE
           /* %JoinFKPK(inserted,Curriculum) */
           inserted.CurriculumID = Curriculum.CurriculumID
     /* %NotnullFK(inserted," IS NULL","select @nullcnt = count(*)
from inserted where"," AND") */

     IF @validcnt + @nullcnt != @numrows
     BEGIN
       SELECT @errno  = 30007,
              @errmsg = 'Cannot update Curriculum_Job_
Classification because Curriculum does not exist.'
       GOTO error
     END
   END

   /* erwin Builtin Trigger */
   /* Job_Classification  Curriculum_Job_Classification on child
update restrict */
   /* ERWIN_RELATION:CHECKSUM="00000000", PARENT_OWNER="",
PARENT_TABLE="Job_Classification"
      CHILD_OWNER="", CHILD_TABLE="Curriculum_Job_Classification"
      P2C_VERB_PHRASE="", C2P_VERB_PHRASE="",
      FK_CONSTRAINT="R_23", FK_COLUMNS="ClassificationID" */
```

```
  IF
    /* %ChildFK(" OR",UPDATE) */
    UPDATE(ClassificationID)
  BEGIN
    SELECT @nullcnt = 0
    SELECT @validcnt = count(*)
      FROM inserted,Job_Classification
        WHERE
          /* %JoinFKPK(inserted,Job_Classification) */
          inserted.ClassificationID = Job_Classification.
ClassificationID
    /* %NotnullFK(inserted," IS NULL","select @nullcnt = count(*)
from inserted where"," AND") */

    IF @validcnt + @nullcnt != @numrows
    BEGIN
      SELECT @errno  = 30007,
             @errmsg = 'Cannot update Curriculum_Job_
Classification because Job_Classification does not exist.'
      GOTO error
    END
  END

  /* erwin Builtin Trigger */
  /* Job_Classification  Curriculum_Job_Classification on child
update restrict */
  /* ERWIN_RELATION:CHECKSUM="00000000", PARENT_OWNER="",
PARENT_TABLE="Job_Classification"
    CHILD_OWNER="", CHILD_TABLE="Curriculum_Job_Classification"
    P2C_VERB_PHRASE="", C2P_VERB_PHRASE="",
    FK_CONSTRAINT="R_6", FK_COLUMNS="ClassificationID" */
  IF
    /* %ChildFK(" OR",UPDATE) */
    UPDATE(ClassificationID)
  BEGIN
    SELECT @nullcnt = 0
    SELECT @validcnt = count(*)
      FROM inserted,Job_Classification
        WHERE
          /* %JoinFKPK(inserted,Job_Classification) */
          inserted.ClassificationID = Job_Classification.
ClassificationID
    /* %NotnullFK(inserted," IS NULL","select @nullcnt = count(*)
from inserted where"," AND") */

    IF @validcnt + @nullcnt != @numrows
    BEGIN
      SELECT @errno  = 30007,
```

```
                @errmsg = 'Cannot update Curriculum_Job_
Classification because Job_Classification does not exist.'
        GOTO error
    END
  END
  /* erwin Builtin Trigger */
  RETURN
error:
    RAISERROR (@errmsg, -- Message text.
                @severity, -- Severity (0~25).
                @state) -- State (0~255).
    rollback transaction
END


go


CREATE TRIGGER tD_Degree ON Degree FOR DELETE AS
/* erwin Builtin Trigger */
/* DELETE trigger on Degree */
BEGIN
  DECLARE    @errno    int,
            @severity int,
            @state    int,
            @errmsg   varchar(255)
    /* erwin Builtin Trigger */
    /* Degree  Curriculum on parent delete restrict */
    /* ERWIN_RELATION:CHECKSUM="00010c21", PARENT_OWNER="",
PARENT_TABLE="Degree"
    CHILD_OWNER="", CHILD_TABLE="Curriculum"
    P2C_VERB_PHRASE="", C2P_VERB_PHRASE="",
    FK_CONSTRAINT="R_24", FK_COLUMNS="DegreeID" */
    IF EXISTS (
      SELECT * FROM deleted,Curriculum
      WHERE
        /*  %JoinFKPK(Curriculum,deleted," = "," AND") */
        Curriculum.DegreeID = deleted.DegreeID
    )
    BEGIN
      SELECT @errno  = 30001,
              @errmsg = 'Cannot delete Degree because Curriculum
exists.'
      GOTO error
    END


    /* erwin Builtin Trigger */
    RETURN
```

```
error:
   RAISERROR (@errmsg, -- Message text.
              @severity, -- Severity (0~25).
              @state) -- State (0~255).
     rollback transaction
END

go

CREATE TRIGGER tI_Degree ON Degree FOR INSERT AS
/* erwin Builtin Trigger */
/* INSERT trigger on Degree */
BEGIN
   DECLARE @numrows int,
           @nullcnt int,
           @validcnt int,
           @errno   int,
           @severity int,
           @state    int,
           @errmsg  varchar(255)


  SELECT @numrows = @@rowcount
  /* erwin Builtin Trigger */
  /* Department  Degree on child insert restrict */
  /* ERWIN_RELATION:CHECKSUM="0001719c", PARENT_OWNER="",
PARENT_TABLE="Department"
    CHILD_OWNER="", CHILD_TABLE="Degree"
    P2C_VERB_PHRASE="", C2P_VERB_PHRASE="",
    FK_CONSTRAINT="R_19", FK_COLUMNS="DepartmentID" */
  IF
    /* %ChildFK(" OR",UPDATE) */
    UPDATE(DepartmentID)
  BEGIN
    SELECT @nullcnt = 0
    SELECT @validcnt = count(*)
      FROM inserted,Department
        WHERE
          /* %JoinFKPK(inserted,Department) */
          inserted.DepartmentID = Department.DepartmentID
    /* %NotnullFK(inserted," IS NULL","select @nullcnt = count(*)
from inserted where"," and") */

    IF @validcnt + @nullcnt != @numrows
    BEGIN
      SELECT @errno  = 30002,
             @errmsg = 'Cannot insert Degree because Department
does not exist.'
```

```
      GOTO error
    END
  END


  /* erwin Builtin Trigger */
  RETURN
error:
    RAISERROR (@errmsg, -- Message text.
               @severity, -- Severity (0~25).
               @state) -- State (0~255).
    rollback transaction
END


go


CREATE TRIGGER tU_Degree ON Degree FOR UPDATE AS
/* erwin Builtin Trigger */
/* UPDATE trigger on Degree */
BEGIN
  DECLARE   @numrows int,
            @nullcnt int,
            @validcnt int,
            @insDegreeID varchar(50),
            @errno    int,
            @severity int,
            @state    int,
            @errmsg   varchar(255)


  SELECT @numrows = @@rowcount
  /* erwin Builtin Trigger */
  /* Degree  Curriculum on parent update restrict */
  /* ERWIN_RELATION:CHECKSUM="00027b9b", PARENT_OWNER="",
PARENT_TABLE="Degree"
    CHILD_OWNER="", CHILD_TABLE="Curriculum"
    P2C_VERB_PHRASE="", C2P_VERB_PHRASE="",
    FK_CONSTRAINT="R_24", FK_COLUMNS="DegreeID" */
  IF
    /* %ParentPK(" OR",UPDATE) */
    UPDATE(DegreeID)
  BEGIN
    IF EXISTS (
      SELECT * FROM deleted,Curriculum
      WHERE
        /*  %JoinFKPK(Curriculum,deleted," = "," AND") */
        Curriculum.DegreeID = deleted.DegreeID
    )
```

```
    BEGIN
      SELECT @errno  = 30005,
             @errmsg = 'Cannot update Degree because Curriculum
exists.'
       GOTO error
    END
  END


  /* erwin Builtin Trigger */
  /* Department  Degree on child update restrict */
  /* ERWIN_RELATION:CHECKSUM="00000000", PARENT_OWNER="",
PARENT_TABLE="Department"
    CHILD_OWNER="", CHILD_TABLE="Degree"
    P2C_VERB_PHRASE="", C2P_VERB_PHRASE="",
    FK_CONSTRAINT="R_19", FK_COLUMNS="DepartmentID" */
  IF
    /* %ChildFK(" OR",UPDATE) */
    UPDATE(DepartmentID)
  BEGIN
    SELECT @nullcnt = 0
    SELECT @validcnt = count(*)
      FROM inserted,Department
        WHERE
          /* %JoinFKPK(inserted,Department) */
          inserted.DepartmentID = Department.DepartmentID
    /* %NotnullFK(inserted," IS NULL","select @nullcnt = count(*)
from inserted where"," AND") */

    IF @validcnt + @nullcnt != @numrows
    BEGIN
      SELECT @errno  = 30007,
             @errmsg = 'Cannot update Degree because Department
does not exist.'
       GOTO error
    END
  END


  /* erwin Builtin Trigger */
  RETURN
error:
   RAISERROR (@errmsg, -- Message text.
              @severity, -- Severity (0~25).
              @state) -- State (0~255).
    rollback transaction
END

go
```

```
CREATE TRIGGER tD_Department ON Department FOR DELETE AS
/* erwin Builtin Trigger */
/* DELETE trigger on Department */
BEGIN
  DECLARE  @errno    int,
           @severity int,
           @state    int,
           @errmsg   varchar(255)
    /* erwin Builtin Trigger */
    /* Department  Course on parent delete restrict */
    /* ERWIN_RELATION:CHECKSUM="0001f42a", PARENT_OWNER="",
PARENT_TABLE="Department"
    CHILD_OWNER="", CHILD_TABLE="Course"
    P2C_VERB_PHRASE="", C2P_VERB_PHRASE="",
    FK_CONSTRAINT="R_21", FK_COLUMNS="DepartmentID" */
    IF EXISTS (
      SELECT * FROM deleted,Course
      WHERE
        /*  %JoinFKPK(Course,deleted," = "," AND") */
        Course.DepartmentID = deleted.DepartmentID
    )
    BEGIN
      SELECT @errno  = 30001,
             @errmsg = 'Cannot delete Department because Course
exists.'
      GOTO error
    END

    /* erwin Builtin Trigger */
    /* Department  Degree on parent delete restrict */
    /* ERWIN_RELATION:CHECKSUM="00000000", PARENT_OWNER="",
PARENT_TABLE="Department"
    CHILD_OWNER="", CHILD_TABLE="Degree"
    P2C_VERB_PHRASE="", C2P_VERB_PHRASE="",
    FK_CONSTRAINT="R_19", FK_COLUMNS="DepartmentID" */
    IF EXISTS (
      SELECT * FROM deleted,Degree
      WHERE
        /*  %JoinFKPK(Degree,deleted," = "," AND") */
        Degree.DepartmentID = deleted.DepartmentID
    )
    BEGIN
      SELECT @errno  = 30001,
             @errmsg = 'Cannot delete Department because Degree
exists.'
      GOTO error
    END
```

```
    /* erwin Builtin Trigger */
    RETURN
error:
   RAISERROR (@errmsg, -- Message text.
                @severity, -- Severity (0~25).
                @state) -- State (0~255).
    rollback transaction
END

go

CREATE TRIGGER tI_Department ON Department FOR INSERT AS
/* erwin Builtin Trigger */
/* INSERT trigger on Department */
BEGIN
   DECLARE @numrows int,
           @nullcnt int,
           @validcnt int,
           @errno    int,
           @severity int,
           @state    int,
           @errmsg  varchar(255)

  SELECT @numrows = @@rowcount
  /* erwin Builtin Trigger */
  /* School  Department on child insert restrict */
  /* ERWIN_RELATION:CHECKSUM="0003db4f", PARENT_OWNER="",
PARENT_TABLE="School"
    CHILD_OWNER="", CHILD_TABLE="Department"
    P2C_VERB_PHRASE="", C2P_VERB_PHRASE="",
    FK_CONSTRAINT="R_20", FK_COLUMNS="SchoolID" */
  IF
    /* %ChildFK(" OR",UPDATE) */
    UPDATE(SchoolID)
  BEGIN
    SELECT @nullcnt = 0
    SELECT @validcnt = count(*)
      FROM inserted,School
        WHERE
          /* %JoinFKPK(inserted,School) */
          inserted.SchoolID = School.SchoolID
    /* %NotnullFK(inserted," IS NULL","select @nullcnt = count(*)
from inserted where"," and") */

    IF @validcnt + @nullcnt != @numrows
    BEGIN
      SELECT @errno  = 30002,
```

```
              @errmsg = 'Cannot insert Department because School
does not exist.'
        GOTO error
      END
    END


  /* erwin Builtin Trigger */
  /* School  Department on child insert restrict */
  /* ERWIN_RELATION:CHECKSUM="00000000", PARENT_OWNER="",
PARENT_TABLE="School"
    CHILD_OWNER="", CHILD_TABLE="Department"
    P2C_VERB_PHRASE="", C2P_VERB_PHRASE="",
    FK_CONSTRAINT="R_2", FK_COLUMNS="SchoolID" */
  IF
    /* %ChildFK(" OR",UPDATE) */
    UPDATE(SchoolID)
  BEGIN
    SELECT @nullcnt = 0
    SELECT @validcnt = count(*)
      FROM inserted,School
        WHERE
          /* %JoinFKPK(inserted,School) */
          inserted.SchoolID = School.SchoolID
    /* %NotnullFK(inserted," IS NULL","select @nullcnt = count(*)
from inserted where"," and") */

    IF @validcnt + @nullcnt != @numrows
    BEGIN
      SELECT @errno  = 30002,
             @errmsg = 'Cannot insert Department because School
does not exist.'
        GOTO error
    END
  END


  /* erwin Builtin Trigger */
  /* School  Department on child insert restrict */
  /* ERWIN_RELATION:CHECKSUM="00000000", PARENT_OWNER="",
PARENT_TABLE="School"
    CHILD_OWNER="", CHILD_TABLE="Department"
    P2C_VERB_PHRASE="", C2P_VERB_PHRASE="",
    FK_CONSTRAINT="R_1", FK_COLUMNS="SchoolID" */
  IF
    /* %ChildFK(" OR",UPDATE) */
    UPDATE(SchoolID)
  BEGIN
    SELECT @nullcnt = 0
```

```
    SELECT @validcnt = count(*)
      FROM inserted,School
        WHERE
          /* %JoinFKPK(inserted,School) */
          inserted.SchoolID = School.SchoolID
    /* %NotnullFK(inserted," IS NULL","select @nullcnt = count(*)
from inserted where"," and") */

    IF @validcnt + @nullcnt != @numrows
    BEGIN
      SELECT @errno  = 30002,
             @errmsg = 'Cannot insert Department because School
does not exist.'
      GOTO error
    END
  END

  /* erwin Builtin Trigger */
  RETURN
error:
  RAISERROR (@errmsg, -- Message text.
             @severity, -- Severity (0~25).
             @state) -- State (0~255).
    rollback transaction
END

go

CREATE TRIGGER tU_Department ON Department FOR UPDATE AS
/* erwin Builtin Trigger */
/* UPDATE trigger on Department */
BEGIN
  DECLARE  @numrows int,
           @nullcnt int,
           @validcnt int,
           @insDepartmentID varchar(50),
           @errno   int,
           @severity int,
           @state    int,
           @errmsg  varchar(255)

  SELECT @numrows = @@rowcount
  /* erwin Builtin Trigger */
  /* Department  Course on parent update restrict */
  /* ERWIN_RELATION:CHECKSUM="0006055a", PARENT_OWNER="",
PARENT_TABLE="Department"
```

```
   CHILD_OWNER="", CHILD_TABLE="Course"
   P2C_VERB_PHRASE="", C2P_VERB_PHRASE="",
   FK_CONSTRAINT="R_21", FK_COLUMNS="DepartmentID" */
 IF
   /* %ParentPK(" OR",UPDATE) */
   UPDATE(DepartmentID)
 BEGIN
   IF EXISTS (
     SELECT * FROM deleted,Course
     WHERE
       /*  %JoinFKPK(Course,deleted," = "," AND") */
       Course.DepartmentID = deleted.DepartmentID
   )
   BEGIN
     SELECT @errno  = 30005,
            @errmsg = 'Cannot update Department because Course
exists.'
     GOTO error
   END
 END


 /* erwin Builtin Trigger */
 /* Department  Degree on parent update restrict */
 /* ERWIN_RELATION:CHECKSUM="00000000", PARENT_OWNER="",
PARENT_TABLE="Department"
   CHILD_OWNER="", CHILD_TABLE="Degree"
   P2C_VERB_PHRASE="", C2P_VERB_PHRASE="",
   FK_CONSTRAINT="R_19", FK_COLUMNS="DepartmentID" */
 IF
   /* %ParentPK(" OR",UPDATE) */
   UPDATE(DepartmentID)
 BEGIN
   IF EXISTS (
     SELECT * FROM deleted,Degree
     WHERE
       /*  %JoinFKPK(Degree,deleted," = "," AND") */
       Degree.DepartmentID = deleted.DepartmentID
   )
   BEGIN
     SELECT @errno  = 30005,
            @errmsg = 'Cannot update Department because Degree
exists.'
     GOTO error
   END
 END
```

```
/* erwin Builtin Trigger */
/* School  Department on child update restrict */
/* ERWIN_RELATION:CHECKSUM="00000000", PARENT_OWNER="",
PARENT_TABLE="School"
   CHILD_OWNER="", CHILD_TABLE="Department"
   P2C_VERB_PHRASE="", C2P_VERB_PHRASE="",
   FK_CONSTRAINT="R_20", FK_COLUMNS="SchoolID" */
IF
   /* %ChildFK(" OR",UPDATE) */
   UPDATE(SchoolID)
BEGIN
  SELECT @nullcnt = 0
  SELECT @validcnt = count(*)
    FROM inserted,School
      WHERE
        /* %JoinFKPK(inserted,School) */
        inserted.SchoolID = School.SchoolID
   /* %NotnullFK(inserted," IS NULL","select @nullcnt = count(*)
from inserted where"," AND") */


  IF @validcnt + @nullcnt != @numrows
  BEGIN
    SELECT @errno  = 30007,
           @errmsg = 'Cannot update Department because School
does not exist.'
    GOTO error
  END
END
/* erwin Builtin Trigger */
/* School  Department on child update restrict */
/* ERWIN_RELATION:CHECKSUM="00000000", PARENT_OWNER="",
PARENT_TABLE="School"
   CHILD_OWNER="", CHILD_TABLE="Department"
   P2C_VERB_PHRASE="", C2P_VERB_PHRASE="",
   FK_CONSTRAINT="R_2", FK_COLUMNS="SchoolID" */
IF
   /* %ChildFK(" OR",UPDATE) */
   UPDATE(SchoolID)
BEGIN
  SELECT @nullcnt = 0
  SELECT @validcnt = count(*)
    FROM inserted,School
      WHERE
        /* %JoinFKPK(inserted,School) */
        inserted.SchoolID = School.SchoolID
   /* %NotnullFK(inserted," IS NULL","select @nullcnt = count(*)
from inserted where"," AND") */
```

```
     IF @validcnt + @nullcnt != @numrows
     BEGIN
       SELECT @errno  = 30007,
               @errmsg = 'Cannot update Department because School
does not exist.'
       GOTO error
     END
  END

  /* erwin Builtin Trigger */
  /* School  Department on child update restrict */
  /* ERWIN_RELATION:CHECKSUM="00000000", PARENT_OWNER="",
PARENT_TABLE="School"
    CHILD_OWNER="", CHILD_TABLE="Department"
    P2C_VERB_PHRASE="", C2P_VERB_PHRASE="",
    FK_CONSTRAINT="R_1", FK_COLUMNS="SchoolID" */
  IF
    /* %ChildFK(" OR",UPDATE) */
    UPDATE(SchoolID)
  BEGIN
    SELECT @nullcnt = 0
    SELECT @validcnt = count(*)
      FROM inserted,School
        WHERE
          /* %JoinFKPK(inserted,School) */
          inserted.SchoolID = School.SchoolID
    /* %NotnullFK(inserted," IS NULL","select @nullcnt = count(*)
from inserted where"," AND") */

    IF @validcnt + @nullcnt != @numrows
    BEGIN
      SELECT @errno  = 30007,
              @errmsg = 'Cannot update Department because School
does not exist.'
       GOTO error
    END
  END

  /* erwin Builtin Trigger */
  RETURN
error:
   RAISERROR (@errmsg, -- Message text.
               @severity, -- Severity (0~25).
               @state) -- State (0~255).
    rollback transaction
END

go
```

```
CREATE TRIGGER tD_Faculty ON Faculty FOR DELETE AS
/* erwin Builtin Trigger */
/* DELETE trigger on Faculty */
BEGIN
  DECLARE  @errno    int,
           @severity int,
           @state    int,
           @errmsg  varchar(255)
    /* erwin Builtin Trigger */
    /* Faculty  Course_Offering on parent delete restrict */
    /* ERWIN_RELATION:CHECKSUM="000227e6", PARENT_OWNER="",
PARENT_TABLE="Faculty"
    CHILD_OWNER="", CHILD_TABLE="Course_Offering"
    P2C_VERB_PHRASE="", C2P_VERB_PHRASE="",
    FK_CONSTRAINT="R_30", FK_COLUMNS="FacultyID" */
    IF EXISTS (
      SELECT * FROM deleted,Course_Offering
      WHERE
        /*  %JoinFKPK(Course_Offering,deleted," = "," AND") */
        Course_Offering.FacultyID = deleted.FacultyID
    )
    BEGIN
      SELECT @errno  = 30001,
             @errmsg = 'Cannot delete Faculty because Course_
Offering exists.'
      GOTO error
    END


    /* erwin Builtin Trigger */
    /* Faculty  Course_Offering on parent delete restrict */
    /* ERWIN_RELATION:CHECKSUM="00000000", PARENT_OWNER="",
PARENT_TABLE="Faculty"
    CHILD_OWNER="", CHILD_TABLE="Course_Offering"
    P2C_VERB_PHRASE="", C2P_VERB_PHRASE="",
    FK_CONSTRAINT="R_12", FK_COLUMNS="FacultyID" */
    IF EXISTS (
      SELECT * FROM deleted,Course_Offering
      WHERE
        /*  %JoinFKPK(Course_Offering,deleted," = "," AND") */
        Course_Offering.FacultyID = deleted.FacultyID
    )
    BEGIN
      SELECT @errno  = 30001,
             @errmsg = 'Cannot delete Faculty because Course_
Offering exists.'
      GOTO error
    END
```

```
    /* erwin Builtin Trigger */
    RETURN
error:
   RAISERROR (@errmsg, -- Message text.
              @severity, -- Severity (0~25).
              @state) -- State (0~255).
    rollback transaction
END

go

CREATE TRIGGER tU_Faculty ON Faculty FOR UPDATE AS
/* erwin Builtin Trigger */
/* UPDATE trigger on Faculty */
BEGIN
  DECLARE   @numrows int,
            @nullcnt int,
            @validcnt int,
            @insFacultyID varchar(50),
            @errno    int,
            @severity int,
            @state    int,
            @errmsg   varchar(255)

  SELECT @numrows = @@rowcount
  /* erwin Builtin Trigger */
  /* Faculty  Course_Offering on parent update restrict */
  /* ERWIN_RELATION:CHECKSUM="0002433c", PARENT_OWNER="",
PARENT_TABLE="Faculty"
    CHILD_OWNER="", CHILD_TABLE="Course_Offering"
    P2C_VERB_PHRASE="", C2P_VERB_PHRASE="",
    FK_CONSTRAINT="R_30", FK_COLUMNS="FacultyID" */
  IF
    /* %ParentPK(" OR",UPDATE) */
    UPDATE(FacultyID)
  BEGIN
    IF EXISTS (
      SELECT * FROM deleted,Course_Offering
      WHERE
        /*  %JoinFKPK(Course_Offering,deleted," = "," AND") */
        Course_Offering.FacultyID = deleted.FacultyID
    )
    BEGIN
      SELECT @errno  = 30005,
             @errmsg = 'Cannot update Faculty because Course_
Offering exists.'
      GOTO error
    END
  END
```

```
/* erwin Builtin Trigger */
/* Faculty  Course_Offering on parent update restrict */
/* ERWIN_RELATION:CHECKSUM="00000000", PARENT_OWNER="",
PARENT_TABLE="Faculty"
   CHILD_OWNER="", CHILD_TABLE="Course_Offering"
   P2C_VERB_PHRASE="", C2P_VERB_PHRASE="",
   FK_CONSTRAINT="R_12", FK_COLUMNS="FacultyID" */
  IF
    /* %ParentPK(" OR",UPDATE) */
    UPDATE(FacultyID)
  BEGIN
    IF EXISTS (
      SELECT * FROM deleted,Course_Offering
      WHERE
        /*  %JoinFKPK(Course_Offering,deleted," = "," AND") */
        Course_Offering.FacultyID = deleted.FacultyID
    )
    BEGIN
      SELECT @errno  = 30005,
             @errmsg = 'Cannot update Faculty because Course_
Offering exists.'
      GOTO error
    END
  END


  /* erwin Builtin Trigger */
  RETURN
error:
  RAISERROR (@errmsg, -- Message text.
             @severity, -- Severity (0~25).
             @state) -- State (0~255).
    rollback transaction
END

go

CREATE TRIGGER tD_Job_Classification ON Job_Classification FOR
DELETE AS
/* erwin Builtin Trigger */
/* DELETE trigger on Job_Classification */
BEGIN
  DECLARE @errno   int,
          @severity int,
          @state    int,
          @errmsg  varchar(255)
```

```
    /* erwin Builtin Trigger */
    /* Job_Classification  Curriculum_Job_Classification on parent
delete restrict */
    /* ERWIN_RELATION:CHECKSUM="00028d10", PARENT_OWNER="",
PARENT_TABLE="Job_Classification"
    CHILD_OWNER="", CHILD_TABLE="Curriculum_Job_Classification"
    P2C_VERB_PHRASE="", C2P_VERB_PHRASE="",
    FK_CONSTRAINT="R_23", FK_COLUMNS="ClassificationID" */
    IF EXISTS (
      SELECT * FROM deleted,Curriculum_Job_Classification
      WHERE
        /*  %JoinFKPK(Curriculum_Job_Classification,deleted," =
"," AND") */
        Curriculum_Job_Classification.ClassificationID = deleted.
ClassificationID
    )
    BEGIN
      SELECT @errno  = 30001,
            @errmsg = 'Cannot delete Job_Classification because
Curriculum_Job_Classification exists.'
      GOTO error
    END


    /* erwin Builtin Trigger */
    /* Job_Classification  Curriculum_Job_Classification on parent
delete restrict */
    /* ERWIN_RELATION:CHECKSUM="00000000", PARENT_OWNER="",
PARENT_TABLE="Job_Classification"
    CHILD_OWNER="", CHILD_TABLE="Curriculum_Job_Classification"
    P2C_VERB_PHRASE="", C2P_VERB_PHRASE="",
    FK_CONSTRAINT="R_6", FK_COLUMNS="ClassificationID" */
    IF EXISTS (
      SELECT * FROM deleted,Curriculum_Job_Classification
      WHERE
        /*  %JoinFKPK(Curriculum_Job_Classification,deleted," =
"," AND") */
        Curriculum_Job_Classification.ClassificationID = deleted.
ClassificationID
    )
    BEGIN
      SELECT @errno  = 30001,
            @errmsg = 'Cannot delete Job_Classification because
Curriculum_Job_Classification exists.'
      GOTO error
    END
```

```
    /* erwin Builtin Trigger */
    RETURN
error:
   RAISERROR (@errmsg, -- Message text.
              @severity, -- Severity (0~25).
              @state) -- State (0~255).
    rollback transaction
END

go

CREATE TRIGGER tU_Job_Classification ON Job_Classification FOR
UPDATE AS
/* erwin Builtin Trigger */
/* UPDATE trigger on Job_Classification */
BEGIN
  DECLARE  @numrows int,
           @nullcnt int,
           @validcnt int,
           @insClassificationID varchar(50),
           @errno   int,
           @severity int,
           @state    int,
           @errmsg  varchar(255)

  SELECT @numrows = @@rowcount
  /* erwin Builtin Trigger */
  /* Job_Classification  Curriculum_Job_Classification on parent
update restrict */
  /* ERWIN_RELATION:CHECKSUM="0002e6e0", PARENT_OWNER="",
PARENT_TABLE="Job_Classification"
    CHILD_OWNER="", CHILD_TABLE="Curriculum_Job_Classification"
    P2C_VERB_PHRASE="", C2P_VERB_PHRASE="",
    FK_CONSTRAINT="R_23", FK_COLUMNS="ClassificationID" */
  IF
    /* %ParentPK(" OR",UPDATE) */
    UPDATE(ClassificationID)
  BEGIN
    IF EXISTS (
      SELECT * FROM deleted,Curriculum_Job_Classification
      WHERE
        /*  %JoinFKPK(Curriculum_Job_Classification,deleted," =
"," AND") */
        Curriculum_Job_Classification.ClassificationID = deleted.
ClassificationID
    )
```

```
    BEGIN
      SELECT @errno  = 30005,
              @errmsg = 'Cannot update Job_Classification because
Curriculum_Job_Classification exists.'
        GOTO error
    END
  END


  /* erwin Builtin Trigger */
  /* Job_Classification  Curriculum_Job_Classification on parent
update restrict */
  /* ERWIN_RELATION:CHECKSUM="00000000", PARENT_OWNER="",
PARENT_TABLE="Job_Classification"
    CHILD_OWNER="", CHILD_TABLE="Curriculum_Job_Classification"
    P2C_VERB_PHRASE="", C2P_VERB_PHRASE="",
    FK_CONSTRAINT="R_6", FK_COLUMNS="ClassificationID" */
  IF
    /* %ParentPK(" OR",UPDATE) */
    UPDATE(ClassificationID)
  BEGIN
    IF EXISTS (
      SELECT * FROM deleted,Curriculum_Job_Classification
      WHERE
        /*  %JoinFKPK(Curriculum_Job_Classification,deleted," =
"," AND") */
        Curriculum_Job_Classification.ClassificationID = deleted.
ClassificationID
    )
    BEGIN
      SELECT @errno  = 30005,
              @errmsg = 'Cannot update Job_Classification because
Curriculum_Job_Classification exists.'
        GOTO error
    END
  END


  /* erwin Builtin Trigger */
  RETURN
error:
  RAISERROR (@errmsg, -- Message text.
              @severity, -- Severity (0~25).
              @state) -- State (0~255).
    rollback transaction
END
go
```

```
CREATE TRIGGER tD_School ON School FOR DELETE AS
/* erwin Builtin Trigger */
/* DELETE trigger on School */
BEGIN
  DECLARE  @errno    int,
           @severity int,
           @state    int,
           @errmsg   varchar(255)
    /* erwin Builtin Trigger */
    /* School  Department on parent delete restrict */
    /* ERWIN_RELATION:CHECKSUM="0002e790", PARENT_OWNER="",
PARENT_TABLE="School"
    CHILD_OWNER="", CHILD_TABLE="Department"
    P2C_VERB_PHRASE="", C2P_VERB_PHRASE="",
    FK_CONSTRAINT="R_20", FK_COLUMNS="SchoolID" */
    IF EXISTS (
      SELECT * FROM deleted,Department
      WHERE
        /*  %JoinFKPK(Department,deleted," = "," AND") */
        Department.SchoolID = deleted.SchoolID
    )
    BEGIN
      SELECT @errno  = 30001,
             @errmsg = 'Cannot delete School because Department
exists.'
      GOTO error
    END


    /* erwin Builtin Trigger */
    /* School  Department on parent delete restrict */
    /* ERWIN_RELATION:CHECKSUM="00000000", PARENT_OWNER="",
PARENT_TABLE="School"
    CHILD_OWNER="", CHILD_TABLE="Department"
    P2C_VERB_PHRASE="", C2P_VERB_PHRASE="",
    FK_CONSTRAINT="R_2", FK_COLUMNS="SchoolID" */
    IF EXISTS (
      SELECT * FROM deleted,Department
      WHERE
        /*  %JoinFKPK(Department,deleted," = "," AND") */
        Department.SchoolID = deleted.SchoolID
    )
    BEGIN
      SELECT @errno  = 30001,
             @errmsg = 'Cannot delete School because Department
exists.'
```

```
      GOTO error
   END


   /* erwin Builtin Trigger */
   /* School  Department on parent delete restrict */
   /* ERWIN_RELATION:CHECKSUM="00000000", PARENT_OWNER="",
PARENT_TABLE="School"
   CHILD_OWNER="", CHILD_TABLE="Department"
   P2C_VERB_PHRASE="", C2P_VERB_PHRASE="",
   FK_CONSTRAINT="R_1", FK_COLUMNS="SchoolID" */
   IF EXISTS (
     SELECT * FROM deleted,Department
     WHERE
       /*  %JoinFKPK(Department,deleted," = "," AND") */
       Department.SchoolID = deleted.SchoolID
   )
   BEGIN
     SELECT @errno  = 30001,
            @errmsg = 'Cannot delete School because Department
exists.'
     GOTO error
   END


   /* erwin Builtin Trigger */
   RETURN
error:
   RAISERROR (@errmsg, -- Message text.
              @severity, -- Severity (0~25).
              @state) -- State (0~255).
   rollback transaction
END

go

CREATE TRIGGER tU_School ON School FOR UPDATE AS
/* erwin Builtin Trigger */
/* UPDATE trigger on School */
BEGIN
  DECLARE   @numrows int,
            @nullcnt int,
            @validcnt int,
            @insSchoolID varchar(50),
            @errno   int,
            @severity int,
            @state    int,
            @errmsg  varchar(255)
```

```
  SELECT @numrows = @@rowcount
  /* erwin Builtin Trigger */
  /* School   Department on parent update restrict */
  /* ERWIN_RELATION:CHECKSUM="00032787", PARENT_OWNER="",
PARENT_TABLE="School"
    CHILD_OWNER="", CHILD_TABLE="Department"
    P2C_VERB_PHRASE="", C2P_VERB_PHRASE="",
    FK_CONSTRAINT="R_20", FK_COLUMNS="SchoolID" */
  IF
    /* %ParentPK(" OR",UPDATE) */
    UPDATE(SchoolID)
  BEGIN
    IF EXISTS (
      SELECT * FROM deleted,Department
      WHERE
        /*  %JoinFKPK(Department,deleted," = "," AND") */
        Department.SchoolID = deleted.SchoolID
    )
    BEGIN
      SELECT @errno  = 30005,
             @errmsg = 'Cannot update School because Department
exists.'
       GOTO error
    END
  END

  /* erwin Builtin Trigger */
  /* School   Department on parent update restrict */
  /* ERWIN_RELATION:CHECKSUM="00000000", PARENT_OWNER="",
PARENT_TABLE="School"
    CHILD_OWNER="", CHILD_TABLE="Department"
    P2C_VERB_PHRASE="", C2P_VERB_PHRASE="",
    FK_CONSTRAINT="R_2", FK_COLUMNS="SchoolID" */
  IF
    /* %ParentPK(" OR",UPDATE) */
    UPDATE(SchoolID)
  BEGIN
    IF EXISTS (
      SELECT * FROM deleted,Department
      WHERE
        /*  %JoinFKPK(Department,deleted," = "," AND") */
        Department.SchoolID = deleted.SchoolID
    )
    BEGIN
      SELECT @errno  = 30005,
             @errmsg = 'Cannot update School because Department
exists.'
```

```
      GOTO error
    END
  END


  /* erwin Builtin Trigger */
  /* School   Department on parent update restrict */
  /* ERWIN_RELATION:CHECKSUM="00000000", PARENT_OWNER="",
PARENT_TABLE="School"
    CHILD_OWNER="", CHILD_TABLE="Department"
    P2C_VERB_PHRASE="", C2P_VERB_PHRASE="",
    FK_CONSTRAINT="R_1", FK_COLUMNS="SchoolID" */
  IF
    /* %ParentPK(" OR",UPDATE) */
    UPDATE(SchoolID)
  BEGIN
    IF EXISTS (
      SELECT * FROM deleted,Department
      WHERE
        /*  %JoinFKPK(Department,deleted," = "," AND") */
        Department.SchoolID = deleted.SchoolID
    )
    BEGIN
      SELECT @errno  = 30005,
             @errmsg = 'Cannot update School because Department
exists.'
      GOTO error
    END
  END


  /* erwin Builtin Trigger */
  RETURN
error:
  RAISERROR (@errmsg, -- Message text.
             @severity, -- Severity (0~25).
             @state) -- State (0~255).
    rollback transaction
END

go

CREATE TRIGGER tD_Student ON Student FOR DELETE AS
/* erwin Builtin Trigger */
/* DELETE trigger on Student */
BEGIN
  DECLARE  @errno    int,
           @severity int,
           @state    int,
```

```
        @errmsg  varchar(255)
    /* erwin Builtin Trigger */
    /* Student  Student_Transcript on parent delete restrict */
    /* ERWIN_RELATION:CHECKSUM="00033391", PARENT_OWNER="",
PARENT_TABLE="Student"
    CHILD_OWNER="", CHILD_TABLE="Student_Transcript"
    P2C_VERB_PHRASE="", C2P_VERB_PHRASE="",
    FK_CONSTRAINT="R_36", FK_COLUMNS="StudentID" */
    IF EXISTS (
      SELECT * FROM deleted,Student_Transcript
      WHERE
        /*  %JoinFKPK(Student_Transcript,deleted," = "," AND") */
        Student_Transcript.StudentID = deleted.StudentID
    )
    BEGIN
      SELECT @errno  = 30001,
             @errmsg = 'Cannot delete Student because Student_
Transcript exists.'
      GOTO error
    END

    /* erwin Builtin Trigger */
    /* Student  Course_Enrollment on parent delete restrict */
    /* ERWIN_RELATION:CHECKSUM="00000000", PARENT_OWNER="",
PARENT_TABLE="Student"
    CHILD_OWNER="", CHILD_TABLE="Course_Enrollment"
    P2C_VERB_PHRASE="", C2P_VERB_PHRASE="",
    FK_CONSTRAINT="R_33", FK_COLUMNS="StudentID" */
    IF EXISTS (
      SELECT * FROM deleted,Course_Enrollment
      WHERE
        /*  %JoinFKPK(Course_Enrollment,deleted," = "," AND") */
        Course_Enrollment.StudentID = deleted.StudentID
    )
    BEGIN
      SELECT @errno  = 30001,
             @errmsg = 'Cannot delete Student because Course_
Enrollment exists.'
      GOTO error
    END

    /* erwin Builtin Trigger */
    /* Student  Course_Enrollment on parent delete restrict */
    /* ERWIN_RELATION:CHECKSUM="00000000", PARENT_OWNER="",
PARENT_TABLE="Student"
    CHILD_OWNER="", CHILD_TABLE="Course_Enrollment"
    P2C_VERB_PHRASE="", C2P_VERB_PHRASE="",
```

```
    FK_CONSTRAINT="R_18", FK_COLUMNS="StudentID" */
    IF EXISTS (
      SELECT * FROM deleted,Course_Enrollment
      WHERE
        /*  %JoinFKPK(Course_Enrollment,deleted," = "," AND") */
        Course_Enrollment.StudentID = deleted.StudentID
    )
    BEGIN
      SELECT @errno  = 30001,
             @errmsg = 'Cannot delete Student because Course_
Enrollment exists.'
      GOTO error
    END


    /* erwin Builtin Trigger */
    RETURN
error:
    RAISERROR (@errmsg, -- Message text.
               @severity, -- Severity (0~25).
               @state) -- State (0~255).
    rollback transaction
END


go


CREATE TRIGGER tU_Student ON Student FOR UPDATE AS
/* erwin Builtin Trigger */
/* UPDATE trigger on Student */
BEGIN
  DECLARE   @numrows int,
            @nullcnt int,
            @validcnt int,
            @insStudentID varchar(50),
            @errno   int,
            @severity int,
            @state    int,
            @errmsg  varchar(255)


  SELECT @numrows = @@rowcount
  /* erwin Builtin Trigger */
  /* Student  Student_Transcript on parent update restrict */
  /* ERWIN_RELATION:CHECKSUM="0003701f", PARENT_OWNER="",
PARENT_TABLE="Student"
    CHILD_OWNER="", CHILD_TABLE="Student_Transcript"
    P2C_VERB_PHRASE="", C2P_VERB_PHRASE="",
    FK_CONSTRAINT="R_36", FK_COLUMNS="StudentID" */
```

```
  IF
    /* %ParentPK(" OR",UPDATE) */
    UPDATE(StudentID)
  BEGIN
    IF EXISTS (
      SELECT * FROM deleted,Student_Transcript
      WHERE
        /* %JoinFKPK(Student_Transcript,deleted," = "," AND") */
        Student_Transcript.StudentID = deleted.StudentID
    )
    BEGIN
      SELECT @errno  = 30005,
             @errmsg = 'Cannot update Student because Student_
Transcript exists.'
      GOTO error
    END
  END

  /* erwin Builtin Trigger */
  /* Student  Course_Enrollment on parent update restrict */
  /* ERWIN_RELATION:CHECKSUM="00000000", PARENT_OWNER="",
PARENT_TABLE="Student"
    CHILD_OWNER="", CHILD_TABLE="Course_Enrollment"
    P2C_VERB_PHRASE="", C2P_VERB_PHRASE="",
    FK_CONSTRAINT="R_33", FK_COLUMNS="StudentID" */
  IF
    /* %ParentPK(" OR",UPDATE) */
    UPDATE(StudentID)
  BEGIN
    IF EXISTS (
      SELECT * FROM deleted,Course_Enrollment
      WHERE
        /* %JoinFKPK(Course_Enrollment,deleted," = "," AND") */
        Course_Enrollment.StudentID = deleted.StudentID
    )
    BEGIN
      SELECT @errno  = 30005,
             @errmsg = 'Cannot update Student because Course_
Enrollment exists.'
      GOTO error
    END
  END

  /* erwin Builtin Trigger */
  /* Student  Course_Enrollment on parent update restrict */
  /* ERWIN_RELATION:CHECKSUM="00000000", PARENT_OWNER="",
PARENT_TABLE="Student"
```

```
        CHILD_OWNER="", CHILD_TABLE="Course_Enrollment"
        P2C_VERB_PHRASE="", C2P_VERB_PHRASE="",
        FK_CONSTRAINT="R_18", FK_COLUMNS="StudentID" */
    IF
        /* %ParentPK(" OR",UPDATE) */
        UPDATE(StudentID)
    BEGIN
        IF EXISTS (
            SELECT * FROM deleted,Course_Enrollment
            WHERE
                /*  %JoinFKPK(Course_Enrollment,deleted," = "," AND") */
                Course_Enrollment.StudentID = deleted.StudentID
        )
        BEGIN
            SELECT @errno  = 30005,
                   @errmsg = 'Cannot update Student because Course_
Enrollment exists.'
            GOTO error
        END
    END

    /* erwin Builtin Trigger */
    RETURN
error:
    RAISERROR (@errmsg, -- Message text.
               @severity, -- Severity (0~25).
               @state) -- State (0~255).
    rollback transaction
END

go

CREATE TRIGGER tI_Student_Grade ON Student_Grade FOR INSERT AS
/* erwin Builtin Trigger */
/* INSERT trigger on Student_Grade */
BEGIN
    DECLARE @numrows int,
            @nullcnt int,
            @validcnt int,
            @errno   int,
            @severity int,
            @state   int,
            @errmsg  varchar(255)

    SELECT @numrows = @@rowcount
    /* erwin Builtin Trigger */
    /* Course_Enrollment  Student_Grade on child insert restrict */
```

```
    /* ERWIN_RELATION:CHECKSUM="0001dd00", PARENT_OWNER="",
PARENT_TABLE="Course_Enrollment"
    CHILD_OWNER="", CHILD_TABLE="Student_Grade"
    P2C_VERB_PHRASE="", C2P_VERB_PHRASE="",
    FK_CONSTRAINT="R_27", FK_COLUMNS="CourseID""SectionID"
"StudentID" */
  IF
    /* %ChildFK(" OR",UPDATE) */
    UPDATE(CourseID) OR
    UPDATE(SectionID) OR
    UPDATE(StudentID)
  BEGIN
    SELECT @nullcnt = 0
    SELECT @validcnt = count(*)
      FROM inserted,Course_Enrollment
        WHERE
          /* %JoinFKPK(inserted,Course_Enrollment) */
          inserted.CourseID = Course_Enrollment.CourseID and
          inserted.SectionID = Course_Enrollment.SectionID and
          inserted.StudentID = Course_Enrollment.StudentID
    /* %NotnullFK(inserted," IS NULL","select @nullcnt = count(*)
from inserted where"," and") */

    IF @validcnt + @nullcnt != @numrows
    BEGIN
      SELECT @errno  = 30002,
             @errmsg = 'Cannot insert Student_Grade because
Course_Enrollment does not exist.'
      GOTO error
    END
  END

  /* erwin Builtin Trigger */
  RETURN
error:
   RAISERROR (@errmsg, -- Message text.
              @severity, -- Severity (0~25).
              @state) -- State (0~255).
    rollback transaction
END

go

CREATE TRIGGER tU_Student_Grade ON Student_Grade FOR UPDATE AS
/* erwin Builtin Trigger */
/* UPDATE trigger on Student_Grade */
```

```
BEGIN
  DECLARE   @numrows int,
            @nullcnt int,
            @validcnt int,
            @insCourseID varchar(50),
            @insSectionID varchar(50),
            @insStudentID varchar(50),
            @errno    int,
            @severity int,
            @state    int,
            @errmsg   varchar(255)

  SELECT @numrows = @@rowcount
  /* erwin Builtin Trigger */
  /* Course_Enrollment  Student_Grade on child update restrict */
  /* ERWIN_RELATION:CHECKSUM="0001d56c", PARENT_OWNER="",
PARENT_TABLE="Course_Enrollment"
    CHILD_OWNER="", CHILD_TABLE="Student_Grade"
    P2C_VERB_PHRASE="", C2P_VERB_PHRASE="",
    FK_CONSTRAINT="R_27", FK_COLUMNS="CourseID""StudentID"
"SectionID" */
  IF
    /* %ChildFK(" OR",UPDATE) */
    UPDATE(CourseID) OR
    UPDATE(SectionID) OR
    UPDATE(StudentID)
  BEGIN
    SELECT @nullcnt = 0
    SELECT @validcnt = count(*)
      FROM inserted,Course_Enrollment
        WHERE
          /* %JoinFKPK(inserted,Course_Enrollment) */
          inserted.CourseID = Course_Enrollment.CourseID and
          inserted.SectionID = Course_Enrollment.SectionID and
          inserted.StudentID = Course_Enrollment.StudentID
    /* %NotnullFK(inserted," IS NULL","select @nullcnt = count(*)
from inserted where"," AND") */

    IF @validcnt + @nullcnt != @numrows
    BEGIN
      SELECT @errno  = 30007,
             @errmsg = 'Cannot update Student_Grade because
Course_Enrollment does not exist.'
      GOTO error
    END
  END
END
```

```
   /* erwin Builtin Trigger */
   RETURN
error:
    RAISERROR (@errmsg, -- Message text.
                @severity, -- Severity (0~25).
                @state) -- State (0~255).
      rollback transaction
END

go

CREATE TRIGGER tI_Student_Transcript ON Student_Transcript FOR
INSERT AS
/* erwin Builtin Trigger */
/* INSERT trigger on Student_Transcript */
BEGIN
    DECLARE @numrows int,
            @nullcnt int,
            @validcnt int,
            @errno   int,
            @severity int,
            @state    int,
            @errmsg  varchar(255)

  SELECT @numrows = @@rowcount
  /* erwin Builtin Trigger */
  /* Student  Student_Transcript on child insert restrict */
  /* ERWIN_RELATION:CHECKSUM="000179c3", PARENT_OWNER="",
PARENT_TABLE="Student"
    CHILD_OWNER="", CHILD_TABLE="Student_Transcript"
    P2C_VERB_PHRASE="", C2P_VERB_PHRASE="",
    FK_CONSTRAINT="R_36", FK_COLUMNS="StudentID" */
  IF
    /* %ChildFK(" OR",UPDATE) */
    UPDATE(StudentID)
  BEGIN
    SELECT @nullcnt = 0
    SELECT @validcnt = count(*)
      FROM inserted,Student
        WHERE
          /* %JoinFKPK(inserted,Student) */
          inserted.StudentID = Student.StudentID
    /* %NotnullFK(inserted," IS NULL","select @nullcnt = count(*)
 from inserted where"," and") */
```

```
      IF @validcnt + @nullcnt != @numrows
      BEGIN
        SELECT @errno  = 30002,
               @errmsg = 'Cannot insert Student_Transcript because
Student does not exist.'
        GOTO error
      END
   END


   /* erwin Builtin Trigger */
   RETURN
error:
    RAISERROR (@errmsg, -- Message text.
               @severity, -- Severity (0~25).
               @state) -- State (0~255).
     rollback transaction
END


go


CREATE TRIGGER tU_Student_Transcript ON Student_Transcript FOR
UPDATE AS
/* erwin Builtin Trigger */
/* UPDATE trigger on Student_Transcript */
BEGIN
   DECLARE   @numrows int,
             @nullcnt int,
             @validcnt int,
             @insCourseID varchar(50),
             @insStudentID varchar(50),
             @errno    int,
             @severity int,
             @state    int,
             @errmsg   varchar(255)


   SELECT @numrows = @@rowcount
   /* erwin Builtin Trigger */
   /* Student   Student_Transcript on child update restrict */
   /* ERWIN_RELATION:CHECKSUM="0001701c", PARENT_OWNER="",
PARENT_TABLE="Student"
     CHILD_OWNER="", CHILD_TABLE="Student_Transcript"
     P2C_VERB_PHRASE="", C2P_VERB_PHRASE="",
     FK_CONSTRAINT="R_36", FK_COLUMNS="StudentID" */
```

```
  IF
    /* %ChildFK(" OR",UPDATE) */
    UPDATE(StudentID)
  BEGIN
    SELECT @nullcnt = 0
    SELECT @validcnt = count(*)
      FROM inserted,Student
        WHERE
          /* %JoinFKPK(inserted,Student) */
          inserted.StudentID = Student.StudentID
    /* %NotnullFK(inserted," IS NULL","select @nullcnt = count(*)
from inserted where"," AND") */

    IF @validcnt + @nullcnt != @numrows
    BEGIN
      SELECT @errno  = 30007,
             @errmsg = 'Cannot update Student_Transcript because
Student does not exist.'
      GOTO error
    END
  END

  /* erwin Builtin Trigger */
  RETURN
error:
  RAISERROR (@errmsg, -- Message text.
             @severity, -- Severity (0~25).
             @state) -- State (0~255).
    rollback transaction
END

go
```

Appendix D: Search for Terms

```perl
1   #Sample program to scan file for a list of matching terms;
2   #write records with matches to an output file for later
    import to a database
3   #
4   use TIME::Local;
5   #open the file containing a list of terms of interest and
    load
6   #them into an array; offset for first row = 0
7   $infile = "mysearchterms.txt";
8   open (IN, $infile) or die "Couldn't open input file
    $infile\n";
9   $terms = 0;
10  while ($input = <IN>) {
11   chomp($input);
12   $searchterms[$i] = $input;
13   $nterms++;
14   }
15  close(IN);
16  $set a flag for first output record
17  $match ="n";
18  #identify the file to be searched
19  $infile = "SystemLog.txt";
20  #identify the output file for records that match search terms
21  $outfile = "Output/SystemLogMatches.txt";
22  #open and process the input file
23  open (IN, $infile) or die "Can't open input file $input\n";
24  $num=0;
25  while ($input = <IN>) {
26   chomp($input);
27  #this sample file contains non-printable characters; remove
    them
28   $input =~ s/[\x7E-\xFF]//g;
29   $num++;
30   for ($i=0; $i < $nterms; $i++) {
31  if ($input =~ /$searchterms[$i]/) {
32   #found a match
33   print "Match on $searchterms[$i] in $input\n";
```

```
34  #open output file on first match
35   if ($match eq "n") {
36   open (OUT, ">$outfile") or die "Can't open output file
     $outfile\n";
37   $match = "y";
38   }
39    $message = "Found $searchterms[$i] in $input";
40    print (OUT "$message\n");
41   }
42  }
43  }
44  close(IN);
45  close(OUT);
```

Appendix E: SQL Server Log Check

```perl
1   #Sample program to review, extract SQL Server log records
2   #
3   use TIME::Local;
4   #note the "\\" useage
5   $infile = "C:\\Program Files\\Microsoft SQL Server\\MSSQL11.
    MSSQLSERVER12\\MSSQL\\log\\SQLAGENT.OUT";
6   open (IN, "$infile") or die "Couldn't open SQL Server Log
    File $infile\n";
7   $num = 0;
8   $mindelay = 10; #set the time delay between checks in minutes
9   $delay = 60 * $mindelay; #compute the number of seconds for
    the time delay
10  START_CHECK:
11  $info = "n";
12  $warn = "n";
13  $err = "n";
14  $time = localtime(time());
15  #extract the date and time
16  $datetime = substr($time,4,12);
17  #change spaces and : in datetime for use in filename
18  $datetime =~ s/ /_/g;
19  $datetime =~ s/:/-/;
20  #open and check SQL Server log for messages
21  while ($input = <IN>) {
22    chomp($input);
23    $input =~ s/[\x00-\x1F\x7E-\xFF]//g; #remove nonprintable
      characters
24    #extract date time stamp from message record (ignoring blank
      lines)
25    if (length($input) > 0) {
26      $currdts = substr($input, 0, 19);
27    }
28    #compare timestamp to last processed; only process later
      records
29    if ($currdts lt $lastdts) {next};
30  #check for information, warning, and error messages
31    if ($input =~ /\?/) { #info record found
```

```perl
32    if ($info eq "n" ) { #first record..open output file
33    $info = "y"; #reset flag with first record found
34    $infofile = "Monitor\\Information_" . $datetime . "_Records";
35    open (INFO, ">$infofile") or die "Can't open output file
      $info";
36    print INFO "$input\n";
37    }
38    else {
39    print INFO "$input\n";
40    }
41    }
42    if ($input =~ /\+/) { #warning record found
43    if ($warn eq "n" ) { #first record..open output file
44    $warn = "y"; #reset flag with first record found
45    $warnfile = "Monitor\\Warning_" . $datetime . "_Records";
46    open (WARN, ">$warnfile") or die "Can't open output file
      $warn";
47    print WARN "$input\n";
48    }
49    else {
50    print WARN "$input\n";
51    }
52    }
53    if ($input =~ /\!/) { #error record found
54    if ($err eq "n" ) { #first record..open output file
55    $err = "y"; #reset flag with first record found
56    $errfile = "Monitor\\Error_" . $datetime . "_Records";
57    open (ERR, ">$errfile") or die "Can't open output file
      $err";
58    print ERR "$input\n";
59    }
60    else {
61    print ERR "$input\n";
62    }
63    }
64    }
65    #save timestamp from last record processed for comparison
      with new cycle
66    $lastdts = $currdts;
67    close (IN);
68    close (INFO);
69    close (WARN);
70    close (ERR);
71    $now = localtime(time());
72    print "Sleeping at $now for $mindelay minutes\n";
73    sleep($delay);
74    goto START_CHECK;
```

Index

Note: Page numbers followed by f refer to figures.

1:M (one-to-many) relationship, 28
    3NF data, 35–36
1NF. *See* First normal form (1NF)
2NF (second normal form), 29, 31
    entity/attribute list, 32f
3NF. *See* Third normal form (3NF)
4NF (fourth normal form), 37
5NF (fifth normal form), 37–39

A

ACID properties, 2–3
ActivePerl, 219
Arrays, 215–216
Associative arrays, 217
Atomicity, ACID properties, 2
Attributes, 16. *See also* Entity/attribute list

B

Backup/recovery service, database, 8–9
    SQL Server, 190–194

C

Change management, 94–95
    SQL Server, 157–158
Chomp function, Perl, 214
Computer, uses, 1
Consistency, ACID properties, 3

D

Database, 1
    accuracy and data availability, 2–3
    ACID properties, 2–3
    backup/recovery, 8–9, 190–194

commit call, 2
    DBMS, 2
    DELETE command, 267
    failover mechanisms, 9–10
    incremental/partial backups of, 9
    INSERT command, 267
    installation, 10–12
        Microsoft Access, 10
        Oracle, 10–11
        SQL Server, 10
    logical data model
        3NF, 42f
        university database, 85, 86f, 87f, 96–108
    MySQL, 3–4
    physical data model. *See* Physical data model
    RDBMS, 3
    rollback call, 2
    service agreements, 9
    SQL, 5–6
    SQLSvrLogs, 171–174
    university. *See* University database
    updates, 2–3
Database administrator (DBA), 93, 95, 210,
        214, 227
    graphical user interface, 4
Database management system (DBMS), 1–3, 117
Data Definition Language (DDL), 18, 95, 114–115
    university, 321–404
Data modeling tools, 18, 93
    erwin
        Change Management, 94–95
        DDL creation, 114–115
        erwin trial software, 95
        logical data model, 96–108
        physical data model, 109–113
        reverse engineering, 93–94
    purpose of, 93

Data normalization, 15–16
   1NF, 25
      attributes with one value, 26, 28–29
      entity/attribute list, 30f
      entity uniqueness, keys for, 25–26
   2NF, 29, 31, 32f
   3NF, 31, 33, 34f
      data model, 35–36, 35f, 36f, 42f
   4NF, 37
   5NF, 37–39
   entity/attribute list
      creation, 17–18
      errors, 20–23
      initial, 19f
      order entry model, 18
      revised, 22f, 27f
   language of, 16–17
   Payroll Deduction, 31
   university database, 75–91
Date, C. J., 25
DBA. *See* Database administrator (DBA)
DBMS (database management system),
      1–3, 117
DDL. *See* Data Definition Language (DDL)
Development environment, complex
      systems, 94
.NET Framework, 233
   advantages, 233
   disadvantages, 234
"." operator, 218
Durability, ACID properties, 3

E

Entity, 16
   relationship, 28
Entity/attribute list
   1NF, 30f
   2NF, 32f
   3NF, 34f
   brainstorming, 17
   creation, 17–18
   errors
      homonym, 20, 23
      mutually exclusive data, 21, 23
      rectifying, 21, 23
      redundant information, 20–21, 23
      synonyms, 20–21, 23
   initial, 19f
   order entry model, 18
   revised, 22f
      with keys, 27f

   university database, 75–76
      1NF, 82f–84f
      initial, 77f–78f
      revised, 79f–80f
Entity/relationship modeling, 16
erwin data modeling tool
   change management, 94–95
   erwin trial software, 95
   reverse engineering, 93–94
   university database
      logical data model, 96–108
      physical data model, 109–113
      SQL Server, 114–115

F

Fagin, Ronald, 37
Failover mechanisms, database, 9–10
Fifth normal form (5NF), 37–39
First normal form (1NF), 25
   attributes with one value, 26, 28–29
   entity/attribute list, 30f
   entity uniqueness, keys for, 25–26
   of university database, 78–85
Foreign keys, 45
Forms wizard, 129
Fourth normal form (4NF), 37

G

Graphical user interface (GUI)
   DBA, 4
   Microsoft Access as, 232
      advantages, 232–233
      capabilities, 232
      disadvantages, 233

H

Hashes, 217–218
Homonym, entity/attribute error, 20, 23

I

Index(es), 45–46, 55–56, 69–72, 91, 177–180
   functions of Perl, 214
An Introduction to Database Systems (book), 25
Isolation, ACID properties, 3

J

Java, 235
   PHP and, 275

L

Logical data model
  3NF, 42f
  university database, 85, 86f, 87f
    using erwin, 96–108

M

Many-to-many (M:M) relationship, 28
Microsoft Access, 10, 117–118
  advantages, 155–156
  database design modifications, 118
  data import mechanism, 119
  features, 117
  forms, 129
    Master screen, 146
    for new customer, 141–146
    for updating data in tables, 129–141
  as GUI, 232
    advantages, 232–233
    capabilities, 232
    disadvantages, 233
  linking to SQL Server/Oracle database, 155
  in office environment, 231
    advantages and disadvantages, 232
    capabilities, 231
  Pass-Through queries, 155–156, 231
  PHP and, 275
  physical data model using, 47
    indexes creation, 55–56
    Referential Integrity constraints in, 51–54
    table creation, 47–50
  query, 119–125
    results, 125–129
    using SQL commands, 125
  Query wizard, 119, 125, 129, 155
  reports, 146–153
  tables in, 118
    loading data into, 118–119
  for team of users, 153–155
Microsoft's Visual Studio, 275
M:M (many-to-many) relationship, 28
Modulus operator (%), 218
Mutually exclusive data, entity/attribute error,
    21, 23
MySQL, 3–4

N

Normalization process, 17, 24, 75. *See also* Data
    normalization

O

One-to-many (1:M) relationship, 28
  3NF data, 35–36
Oracle, 10–11
  physical data model using, 72
Order entry model, 18

P

Pass-Through queries, 155–156, 231
Perl, 213
  applications and uses, 226–227
  "\" character in, 220
  functions
    arrays in, 215–216
    chomp, 214
    hashes, 217–218
    if/then/else, 215
    index, 214
    int, 218
    length, 214
    modulus operator, 218–219
    "." operator, 218
    sleep, 215
    split, 214
    substitute operator, 215
    substr, 214
    system, 215, 226
    while loop, 214
  key matching features, 221–222
  loading data into tables, 227–229
  versus Python, 219
  scripts to monitoring
    SQL Server logs, 222–224, 224f
    Windows logs, 225, 226f
  to search file, 215f, 216–217, 217f, 405–406
    in Oracle database, 216–217
  search patterns, 214
  Warning and Error log messages, 278
  in Windows *versus* Unix, 219–221
PHP, 234, 275–276
  advantages, 234
  configuration testing, 277
  disadvantages, 235
  features, 276
  format file command, 278
  Handler Mapping, 277
  IIS and, 276–277
  installation, 277
  and Java, 275
  and Microsoft Access, 275

PHP (*Continued*)
   user interface and, 275
   web-based application, 276
      error messages, 294–295, 309–319
      system components, 276–279
      warning messages, 292–294, 297–307
   web-based interface, 279
      home page user options, 283
      review/check error records, 292
      review/check warning records, 283–291
      user authentication, 281–282
      user logon options, 280–281
Physical data model, 41, 46f
   access paths, 42–44
   indexes, 45–46
   table
      creation, 46
      key and column data types, 44–45
   university database, 88–91
      Referential Integrity constraints, 241–244
      tables creation, 237–240
      using erwin, 109–113
   using Microsoft Access, 47
      indexes creation, 55–56
      Referential Integrity constraints in, 51–54
      table creation, 47–50
   using SQL Server
      database creation, 56–59
      indexes in, 69–72
      Referential Integrity constraints in, 62–68
      table creation, 60–62
Production environment, complex systems, 95
Python, 219

Q

Query wizard, 119, 125, 129, 155

R

Redundant array of inexpensive disks (RAID), 12, 159
Redundant information, entity/attribute error, 20–21, 23
Referential Integrity, 6–7
   constraints, 3, 51–54, 62–68, 180–184, 241–244
Relational database management system (RDBMS), 3, 117. *See also* Microsoft Access; Structured Query Language (SQL) Server
Reports, Microsoft Access, 146–153
Reverse engineering, 93–94

S

Second normal form (2NF), 29, 31
   entity/attribute list, 32f
Sleep function, Perl, 215
Split function, Perl, 214
SQL. *See* Structured Query Language (SQL)
SQL Server Agent, 208–210
SQL Server Management Studio, 56, 68, 157, 170, 184, 204, 210
SQLSvrLogs database, 171–174, 207
Stored Procedure, 207–208
Structured Query Language (SQL)
   language, 5–6
   for query creation, 125
Structured Query Language (SQL) Server, 2, 10, 157
   advantages, 157
   authorized users, 186–190
   Change Management, 157–158
   databases
      backup/recovery services, 190–194
      creation, 170
   installation
      on laptop, 159
      preinstallation considerations, 158–159
      prerequisites, 159
      on server, 159
      software, 160–169
   loading data into tables, 195–201
   logs, 222
      check, 407–408
      Perl scripts to monitoring, 222–224, 224f
   manual queries and edits, 204–207
   Microsoft Access to, 155
   physical data model using
      database creation, 56–59
      indexes in, 69–72
      Referential Integrity constraints in, 62–68
      table creation, 60–62
   SQL Server Agent, 208–210
   SQLSvrLogs, 171–174, 207
   Stored Procedure, 207–208
   university database, 114–115, 174
      indexes, 177–180
      Referential Integrity constraints, 180–184
      table creation, 174–177
   user roles, 184–186
   View creation, 202–204
Substitute operator, Perl, 215
Substr function, Perl, 214
Synonyms, entity/attribute errors, 20–21, 23

T

Table
creation
using Microsoft Access, 47–56
using SQL Server, 56–72, 174–177
indexes in, 45–46
keys in physical data model, 44–45
Test environment, complex systems, 94
Third normal form (3NF), 31, 33. *See also* Data
normalization
data model, 35–36
logical, 42f
physical, 41–44
entity/attribute
diagram, 35f, 36f
list, 34f
of university database, 78–87
Transact-SQL, 186

U

Unique identifiers, 81
University database
1NF, 78–85
3NF, 78–87
entity/attribute list, 75–76
1NF, 82f–84f
initial, 77f–78f
revised, 79f–80f

logical data model, 85, 86f, 87f
using erwin, 96–108
physical data model, 88–91
using erwin, 109–113
SQL Server, 114–115, 174
indexes, 177–180
Referential Integrity constraints, 180–184
table creation, 174–177
user roles, 184
University database application, 237
master screen, 271–272
Referential Integrity constraints, 241–244
tables creation, 237–240
for university administrators, 272–273
window/screen creation
for adding new students, 244–260
for assigning grades, 268–271
for enrollment of students, 260–268
for entering midterm/final grades, 271
University DDL, 321–404

V

View creation, SQL Server, 202–204

W

While loop, Perl, 214
Windows Event Viewer, 225